A Theory of Dynamic Preferences

"A paradigm shift in understanding choice. Pirinsky shows that what looks like irrationality is often exploration in disguise. The book's scope is impressive—from genetic mutation to political ideology—yet the core insight remains clear: we explore to survive, and biases evolved to ensure we explore enough. A bold reconceptualization of decision theory. Economics has needed this book."

—Murillo Campello *Cordell Eminent Scholar in Finance, University of Florida*

"This book bridges economics, psychology, and evolutionary science, offering a compelling look at how our preferences develop and why exploration lies at the heart of human decision-making. A must-read for anyone curious about the hidden logic behind seemingly irrational behavior."

—Alexander Chernev *Professor of Marketing, Northwestern University, author of* Customer Science

"In this book, Christo Pirinsky lucidly blends economics and behavioral science to reveal how preferences evolve through exploration. Challenging static utility models, he masterfully reframes illusions, irrational behaviors, self-sabotage, and even superstitions as adaptive mechanisms for navigating uncertainty. The result is a bold framework with a provocative takeaway: choice isn't about knowing what you want. It's about finding out."

—John A. List *Griffin Distinguished Service Professor, Department of Economics, University of Chicago*

Christo A. Pirinsky

A Theory of Dynamic Preferences

Using Economics and Behavioral Sciences to Explore Bias, Irrationality, and Choice

palgrave
macmillan

Christo A. Pirinsky
Business Administration and Finance
University of Central Florida
Orlando, FL, USA

ISBN 978-3-032-13333-5 ISBN 978-3-032-13334-2 (eBook)
https://doi.org/10.1007/978-3-032-13334-2

This Palgrave Macmillan imprint is published by the registered company Springer Nature Switzerland AG.
The registered company address is: Gewerbestrasse 11, 6330 Cham, Switzerland

Preface

You have a choice: to spend time with the people you like, to watch your favorite show, or to enjoy your signature coffee drink. The idea that our preferences determine our choices is a fundamental assumption in economics and decision sciences. A deeper examination, however, suggests that we can evaluate only the outcomes that we have experienced in some form or another. Do you know whether you would like a person you have never met, a film you don't know anything about, or a drink you have never tasted? Some of the most important decisions in life are made with little guidance from our innate preferences. How are these decisions made? If preferences are not important here, do they matter at all? If they do, are they always moving our lives in the "right direction"?

This book develops a theory of choice based on the idea that preferences provide important information about the evolutionary advantages of the options we face. To access this information, however, living organisms need to explore the environment and learn the attractiveness (rewards) of these options. Propensity for exploration is partially motivated by inherited traits such as curiosity and boredom. A great deal of exploration, however, is incentivized through the belief system of individuals. Exploration happens at different levels. At a higher level, it is directed toward the environment. At a deeper level, exploration is directed toward one's own preferences. Shifts in the environment could make inherited preferences suboptimal, as people could become attracted to dangerous behaviors and pushed away from beneficial behaviors. This creates the need for exploration of one's own preferences.

The theory provides an insight into the origin and evolution of individual preferences. It suggests that many seemingly irrational phenomena, such as biased perceptions, self-sabotaging behaviors, and superstitious beliefs, could be rationalized as a mechanism guiding individual exploration. Individual and group behavior could be understood better if we do not regard people as creatures who always know what they like, want, and aspire to. We are designed to constantly explore an unknown and vastly mysterious world and, in the process, discover and develop who we are.

Acknowledgments I am very grateful to the editor, Bronwyn Geyer, as well as the whole editorial team at Palgrave Macmillan, a part of Springer Nature, for their guidance and constructive suggestions. I am indebted to Murillo Campello, Alexander Chernev, and John A. List for their time and support while working on the manuscript. Their encouragement means a great deal to me. While working on the book, I also received valuable feedback from Cuneyt Akcora, Vladimir Atanasov, Robert Davidson, Vladimir Gatchev, Murat Kantarcioglu, Kosta Kushlev, Roger Loh, Jordan Milev, Carrie Pan, Ajai Singh, and numerous other colleagues. I am particularly grateful to Charles Cuny for his detailed and thoughtful comments on the manuscript. I would like to thank Valerie Appleby for her feedback at earlier stages of the project.

Competing Interests The author has no competing interests to declare that are relevant to the content of this manuscript.

Contents

About the Author

Christo Pirinsky, Ph.D., is a Professor of Financial Economics, a Truist Fellow, and the Director of the FinTech Program at the University of Central Florida College of Business Administration in Orlando, Florida. Prior to joining the university, he served as an economist at the U.S. Securities and Exchange Commission in Washington, DC. In addition to his regulatory work, he was a full-time faculty member at major academic institutions, including Texas A&M University, Rutgers University, and George Washington University.

Over the past 20 years, he has been studying decision-making processes from various perspectives: individual, organizational, and, more recently—algorithmic (machine learning). Part of his work also examines the decisions made by corporate executives to engage in critical activities such as research and development and corporate acquisitions. His latest research and teaching interests focus on machine learning and data analytics applied to business decisions. His research has been published in top-tier academic journals across various disciplines, including the *Journal of Finance*, *Journal of Financial Economics*, *Research Policy*, and *Accounting Review*, among others. Professor Pirinsky's work has been presented at numerous conferences and seminars worldwide and has been featured in the media.

List of Figures

CHAPTER 1

Introduction

Contents

This book develops a theory of choice based on the idea that individual preferences are shaped by two processes. The first one is a long-term evolutionary process directing individual choices toward activities that increase their chance for survival. In this process, beneficial factors (e.g., consumption of high-calorie food, sex) are associated with positive sensory and emotional responses, while disadvantageous factors (e.g., exposure to dangerous predators, extreme weather) are associated with negative responses. These differences in responses allow individuals to rank all possible outcomes based on their level of attractiveness, which in turn defines a set of preferences over these outcomes. I refer to them as primary preferences (see Chap. 2).

The second process affecting our preferences is short-term and reflects our more recent history. When the environment changes, inherited preferences could become out-of-tune with survival. In the new environment, people could be drawn to self-destructive behaviors and pushed away from beneficial behaviors. For example, over-eating could have been optimal

C. A. Pirinsky, *A Theory of Dynamic Preferences*,
https://doi.org/10.1007/978-3-032-13334-2_1

when the supply of food was scarce and unpredictable. However, such behavior could become harmful when food is abundant. This creates the need for deeper exploration of our own preferences. The knowledge gained from deeper exploration leads to a correction of our primary preferences. I refer to the new updated set of preferences as revised preferences (see Chap. 9). We can think about primary preferences as being shaped by genetics and about revised preferences as being shaped by the environment.

Since people cannot inherit the sensory responses (rewards, utilities) associated with every single action, they need to explore their environment to discover what their primary preferences are. Given its importance, most living organisms have developed mechanisms incentivizing exploration. One such mechanism is the emergence of higher-level rewards for exploration activities. I refer to it as propensity for exploration (PEX). Curiosity and boredom, evident in humans as well as animals, are emotions facilitating these rewards. Data scientists refer to such exogenous objects as hyperparameters. However, while data scientists can change a hyperparameter and retrain their algorithm, a person cannot alter their genetic predispositions and relive their life. As a result, humans have developed an alternative mechanism for fine-tuning their propensity for exploration—the adoption of biased perceptions of reality.

Building on recent advances in biology, physiology, and machine learning, Chap. 3 introduces the ABC-model of exploration. The model states that the likelihood for engaging in exploration could be modeled with the quantity A*(B – C), where B is the expected benefit of exploration and refers to factors such as the number of future encounters with the option; C is the expected cost of exploration and refers to factors such as distance to the option; and A is an affinity parameter governing the sensitivity of the exploration decision to its expected net benefits. The estimated value from the ABC-model could be converted into a decision through the introduction of a threshold parameter, where a person engages in exploration only when the estimated value exceeds the threshold.

Parameter A is further assumed to depend on both a person's innate propensity for exploration (PEX) as well as their beliefs about the exploration process (β). Thus, the exploration decision could be reduced to the quantity (PEX*β)*(B – C). While people cannot change their innate propensity for exploration, they could alter its perceived net benefits by adopting biased perceptions of reality. When $\beta > 1$, people would tend to explore more; and when $\beta < 1$, people would tend to explore less. Thus, beliefs serve the important purpose of fine-tuning inherited attitudes toward exploration. To be an effective tuning mechanism, beliefs need to be biased. I refer to this proposition as the Exploration Tuning Hypothesis.

While the inherited PEX could be either abnormally high or abnormally low, the latter possibility is far more likely. Exploration is inherently dangerous, and the risks of over-exploration are expected to outweigh the risks of under-exploration. As a result, the forces of natural selection would tend to under-incentivize exploration genetically. In response, people would develop alternative ways to motivate exploration.

One effective mechanism for incentivizing exploration is the adoption of an *unrealistically* positive outlook on the outcomes of the exploration process or positive illusions. Positive illusions encompass a wide range of behavioral biases such as excessive optimism, overconfidence, the illusion of control, and others. It is well-documented that most people exhibit positive illusions. Yet, the evolutionary advantage of these biases has been difficult to identify. By being unrealistically positive about the unknown, optimistic individuals are more likely to make costly mistakes. One important advantage of these biases, however, is that they allow people to explore aspects of the environment they know little about. Well-documented patterns of these biases support this interpretation. Chapter 4 analyzes positive illusions as a belief system incentivizing exploration.

The ABC-model implies that individual choices go through two stages (see Fig. 1.1). At stage one, people review a wide set of available alternatives and focus on a subset of them (exploration). At stage two, people select one of the explored options (exploitation). Note that, at this stage, the rewards or utilities associated with explored options are already known. As a result, locally (for a specific choice), exploitation reduces to the concept of choice in classical utility theory.

There are two ways to explore: directly, through trial-and-error, and indirectly, without interacting with the environment. In both cases, one's ability to evaluate, acquire, and apply the relevant information is an important factor for exploration success. Direct exploration could be directed or random, depending on whether the agent targets a specific outcome or makes a random selection (see Fig. 1.2). Chapter 5 discusses direct exploration. It argues that randomization, or one's ability to engage in completely random actions, is an important element of exploration.

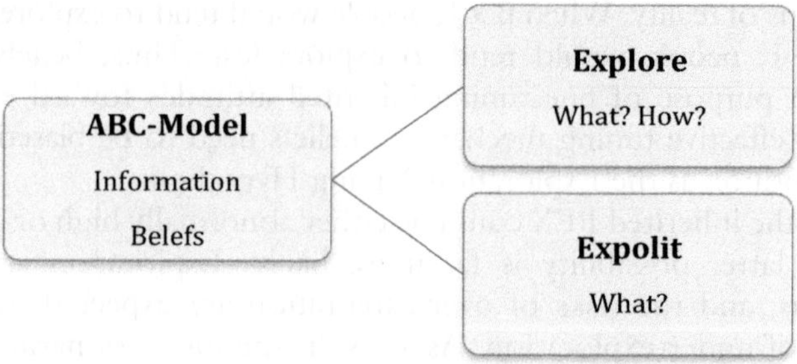

Fig. 1.1 The exploration decision. The figure depicts the exploration-exploitation dilemma embedded in every individual choice

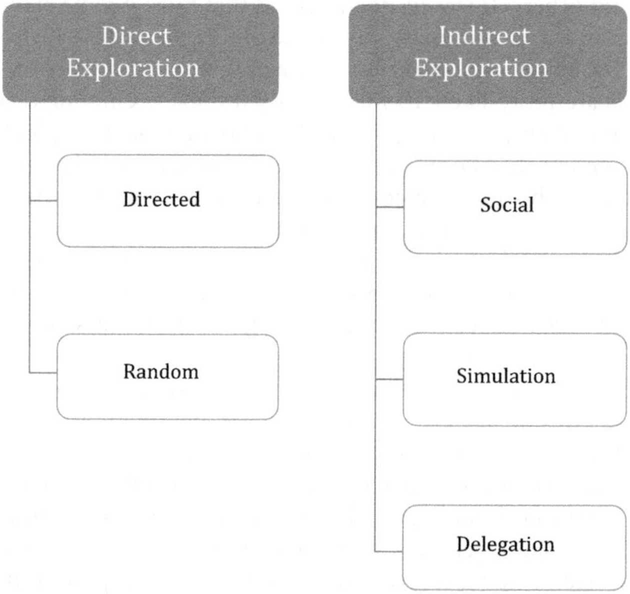

Fig. 1.2 Types of exploration. The figure presents five exploration strategies, classified into two types—direct and indirect exploration

Operationalizing randomization, however, is not trivial. Traditional approaches (e.g., coin flipping) and modern mechanisms (e.g., random number generators) are not easily applicable in everyday life situations. I argue that robust behavioral biases, such as context-dependent choice, could be justified as mechanisms for the promotion of exploration through randomization. Many widespread superstitious beliefs also promote exploration by introducing random elements to individual choices (e.g., divination).

Direct exploration could be costly, risky, and slow. As a result, living organisms have developed alternative, less direct forms of exploration. Chapters 6 through 8 analyze three forms of indirect exploration—social exploration, exploration through simulation, and exploration through delegation (see Fig. 1.2).

Social exploration infers the rewards of various options from the behavior of others. More similar individuals are expected to generate more relevant information because they are more likely to exhibit similar preferences. Such individuals, however, are also more likely to have similar experiences. As a result, the information they generate would be less useful. Thus, the value of social information is maximized for individuals that exhibit a moderate level of similarity to the observer. Chapter 6 also notes that social exploration often leads to conformist behavior, some of which could be suboptimal. These negative externalities create incentives for people to develop non-conformist tendencies. The chapter discusses some of them, such as the need for rebellion and differentiation.

Another effective way of exploring the environment is through simulations. Simulations are stylized representations of real processes that maintain their core properties. For example, a flight simulator mimics the cockpit of an aircraft and could be used for training and exploration of the aircraft navigation process. Simulations could be physical, computer-based, or mental, depending on whether they are generated in the physical world, a computer, or the mind. Simulations are ubiquitous. Job interviews often simulate a hypothetical working environment. Dating scenes simulate what life would look like with a potential partner. Our minds simulate numerous scenarios before making an important decision. The main purpose of these simulations is to explore aspects of the environment that would be very difficult or impossible to explore with other means.

People can also explore their environment through delegation. The action space could be divided into three areas: explored states (E), known unexplored states (U), and unknown unexplored states (U2). Most forms of exploration focus on known but unfamiliar options. Delegation could be an effective tool for the exploration of unknown unexplored states, because what is unknown to some people could be familiar to others. People can delegate responsibilities to others by accepting their recommendations or advice. Indeed, demand for exploration could explain the recent growth of the advisory industry both at the personal and the business level.

If the environment is stable, primary preferences are expected to direct individuals toward actions that are beneficial for survival and away from actions that diminish their chances for survival. This is because preferences that are not aligned with survival would be less likely to be passed on to the next generation. However, when the environment changes, preferences could become out of tune with survival. As a result, learning about the optimality of our own preferences becomes important. I refer to this learning process as deep exploration, and the system of preferences that incorporates this knowledge as revised preferences. Chapter 9 elaborates on deep exploration.

We cannot learn about the optimality of our own preferences through our personal experiences alone. As a result, societies make a collective effort to understand better their preferences. The knowledge generated is then integrated into society's culture and transferred from one generation to the next in oral and written forms. Thus, cultural beliefs serve the important purpose of fine-tuning individual preferences by directing them toward beneficial alternatives and away from harmful alternatives. I refer to this proposition as the Preference Tuning Hypothesis.

When people start questioning the optimality of their primary preferences, they would be more prone to share their experiences, especially the ones they regard as positive or negative. Sharing invites feedback, which enables a person to compare their reward system to the reward systems of others. Various social phenomena, such as bragging and complaining, could be rationalized as mechanisms promoting learning about our own preferences.

The environment changes for a variety of reasons. Some are completely random, while others are related to our preferences. Such endogenous changes could distort the optimality of primary preferences. For example, the rewards of beneficial outcomes are expected to increase with their scarcity. This is necessary to incentivize living organisms to acquire valuable resources. However, people are naturally inclined to increase their access to high-reward options. By making high-reward options more available, societies effectively reduce the value of these options. This makes the attractiveness or utility of high-reward alternatives unjustifiably high. I refer to this possibility as the Reward Inflation Hypothesis. Chapter 10 analyzes reward inflation of some valuable resources such as food, security, social connections, and wealth.

Reward inflation could lead to over-consumption, which could be harmful. This suggests that a hedonistic approach to life would not be optimal because it puts too much emphasis on the acquisition of high-reward resources. As a result, societies are expected to develop social norms for abstinence from these options. However, an ascetic approach to life would not be optimal either because it completely disregards high-reward options. Thus, an optimal policy in life would be to follow the middle path between two extremes—one of excess and the other of deficiency. This provides a justification of the golden mean philosophical doctrine, advocated in most cultures and spiritual teachings around the world.

Exploration is a collective effort. Most social species often work together to explore and exploit resources in their environment. This is because a group of individuals exhibits greater ability to explore than a single individual. I contend that the exploration potential of a group is determined by two factors: 1) its ability to generate diverse opinions and 2) the expertise to evaluate critically these opinions and identify the best ones. Chapter 11 presents evidence that group exploration across numerous domains tends to follow these principles.

Similarly to the way individuals explore their environment, societies explore the rules (policies) governing their behavior. These rules are commonly referred to as institutions. The framework developed in this book provides an insight into institutional change. It argues that the likelihood that a person supports a particular policy depends on their perceived benefits and costs of the policy, as well as their propensity for exploration. Unconditionally, people who are more open to change would be more likely to support new policies, regardless of their content. This suggests that institutional change tends to favor the preferences of voters who are more open to change.

A long line of research in political science suggests that people who are more open to change tend to identify with liberal political ideologies, while people who are less open to change tend to identify with conservative political ideologies (reviewed in Chap. 12). Thus, the analysis predicts that the liberal political ideology would be more progressive, i.e., institutional change would be more likely to favor its preferences. Interestingly, this tendency is not related to the values of liberal voters; it is merely an artifact of their greater tolerance for change. The framework developed in this book also predicts that, by being disadvantaged, conservative voters are more likely to develop biased beliefs about the relative advantages of conservative policies to achieve a competitive representation in the political process. Chapter 12 elaborates on the link between political preferences and policy exploration.

Chapter 13 discusses some implications of the theory. The framework developed in this book contributes to our understanding of biased perception, inconsistent preferences, and other forms of seemingly irrational behaviors. It is well-documented that people exhibit numerous behavioral biases, and the evolutionary advantages of these biases have been difficult to identify. This chapter argues that one important advantage of these biases is that they allow people to explore aspects of the environment they know very little about. Many well-documented patterns of these biases support this interpretation.

Preference exploration also provides an explanation of economic (hyper) activity. Entrepreneurs start new businesses not only because they believe they have a great idea but also because they would like to explore their abilities to develop and commercialize new ideas. Managers experiment with a new product line not only because they believe it would be profitable, but also because they would like to discover the relative advantages of their enterprise. We buy things not only to consume them but also to learn about them. In a marketplace with an increasingly large number of products and services, the motivation for exploration could be as strong as the motivation for consumption.

Exploration happens at multiple levels. Social groups engage in collective exploration of their environment. Individuals explore the outside world as well as their own dispositions. Organ systems within the body also explore their environment to optimize their performance. This raises the question of whether exploration happens at the gene level as well. Chapter 14 explores this possibility. It argues that existing patterns of gene mutations are consistent with the idea that genes could engage in the exploration of alternative configurations.

Exploration is also fundamentally linked to an individual's ability to collect, process, and interpret available information, or their intelligence. There are different forms of intelligence as well as different forms of exploration. This creates an opportunity for matching, where people with different abilities commit to different exploration methods. For example, people with greater social and emotional intelligence would find social exploration more useful, while people with greater analytical abilities would find model-based exploration more suitable. Chapter 15 elaborates on the implications of both natural intelligence and artificial intelligence for exploration.

The theory has implications for economic analysis. The concept of preferences plays a central role in economics and decision sciences.

Researchers usually model preferences with a utility function, assigning numerical values to different outcomes conditional on the level of satisfaction they provide. Classical utility theory is incomplete in two directions. First, it assumes that individuals inherit complete information about the utilities associated with all possible outcomes. The genetic transfer of such vast amounts of information is practically impossible. Second, utility theory is agnostic with respect to the origin of preferences. Since economic behavior ultimately reduces to preferences, without adopting a dynamic view on preferences, it would be difficult to understand economic change. The book provides two important insights into the origin of preferences. First, preferences are linked to survival. Second, the link between preferences and survival is not perfect. As a result, the accumulation of knowledge about the optimality of one's preferences becomes an important factor for survival.

The theory contributes to our understanding of biased beliefs and a wide host of seemingly irrational behaviors. Such behaviors are prevalent in human society (Thaler & Sunstein, 2008; Kahneman, 2011; Altman, 2017). Yet, they have been difficult to rationalize. Biased beliefs are more likely to lead to costly mistakes, and it is unclear how these beliefs can survive in competition with accurate beliefs. One of the central ideas in this book is that biased perceptions could be an effective mechanism for fine-tuning inherited dispositions. Inherited traits are often imperfect and inflexible. Individual and group beliefs evolve to correct their deficiencies. Importantly, to be effective correction mechanism beliefs need to be biased. Nurture complements nature and mitigates the effect of genetics on individual behavior.

The framework developed in this book builds on ideas from recent research in biology, physiology, and machine learning on reward systems and exploration. A long line of literature in organizational studies, starting with the seminal work of March (1991), analyzes the exploratory activities of firms. This research has recognized the importance of exploration for the ability of firms to adapt and stay ahead of the competition. Firms, however, are not living organisms with well-defined objectives, but rather a complex nexus of contractual relationships among various parties. As a result, the insights derived from this literature do not translate to human behavior.

There is also literature in economics studying information search in various markets going back to the seminal work of Stigler (1961). In a recent article, Wright et al. (2021) surveyed the literature on directed search and competitive search equilibrium. In this literature, the search usually provides information about external conditions and not about the person engaging in the search. As noted above, in economic analysis, preferences are generally regarded as exogenous. A theory of dynamic preferences requires learning that is not only extrospective but also introspective. The framework developed in this book outlines some of the basic principles of such theory.

The theory falls broadly within the framework of evolutionary economics (Alchian, 1950; Nelson & Winter, 1985). Evolutionary economic theory views economic development as a process guided by the forces of natural selection. The basic unit of selection in most evolutionary economic models, however, is the firm and not the individual. More recently, Andrew Lo applies evolutionary ideas to the analysis of financial markets (Lo, 2004, 2017). He proposed the adaptive market hypothesis, according to which better investment strategies out-compete worse investment strategies following the laws of natural selection. The analysis presented here echoes the ideas in the adaptive market hypothesis. The mediating factor in the analysis, however, is individual preferences.

Existing research has identified numerous factors affecting individual preferences. We know that genetics matters (Hamilton, 1964; Allen, 1984), and so does the environment (Rende et al., 1990; Meaney, 2004). Preferences are often influenced by our peers (Bertrand et al., 2000; Duflo & Saez, 2002; Georgarakos et al., 2014) and shaped by habits and conventions (Frey, 1997; Graybiel, 2008; Duhigg, 2012). Some researchers have emphasized the role of markets and other economic institutions in the evolution of values, tastes, and personalities (Bowles, 1998, 2016). Others have noted the importance of ethical considerations (Sen, 1987; Andreoni, 1990). There is also evidence that people often adjust their desires to align with outcomes they cannot achieve (Elster, 2016). Despite the long history of research on the subject, we still lack a complete picture of preference formation and adaptation. As Bowles (1998) notes, "[w]e know surprisingly little about how we come to have the preferences we do." This book makes a step in this direction. By connecting evolutionary psychology, adaptation, and decision science, it provides a framework for understanding how preferences form, why they shift, and how they can be realigned.

The concept of preference revision is related to the idea of multiple layers of preferences, also known as meta-preferences (Frankfurt, 1971; Jeffrey, 1974). While first-order preferences are preferences about things, higher-order preferences are preferences about preferences. For example, a smoker might have a first-order desire to smoke but a second-order desire not to have the desire to smoke. Once first-order preferences are set, people exhibit limited capacity to act on their desired second-order preferences. George (2001) argues that markets and advertisers often help first-order preferences dominate second-order preferences. According to the framework developed in this book, primary preferences could be suboptimal. This prompts individuals to explore the optimality of their own preferences. Once the accumulated evidence for suboptimality is strong enough, people and societies revise their primary preferences.

References

Alchian, A. A. (1950). Uncertainty, evolution, and economic theory. *Journal of Political Economy, 58*(3), 211–221.

Allen, G. E. (1984). The roots of biological determinism: Review of The mismeasure of man by Stephen Jay Gould. *Journal of the History of Biology, 17*(1), 141–145.

Altman, M. (Ed.). (2017). *Handbook of behavioural economics and smart decision-making*. Edward Elgar Publishing.

Andreoni, J. (1990). Impure altruism and donations to public goods: A theory of warm-glow giving. *The Economic Journal, 100*(401), 464–477.

Bertrand, M., Luttmer, E., & Mullainathan, S. (2000). Network effects and welfare cultures. *Quarterly Journal of Economics, 115*, 1019–1057.

Bowles, S. (1998). Endogenous preferences: The cultural consequences of markets and other economic institutions. *Journal of Economic Literature, 36*(1), 75–111.

Bowles, S. (2016). *The moral economy: Why good incentives are no substitute for good citizens*. Yale University Press.

Duflo, E., & Saez, E. (2002). Participation and investment decisions in a retirement plan: The influence of colleagues' choices. *Journal of Public Economics, 85*, 121–148.

Duhigg, C. (2012). *The power of habit: Why we do what we do in life and business*. Random House.

Elster, J. (2016). *Sour grapes*. Cambridge University Press.

Frankfurt, H. G. (1971). Freedom of the will and the concept of a person. *Journal of Philosophy, 68*, 5–20.

Frey, B. S. (1997). *Not just for the money*. Edward Elgar.

Georgarakos, D., Haliassos, M., & Pasini, G. (2014). Household debt and social interactions. *The Review of Financial Studies, 27*(5), 1404–1433.

George, D. (2001). *Preference pollution: How markets create the desires we dislike*. University of Michigan Press.

Graybiel, A. M. (2008). Habits, rituals, and the evaluative brain. *Annual Review of Neuroscience, 31*(1), 359–387.

Hamilton, W. D. (1964). The genetical evolution of social behaviour. I. *Journal of Theoretical Biology, 7*(1), 1–16.

Jeffrey, R. C. (1974). Preference among preferences. *Journal of Philosophy*, *71*, 377–391.

Kahneman, D. (2011). *Thinking, fast and slow*. Farrar, Straus and Giroux.

Lo, A. W. (2004). The adaptive markets hypothesis: Market efficiency from an evolutionary perspective. *Journal of Portfolio Management*, *5*(30), 15–29.

Lo, A. W. (2017). *Adaptive markets: Financial evolution at the speed of thought*. Princeton University Press.

March, J. G. (1991). Exploration and exploitation in organizational learning. *Organization Science*, *2*(1), 71–87.

Meaney, M. (2004). The nature of nurture: Maternal effects and chromatin remodeling. In J. T. Cacioppo & G. G. Berntson (Eds.), *Essays in social neuroscience*. MIT Press.

Nelson, R. R., & Winter, S. G. (1985). *An evolutionary theory of economic change*. Harvard university press.

Rende, R. D., Plomin, R., & Vandenberg, S. G. (1990). Who discovered the twin method? *Behavior Genetics*, *20*(2), 277–285.

Sen, A. (1987). *On ethics and economics*. Basil Blackwell.

Stigler, G. J. (1961). The economics of information. *Journal of Political Economy*, *69*(3), 213–225.

Thaler, R. H., & Sunstein, C. R. (2008). *Nudge: Improving decisions about health, wealth, and happiness*. Yale University Press.

Wright, R., Kircher, P., Julien, B., & Guerrieri, V. (2021). Directed search and competitive search equilibrium: A guided tour. *Journal of Economic Literature*, *59*(1), 90–148.

CHAPTER 2

Primary Preferences

Good decisions come from experience. Experience comes from making bad decisions.

—Unknown

Source: The true origination of this quote has not been determined, but it is commonly misattributed to Mark Twain

Contents

Introduction

Our life is a result of our choices. At least, we prefer to think that way because we like the idea that we are in control of what happens to us. This also brings a sense of purpose to our lives. If everything is

C. A. Pirinsky, *A Theory of Dynamic Preferences*,
https://doi.org/10.1007/978-3-032-13334-2_2

predetermined, then understanding how things come about has no consequences. Yet, if we have even modest freedom to choose, a better understanding of the world and our interactions with it could help us make better decisions. Perhaps, this is why freedom of choice is an underlying assumption in most social sciences. It is also the first assumption of this book.

When people are free to choose, they want to know what choices are better than others and then choose the preferred ones according to some consistent criterion. Thus, most theories of choice are built on the idea that individuals have preferences that allow them to rank and compare all possible outcomes they choose from. This is the second assumption of this book.

The third assumption of the book is that preferences are operationalized through an elaborate system of rewards. A long line of research in neuroscience suggests that such system exists in most living organisms, and it associates activities that are beneficial for survival with positive sensory and emotional responses (pleasure, joy), while activities that are disadvantageous for survival with negative responses (pain, fear). Since rewards allow people to rank all possible outcomes, they define a system of preferences. I refer to it as primary preferences. Primary preferences play an important role in the evolutionary survival of organisms by maximizing contact with beneficial stimuli and minimizing contact with harmful stimuli in the environment.

The fourth assumption of the book is that since people cannot inherit the sensory responses associated with every single action, they need to explore their environment to discover what their primary preferences are. Thus, exploration enables a dual learning process: one outward, toward the environment, and another inward—toward our own preferences.

Building on recent advances in biology, neuroscience, and psychology, this chapter corroborates the above four assumptions. It presents evidence that preferences are operationalized through a complex system of rewards and living organisms need to explore their environment to learn the attractiveness (rewards) of the various options they face. Thus, individual choice is embedded in a more fundamental choice of when and what to explore. As the above quote suggests, learning and growth often come from mistakes and negative experiences. These experiences, however, provide valuable information that ultimately leads to better decision-making in the future.

Rational Choice

The concept of choice is meaningful only if individuals know what they want or like. Not surprisingly, the analysis of choice has evolved around the idea that people exhibit clear preferences about the various options they face. Preferences allow individuals to rank all available options based on their level of attractiveness and select the one they like best. Preferences are also assumed to be rational, which is usually reduced to two properties—completeness and transitivity.

Completeness means that people can evaluate (or compare) the attractiveness of any two alternatives they face. Specifically, if a person is provided with two options: an apple (A) and a banana (B), they will either prefer A to B, B to A, or they will be indifferent between A and B. Transitivity means that if a person prefers A to B and B to C, then they will necessarily prefer A to C. Also, if a person is indifferent between A and B, and indifferent between B and C, then they will necessarily be indifferent between A and C.

It is easy to show that when preferences are complete and transitive, one can always create a definitive ranking among a set of possible outcomes. A rational person, then, is expected to (1) always choose the highest-ranked alternative in the set and (2) make consistent choices over time. There has been mounting evidence, however, that human behavior often violates these conditions. In other words, people do not seem to behave rationally.

For example, individual preferences tend to be context-dependent, i.e., the value of an option depends on the other options available in a choice set, or the "context". Empirical research across several fields, including law, economics, and psychology, has confirmed that choices are susceptible to contextual influences (Kahneman & Tversky, 1984; Tetlock, 1985; Tversky & Simonson, 1993; Kelman et al., 1996). One widely discussed case of context-dependent preferences is "loss aversion", or the fact that the same situation tends to be perceived as worse if it is framed as a loss, rather than a gain (Kahneman & Tversky, 1979). Context-dependent preferences contradict the rational paradigm because they frequently lead to inconsistent behavior.

Extensive evidence in economics and sociology also suggests that people tend to emulate the behavior of better-performing peers, an idea that could be traced back to the works of Adam Smith and Thorsten Veblen (Smith, 1776; Veblen, 1899). According to Veblen (1899), "[t]he motive is emulation—the stimulus of an invidious comparison which prompts us to outdo those with whom we are in the habit of classing ourselves." This "keeping up with the Joneses" effect exists in various domains ranging from individual consumption and investment decisions to highly-consequential choices (Grinblatt et al., 2008; Georgarakos et al., 2014; Hong et al., 2014; Ager et al., 2022). Empirical research confirms that individual subjective well-being depends heavily on the consumption of others (see, for example, Luttmer, 2005; Kuhn et al., 2011; Bertrand & Morse, 2016). This research also finds, however, that when people follow the behavior of others, they are prone to mistakes. Thus, social influence is not consistent with rational preferences either.

Individual decisions are also significantly affected by emotions. The vast majority of the brain's activities consist of unconscious evaluations of events and situations that trigger emotional responses (Markwica, 2018). It is now well accepted that emotions significantly affect consumer and investor behavior, and could cause significant price disturbances in product and capital markets (Baker & Wurgler, 2007; Gillitzer & Prasad, 2018). Such behavior is also difficult to reconcile with rational choice as it appears erratic and, often, self-destructive.

The evidence against rationality extends beyond the above examples (see e.g., Kahneman, 2011). It presents a major challenge to our understanding of choice because it is inconsistent with evolutionary dynamics (see e.g., Eriksson, 2011). It is unclear how "irrational" behavior can survive in competition with rational behavior. Life is highly competitive, and even modest disadvantages would prevent individuals from passing on their traits to the next generation. Yet, most of these biases survive competitive interactions and persist.

When a theory is contradicted by facts, a critical examination of its underlying assumptions is necessary. The main assumption behind the rational choice theory is the completeness of individual preferences, or our ability to compare and rank consistently any two possible outcomes at any point in time. A closer examination suggests that this assumption is far from obvious. Throughout our lifetime, we constantly encounter unfamiliar outcomes and situations. A definite comparison of these alternatives is extremely difficult. The relative attractiveness of an object also depends on completely random factors, such as our current state of mind, as well as the state of the object.

If you need to choose between an apple and a banana, which one would you pick? Even if you like apples better than bananas, this does not automatically imply that you would like this particular apple better than this particular banana. The apple might not look appetizing, or the banana might look better than average. Hunger could also steer a person toward the banana, which is a more calory-dense fruit than the apple. It seems that the only way to know with certainty which fruit you would prefer in the current situation would be to try both of them. But in this case, you would not be making a choice. And if you choose one of them, you will never know whether you would have liked the other one better. There seems to be a fundamental uncertainty about the relative attractiveness of the options we face.

The inherent limitations of our ability to compare outcomes were well articulated by the ancient Greek philosopher Heraclitus, who lived at the outset of the fifth century BC. He famously commented that: no man ever steps in the same river twice; for it's not the same river and he's not the same man (Stern, 1991). This observation applies to consecutive choices as well. No person ever chooses among the same options twice. First, because they would never be the same options, and second, because he would never be the same person.

It seems that the completeness assumption of individual preferences is always violated. Perhaps a more fundamental property of preferences is that they are incomplete. They become more complete with the choices we make. These choices inevitably change our own preferences because they have an element of learning and self-discovery. Evolving preferences also result in choices that would appear inconsistent to an observer who fails to recognize that preferences change with the choices we make.

Utility Theory

Preferences could be conveniently modeled with a function mapping various outcomes to a quantity assessing the degree of attractiveness (or utility) of each outcome. Such function is commonly referred to as utility function, and the theory of mapping utility to preferences as utility theory.

Consider a set of alternatives among which a person has a preference ordering. A utility function represents that ordering, if it is possible to assign a real number to each alternative in such a manner that an alternative A is assigned a number greater than an alternative B if and only if the individual prefers alternative A to alternative B. In this situation, the most preferred alternative must be also the alternative that maximizes the corresponding utility function. In this setting, the problem of choice can be reduced to the problem of maximizing a real-valued utility function.

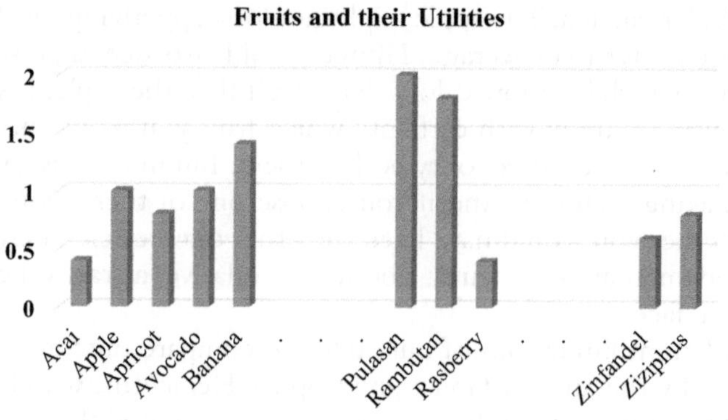

Fig. 2.1 The utility of fruits. The figure presents a list of fruits and the utilities associated with them for a hypothetical person

Figure 2.1 presents the hypothetical utilities associated with various fruits, sorted in alphabetical order. These utilities define a complete set of preferences. They indicate, for example, that this person exhibits preference for tropical fruits, such as pulasan, rambutan, and bananas. (S)he also appears indifferent between apples and avocados because these fruits are associated with the same utilities (yes, avocados are botanically considered fruits). The utility representation also implies that this individual knows with certainty how (s)he values every single fruit in the world in relative terms. (S)he knows the tastes of acai berry, apricots, and ziziphus. Furthermore, (s)he knows that (s)he likes ziziphus fruit exactly twice as much as the acai berry, and so on. While one can easily construct a utility function over all fruits in the world, finding a real person with its implied preferences would be almost impossible.

The utility function on Fig. 2.1 also does not factor in quantities. For example, this person might prefer an apple to a banana, but (s)he could prefer two apples to a single banana. The incompleteness of individual preferences becomes even more apparent once we incorporate quantities into the utility function. If a person does not know how to compare apples to rambutans, they would know even less how to compare 1.3*apples to 0.7*rambutans.

The concept of utility maximization could be linked to the philosophical doctrine of hedonism, emphasizing the prioritization of pleasure in one's actions and thoughts. The ideas of hedonism were put forward by the ancient Greek philosophers Aristippus and Epicurus (Inwood & Gerson, 1994). A disciple of Socrates, Aristippus believed that people should strive toward sentient pleasures. Epicurus asserted that the highest purpose of philosophy was to attain *ataraxia* (inner tranquility) and *aponia* (freedom from pain).

During the Renaissance, the ideas of hedonism evolved into the ethical position of utilitarianism, most notably in the works of Jeremy Bentham. In his work, Bentham (1789) made the assumption that people always act to maximize their pleasure (he treated pain as negative pleasure). Bentham's work opens with a statement of the principle of utility, arguing that "[n]ature has placed mankind under the governance of two sovereign masters, pain and pleasure." In the book, Bentham also introduces a method of calculating the value of pleasures and pains, which became known as the hedonic calculus. The calculation includes several quantities characterizing pleasurable experiences, such as their intensity, duration, certainty, timing, as well as their impact on other people. Bentham's analysis may now be seen as a predecessor of mathematical utility theory.

The modern formulation of utility theory could be traced to an article by the mathematician Daniel Bernoulli, published in 1738 (Bernoulli, [1738] 1954). Bernoulli argued that people choose among various outcomes by comparing the utility derived from those outcomes, rather than their monetary value. Axiomatic utility theory was later developed by Ramsey (1931), von Neumann & Morgenstern (1944), and Savage (1954).

Utility theory represents a tractable way to model preferences. The utility function, as a numeric representation of preferences, does not need to link directly to pleasure and pain. One can design internally consistent axiomatic preferences that are unrelated to hedonic experiences. It seems that the choices of living organisms, however, are fundamentally linked to the pleasure (or rewards) these choices entail. Pleasure comes in various forms, and so does pain. We enjoy food, seeing a beautiful sunset, or engaging in an intellectually satisfying conversation, and we are adversely affected by a wide set of emotions such as fear, anger, or anxiety.

The System of Rewards

Extensive research in neuroscience shows that the choices of living organisms are fundamentally linked to pleasure. The mapping from experiences to pleasure is achieved through the reward system—a collection of brain structures and neural pathways that are responsible for reward-related cognition (Berridge & Kringelbach, 2015). Rewards are the attractive and motivational properties of stimuli that induce approach and consummatory behavior. A ubiquitous artifact of living systems, rewards closely resemble the concept of utility. In a recent review article, Schultz (2015) comments that: "*Rewards are the most crucial objects for life. Their function is to make us eat, drink, and mate. Species with brains that allow them to get better rewards will win in evolution. This is what our brain does, acquire rewards, and do it in the best possible way. It may well be the reason why brains have evolved. Brains allow multicellular organisms to move about the world.*"

The research on reward systems was influenced by the early work of psychologist Edward Thorndike, who proposed a principle commonly known as the law of effect (Thorndike, 1927; Athalye et al., 2018). According to this principle, behaviors with satisfying outcomes are more likely to reoccur, while behaviors with unsatisfying outcomes are less likely to happen again. In an experiment that Thorndike conducted, he placed a hungry cat inside a box, where the animal could escape and reach a food source only by operating the latch of a door. At first, the cats would scratch the walls of the box and, only by accident, would activate the latch to open the door. On successive trials, however, the behavior of the animal would become automatic, where it would operate the latch without hesitation. The occurrence of the satisfying outcome induced repetitive behavior, causing the outcome.

Rewards are motivating and make us exert effort. If you work hard and then receive a promotion or a pay raise, you will be more likely to continue to put in more effort. The law of effect also implies that punishment leads to deterrence. If you speed and then get a traffic ticket, you will be less likely to speed in the future.

As suggested by Thorndike's experiment, rewards can generate learning. Learning allows biological organisms to assess the rewards of complex outcomes at a relatively low cost, which in turn enhances their evolutionary fitness.

Pavlovian learning (classical conditioning) occurs automatically, without the subject's own active participation. It works by associating one stimulus with something that already leads to a response. The Russian physiologist Ivan Pavlov discovered classical conditioning while studying the digestive systems of dogs. Pavlov noticed that the animals in his experiment salivated any time they saw the lab assistants who fed them. To investigate further, Pavlov began ringing a bell whenever the dogs were fed. He observed that an association formed between the sound of the bell and the presentation of food, and the dogs began to salivate whenever they heard the sound of the bell.

Operant learning (operant conditioning) requires an own action for the occurrence of a reward (e.g., pushing a button). Operant conditioning was first described by behaviorist B.F. Skinner, which is why it is sometimes referred to as Skinnerian conditioning (Staddon & Cerutti, 2003). Through operant conditioning, behavior that is rewarded is likely to be repeated, while behavior that is punished is less likely to happen. Both operant learning and Pavlovian learning occur frequently together and constitute the building blocks for behavioral reactions to rewards.

Rewards could be also classified into intrinsic and extrinsic. Intrinsic rewards are unconditioned rewards that are inherently pleasurable. Examples of intrinsic rewards include the pleasure of enjoying your favorite meal, attending an art exhibit, or having an interesting conversation. Extrinsic rewards are conditioned rewards that are attractive and motivate behavior but are not inherently pleasurable. Extrinsic rewards, however, may also elicit pleasure because of a learned association with an intrinsic reward (e.g., euphoria from getting a new job or promotion).

Although sensory receptors detect a wide range of signals from the environment, this sensory information is not externally labeled as rewarding. Rewards are produced through an elaborate system of brain activities (Newsome et al., 1989; Singh et al., 2010). The experiences of pleasure and pain could be also quite different across various types of activities. The experiences of eating delicious food, listening to music, or seeing an old friend seem uniquely different. Interestingly, however, all these activities produce strikingly similar patterns of brain activity, suggesting that the brain converts a diverse set of rewards into a "common currency" and optimizes based on it (Berridge & Kringelbach, 2015). Living organisms also consider both expected rewards as well as their uncertainty (risk) when making decisions (Preuschoff et al., 2006).

Primary Preferences

The reward system allows living organisms to rank all possible outcomes based on their level of attractiveness. As such, it defines a set of preferences over these outcomes. I refer to it as primary preferences. Primary preferences play an important role in the evolutionary survival of organisms by maximizing contact with beneficial stimuli and minimizing contact with harmful stimuli in the environment. Thus, primary preferences are not an abstract construct, but an artifact of living organisms shaped by natural selection.

The fact that individual choices are guided by a system of rewards opens the question of how choices are operationalized in living organisms. A straightforward possibility for them would be to inherit a complete record with the relative attractiveness of all available options. Decisions then would involve simply "looking up" the corresponding rewards of these options and choosing the one with the highest value. Such an approach, however, would require enormous cognitive resources. The world is extremely complex and includes an unlimited number of objects, circumstances, and situations. Obtaining and utilizing a complete record of the rewards of all possible actions is practically impossible. Such records could also quickly become obsolete because of mutations of both the environment and the decision-maker.

For these reasons, living organisms do not inherit information about the rewards of individual outcomes but about the basic elements (substances) comprising these outcomes. Based on this information, they can infer the relative attractiveness of a particular outcome through experience. For example, if you like fat and carbohydrates, you would very likely like pasta. If you like to laugh, then you would probably enjoy a comedy film. Thus, people need to explore their environment to infer the rewards associated with various alternatives. They could do this either directly—for example, by ordering a pasta dish; or indirectly—for example, by reading a review about it. Regardless of the approach, living organisms need to explore their environment to discover what their primary preferences are.

Concepts

Preferences. *An attitude toward a set of options enabling an individual to rank them based on their level of attractiveness or desirability. For example, someone prefers A over B if they would rather choose A than B.*

Utility function. *A mathematical function (mapping) from a set of possible outcomes to a real number indicating the degree of attractiveness of each outcome (or its utility).*

Hedonism. *A philosophical view that prioritizes the pursuit of pleasure and the avoidance of pain as a primary human motivation.*

System of rewards. *A collection of neural structures that are responsible for the attractive and motivational property of a stimulus (the reward). The reward system induces behavior toward stimuli associated with positively-valenced emotions (e.g., pleasure, joy) and away from stimuli associated with negatively-valenced emotions (e.g., pain, fear).*

Primary preferences. *A system of preferences generated by the innate reward system of a living organism, whereas outcomes are ranked based on their level of (expected) reward.*

Exploration/Exploitation. *Exploration refers to the act of obtaining information about the relative attractiveness (reward) of a particular action. Exploitation refers to the act of choosing among (explored) options the one with the highest reward. An agent needs to exploit what (s)he already knows to obtain more rewards, but (s)he also needs to explore more options to make better choices in the future. Thus, one needs to identify a balance between exploration and exploitation in any situation (the exploration-exploitation tradeoff).*

Exploration Vs. Exploitation

Since primary preferences determine our choices only over familiar outcomes, one needs to explore the environment before making a choice. More formally, exploration could be defined as any action that generates knowledge about the rewards associated with various options, while exploitation is any action capitalizing on this knowledge. Because individuals do not have complete knowledge about the environment, they need to explore which actions earn high rewards.

When exploring, a person sacrifices immediate rewards but learns more about the environment, so that they can obtain higher rewards later. When exploiting, i.e., taking the action, which currently looks best, a person sacrifices the knowledge that they could have obtained upon exploring some of the options they are unfamiliar with. Thus, the exploration-exploitation choice always takes the form of a tradeoff, whereas commitment to one of them is always at the expense of the other.

To illustrate the exploration-exploitation tradeoff, let's consider three examples: choosing a restaurant, choosing a mate, and choosing a career. Exploring the restaurant scene is relatively straightforward. There are different ways one could do that. People could engage in direct exploration by simply visiting a new place or trying something new from the menu of an old restaurant. This option is risky because people might not like what they have ordered; they could be also allergic to certain ingredients in the meal. Alternatively, people could ask the chef about the ingredients in a particular dish, and based on this information, they could infer whether they would like it or not. This option is not as informative as the first one, but is safer.

When choosing a mate, exploration is more difficult. It could take many years to learn whether a person would be a good friend, husband, or parent. This is why humans (and other species) have developed alternative mechanisms for exploration of their potential partners. Elaborate courting rituals exist with the main purpose of getting to know a potential partner better before establishing a connection. For example, people usually go on multiple dates with a potential partner before entering a relationship.

Career exploration is also challenging. The modern world offers numerous employment opportunities. You cannot take a potential employer "on a date." The interview process allows both employers and potential employees to learn more about each other, but this process is very noisy. After all, people themselves might not know whether a particular career would be the "right" choice for them. Career exploration is as external, as it is internal.

In his commencement address to the graduates at Stanford University on June 12, 2005, Steve Jobs commented on the importance of career exploration and the process of self-discovery (Jobs 2005). Jobs encouraged the graduates to have the courage to follow their intuition, and not to be distracted by the opinions of others. He also commented that the value of exploration cannot be understood in real time because its benefits come later. According to Jobs, one cannot "connect the dots" looking forward; only when looking backward. In his address, Jobs provides one interesting example from his own life. While in college, he felt drawn to calligraphy and decided to take a calligraphy course. What he learned in this course turned out to be extremely useful for the design of the beautiful typography of the Mac computer. Maybe his decision to study calligraphy in college was not completely random and was influenced by Job's intuition or somebody else's advice. This decision was an exploration that helped him "connect the dots." Of course, explorations generate many dots, some of which are never connected. This is the nature and the inherent cost of every exploration.

The above examples also provide an insight into the value of exploration. In general, the value of exploration is higher when it is (1) more beneficial and (2) less costly to implement. For example, exploration would be more beneficial early in the course of one's life or in a situation because in these cases, the knowledge it generates could be utilized many times in the future. Exploration would be more costly when people have discovered high-reward options. For example, trying out a new restaurant would be less attractive when you already have a set of excellent options to choose from.

It is also important to note that exploration and exploitation overlap. Everything you are aware of is already explored to a degree. The very fact that you know about its existence already provides some information about it. Nothing, however, is fully explored. Even when we are choosing among familiar outcomes, we keep learning about them (and ourselves) with every iterative choice we make. Paraphrasing Heraclitus, this is because they are never the same options, and we are never the same person.

Exploration is an important factor in most ecosystems and takes many forms (Hills et al., 2015). Animals need to explore their environment to decide where to forage, with whom to mate, or where to breed. There is mounting evidence that living organisms strategically solve the exploration-exploitation dilemma among species as diverse as birds (Korf, 1985), fish (Sutton & Barto, 1998), and mammals (Hills, 2006; Stephens et al., 2008). The balancing of exploitation and exploration has been even documented in basic life forms, such as fungi deciding whether to concentrate on a local site or to sample more distant resources (Watkinson et al., 2005).

Humans face the exploration-exploitation dilemma in virtually every decision they make. Furthermore, they explore a wide range of domains such as the physical space, social networks, and the Internet. People even engage in internal exploration of their memory (Hills et al., 2015). Exploration is also an important decision in scientific research, where a scientist needs to decide between exploring a new methodology and using an old, well-established one.

Exploration is an important factor for firm innovation and economic development more broadly (Arrow, 1962; March, 1991; Manso, 2011; Lucas Jr. &

Moll, 2014). According to Arrow (1962), “learning associated with repetition of essentially the same problem is subject to sharply diminishing returns.” The accumulation of knowledge in the economy has been also fundamentally linked to experimentation (Romer, 1994; Aghion & Howitt, 1998).

Exploration has been also recognized as an important element in reinforcement learning algorithms. In reinforcement learning, the agent is not told which actions to take but instead must discover which actions yield the most reward by trying them. For example, a robot could be programmed to receive a positive reward for successfully grasping an object and a negative reward for dropping it. To obtain more rewards, a reinforcement learning agent must choose familiar actions that generate the highest rewards (greedy actions). To discover such actions, however, it has to try actions that it has not selected before. The agent has to exploit what it already knows, but it also has to explore the unknown to make better decisions in the future (Sutton & Barto, 1998; Amin et al., 2021).

Recent research in Physics has suggested that exploration could be even deeply wired in the very existence of the Universe. It is remarkable that all constants and laws of physics appear remarkably fine-tuned, so that even small deviations from their values might not be able to sustain the formation of matter and life. In a recent article, Bassani and Magueijo (2025) develop the idea that this fine-tuning could take place in a series of simulations, where the success (reward) of a particular simulation is related to the creation of matter. We might be living in an exploring Universe.

Conclusion

This chapter argues that individual choice is embedded in a more fundamental choice of when and what to explore. Before a person chooses from a consideration set, they need to decide what this set is. To navigate the explored territories in their lives, individuals are provided with an important tool—their primary preferences. Preferences direct individuals toward choices that are beneficial for survival and away from choices that are harmful. To assess the relative attractiveness of an option, however, an individual needs first to explore it.

The exploration decision is more complex than the exploitation decision. Primary preferences cannot evaluate options without any structural information about them. As a result, exploration needs to be guided by higher-level rewards. The next chapter argues that exploration decisions can be characterized effectively by a small number of inputs (parameters).

References

Ager, P., Bursztyn, L., Leucht, L., & Voth, H. J. (2022). Killer incentives: Rivalry, performance and risk-taking among German fighter pilots, 1939–45. *The Review of Economic Studies, 89*(5), 2257–2292.

Aghion, P., & Howitt, P. (1998). *Endogenous growth theory*. MIT Press.

Amin, S., Gomrokchi, M., Satija, H., van Hoof, H., & Precup, D. (2021). A survey of exploration methods in reinforcement learning. arXiv preprint https://arxiv.org/abs/2109.00157

Arrow, K. J. (1962). The economic implications of learning by doing. *Review of Economic Studies, 29*, 155–173.

Athalye, V. R., Santos, F. J., Carmena, J. M., & Costa, R. M. (2018). Evidence for a neural law of effect. *Science, 359*(6379), 1024–1029.

Baker, M., & Wurgler, J. (2007). Investor sentiment in the stock market. *Journal of Economic Perspectives, 21*(2), 129–151.

Bassani, P. M., & Magueijo, J. (2025). How to make a Universe. arXiv preprint https://arxiv.org/abs/2502.00081

Bentham, J. (2009). An introduction to the principles of morals and legislation (1789). In *Dover philosophical classics*. Dover Publications Inc.

Bernoulli, D. ([1738] 1954). Exposition of a new theory on the measurement of risk. *Econometrica, 22*, 23–36.

Berridge, K. C., & Kringelbach, M. L. (2015). Pleasure systems in the brain. *Neuron, 86*(3), 646–664.

Bertrand, M., & Morse, A. (2016). Trickle-down consumption. *Review of Economics and Statistics, 98*(5), 863–879.

Eriksson, L. (2011). *Rational choice theory: Potential and limits*. Bloomsbury Publishing.

Georgarakos, D., Haliassos, M., & Pasini, G. (2014). Household debt and social interactions. *The Review of Financial Studies, 27*(5), 1404–1433.

Gillitzer, C., & Prasad, N. (2018). The effect of consumer sentiment on consumption: Cross-sectional evidence from elections. *American Economic Journal: Macroeconomics, 10*(4), 234–269.

Grinblatt, M., Keloharju, M., & Ikäheimo, S. (2008). Social influence and consumption: Evidence from the automobile purchases of neighbors. *Review of Economics and Statistics, 90*, 735–753.

Hills, T. T. (2006). Animal foraging and the evolution of goal-directed cognition. *Cognitive Science, 30*, 3–41.

Hills, T. T., Todd, P. M., Lazer, D., Redish, A. D., & Couzin, I. D. (2015). Exploration vs. exploitation in space, mind, and society. *Trends in Cognitive Sciences, 19*(1), 46–54.

Hong, H., Jiang, W., Wang, N., & Zhao, B. (2014). Trading for status. *The Review of Financial Studies, 27*(11), 3171–3212.

Inwood, B., & Gerson, L. P. (1994). *The epicurus reader: Selected writings and testimonia*. Hackett Publishing Company.
Jobs, S. (2005). Steve Jobs to 2005 graduates: 'Stay hungry, stay foolish'. *Stanford Report*, June 12, 2005, http://news.stanford.edu/2005/06/14/jobs-061505/
Kahneman, D. (2011). *Thinking, fast and slow*. Macmillan.
Kahneman, D., & Tversky, A. (1979). Prospect theory: An analysis of decision under risk. *Econometrica*, *47*(4), 263–291.
Kahneman, D., & Tversky, A. (1984). Choices, values, and frames. *American Psychologist*, *39*(4), 341.
Kelman, M., Rottenstreich, Y., & Tversky, A. (1996). Context-dependence in legal decision making. *Journal of Legal Studies*, *25*(2), 287–318.
Korf, R. E. (1985). Depth-first iterative-deepening: An optimal admissible tree search. *Artificial Intelligence*, *27*(1), 97–109.
Kuhn, P., Kooreman, P., Soetevent, A., & Kapteyn, A. (2011). The effects of lottery prizes on winners and their neighbors: Evidence from the Dutch post-code lottery. *American Economic Review*, *101*(5), 2226–2247.
Lucas Jr, R. E., & Moll, B. (2014). Knowledge growth and the allocation of time. *Journal of Political Economy*, *122*(1), 1–51.
Luttmer, E. (2005). Neighbors as negatives: Relative earnings and well-being. *Quarterly Journal of Economics*, *120*(3), 963–1002.
Manso, G. (2011). Motivating innovation. *The Journal of Finance*, *66*(5), 1823–1860.
March, J. G. (1991). Exploration and exploitation in organizational learning. *Organization Science*, *2*(1), 71–87.
Markwica, R. (2018). *Emotional choices: How the logic of affect shapes coercive diplomacy*. Oxford University Press.
Newsome, W. T., Britten, K. H., & Movshon, J. A. (1989). Neuronal correlates of a perceptual decision. *Nature*, *341*, 52–54.
Preuschoff, K., Bossaerts, P., & Quartz, S. R. (2006). Neural differentiation of expected reward and risk in human subcortical structures. *Neuron*, *51*(3), 381–390.
Ramsey, F. P. (1931). Truth and probability. In F. P. Ramsey & R. B. Braithwaite (Eds.), *Foundations of mathematics and other logical essays*. K. Paul.
Romer, P. M. (1994). The origins of endogenous growth. *Journal of Economic Perspectives*, *8*(1), 3–22.
Savage, L. J. (1972 [1954]). *The foundations of statistics*. Dover.
Schultz, W. (2015). Neuronal reward and decision signals: From theories to data. *Physiological Reviews*, *95*(3), 853–951.
Singh, S., Lewis, R. L., Barto, A. G., & Sorg, J. (2010). Intrinsically motivated reinforcement learning: An evolutionary perspective. *IEEE Transactions on Autonomous Mental Development*, *2*(2), 70–82.
Smith, A. (1776). *An inquiry into the nature and causes of the wealth of nations*, Vol. I and II (R. H. Campbell, & A. S. Skinner, Eds.). Indianapolis.

Staddon, J. E., & Cerutti, D. T. (2003). Operant conditioning. *Annual Review of Psychology*, *54*(1), 115–144.

Stephens, D. W., Brown, J. S., & Ydenberg, R. C. (Eds.) (2008). *Foraging: Behavior and ecology*. University of Chicago Press.

Stern, D. G. (1991). Heraclitus' and Wittgenstein's river images: Stepping twice into the same river. *The Monist*, *74*(4), 579–604.

Sutton, R. S., & Barto, A. G. (1998). *Reinforcement learning: An introduction*. MIT Press.

Tetlock, P. E. (1985). Accountability: The neglected social context of judgment and choice. *Research in Organizational Behavior*, *7*, 297–332.

Thorndike, E. L. (1927). The law of effect. *The American Journal of Psychology*, *39*(1/4), 212–222.

Tversky, A., & Simonson, I. (1993). Context-dependent preferences. *Management Science*, *39*(10), 1179–1189.

Veblen, T. (1899). *The theory of the leisure class: An economic study of institutions*. Penguin.

von Neumann, J., & Morgenstern, O. (1944). *Theory of games and economic behavior*. Princeton University Press.

Watkinson, S. C., Boddy, L., Burton, K., Darrah, P. R., Eastwood, D., Fricker, M. D., & Tlalka, M. (2005). New approaches to investigating the function of mycelial networks. *Mycologist*, *19*, 11–17.

CHAPTER 3

Born to Explore

You enter the forest at the darkest point, where there is not path. Where there's a way or path, it is someone else's path.

—Joseph Campbell

Source: Campbell, J. (2009). Pathways to Bliss: Mythology and Personal Transformation (EasyRead Large Edition, 2009) (**p. xxvi**)

Contents

C. A. Pirinsky, *A Theory of Dynamic Preferences*,
https://doi.org/10.1007/978-3-032-13334-2_3

Introduction

Every culture has its own myths. What is surprising is that it is essentially the same myth. The same symbolic narratives mysteriously reappear across societies that have been completely isolated over space and time. Joseph Campbell refers to this reoccurring plot as the monomyth. The story of the monomyth is usually centered around the life and pursuits of a heroic protagonist who needs to overcome an unknown power. In his book *The Hero with a Thousand Faces*, Campbell (1949) describes the structure of the monomyth as follows: "[a] hero ventures forth from the world of common day into a region of supernatural wonder: fabulous forces are there encountered, and a decisive victory is won: the hero comes back from this mysterious adventure with the power to bestow boons on his fellow men."

At the beginning of the hero-narrative, the protagonist lives an ordinary life and receives a call to go on an adventure. In the ancient Mesopotamian Epic of Gilgamesh, Gilgamesh was a powerful king who after witnessing the killing of his best friend sets off on a journey to seek immortality. In the story of Odysseus, Odysseus is called by King Menelaus to help the Greeks in the Trojan War. In the myth of Beowulf, the young Beowulf, a prince of the Geats (a region in southern Sweden), learns that the Danish kingdom is terrorized by a monster Grendel and feels destined to help the Danish people. The call for adventure is dangerous and the protagonist is often looking for reasons to reject it. For Odysseus, the excuse was to stay home and help his wife Penelope raise their newborn son. Nevertheless, Odysseus is provoked to leave his current life behind; and so are the other heroes.

One explanation of the commonality in world mythology is that it reflects the path of personal development that every person undergoes. We are all the heroes of our own lives. One's life journey from childhood to adulthood usually involves confronting challenges, forming relationships, and ultimately embracing responsibility as an adult. The journey starts with a call for exploration of the unknown. Yet, accepting the call and embracing the journey is not easy. Fear, insecurity, and habits tend to hold people back in their current circumstances. Personal growth is inevitably linked to our ability and willingness to explore the unlimited possibilities of the unknown.

This chapter looks deeper into the motivation of exploration. Recent research shows that the incentive for exploration could be fundamentally linked to two factors—an innate propensity for exploration (PEX) and the perceived benefits and costs of the exploration process. Building on this evidence, this chapter introduces the ABC-model of exploration. It states that the likelihood for the exploration of an option increases with the quantity $A^*(B - C)$, where B is the expected benefit of the exploration, C is the expected cost of the exploration, and A is a parameter guiding one's affinity for exploration. The chapter also justifies the important role of beliefs for the motivation of exploration. It contends that the affinity for exploration A could be expressed as the product of one's innate propensity for exploration (PEX) and beliefs about the exploration process β, thus $A = PEX^*\beta$.

Propensity for Exploration (PEX)

The point of departure of the theory is that exploration cannot be incentivized within the existing reward system. Choosing an action that achieves the highest expected reward is, by definition, an exploitation. Thus, exploration needs to be incentivized by a higher-level reward system that rewards exploratory activities. I refer to it as propensity for exploration or PEX.

There is evidence that living organisms value information as a good in itself. This motivates them to collect information even when its potential benefits are unknown (Gottlieb & Oudeyer, 2018). Pure information preferences have been also documented in numerous species in the animal world (Eliaz & Schotter, 2007; Vasconcelos et al., 2015). For example, monkeys showed strong interest in viewing informative (rather than uninformative) cues, even when they cannot take actions based on these cues. Moreover, these preferences were encoded by neurons implicated in reward and motivation in the orbitofrontal cortex and midbrain dopamine cells, supporting the idea that animals assign intrinsic value to information (Bromberg-Martin & Hikosaka, 2009; Blanchard et al., 2015). Experiments with starlings also show that in a choice between two food sources, the birds prefer the option that yields richer information, even if such information cannot be used to alter forthcoming events (Vasconcelos et al., 2015).

The fact that animals and humans seek information even when it serves no particular purpose is closely related to the concept of curiosity, or the intrinsic desire to know or learn something (Gottlieb & Oudeyer, 2018). Curiosity has long been recognized as an important motive that influences human behavior throughout the lifespan (Loewenstein, 1994).

One of the main explanations for curiosity in the literature is that gaining information about novel stimuli is intrinsically rewarding (Berlyne, 1950; Lehman & Stanley, 2011; Dubey & Griffiths, 2020). Recent research in neuroscience also confirms that novel stimuli activate reward-responsive areas in the brain (Ranganath & Rainer, 2003; Wittmann et al., 2008; Düzel et al., 2010). Gottlieb and Oudeyer (2018) present further evidence that curiosity is associated with increased functional MRI activation in midbrain reward structures, suggesting that information is intrinsically motivating.

Recent models in reinforcement learning have also demonstrated the usefulness of novelty-seeking as an efficient exploration strategy (Lehman & Stanley, 2011; Amin et al., 2021). In classic reinforcement learning algorithms, the agent evaluates various outcomes based on their expected external rewards. The rate of learning of these algorithms, however, is often prohibitively slow. In contrast, an algorithm utilizing intrinsic information rewards motivates the agent to explore the environment even when the material rewards are rare or unknown. There is evidence that such strategies often lead the agent to discover a variety of effects, which in turn lead to further discoveries (Baranes & Oudeyer, 2013; Gottlieb & Oudeyer, 2018).

Research has suggested that the relation between knowledge and curiosity exhibits an inverted U-shaped pattern: it peaks when one has moderate amount of knowledge about a stimulus, but it diminishes when one knows too little or too much about it (Kang et al., 2009; Baranes et al., 2014). Several studies have confirmed that people indeed exhibit the highest curiosity for topics they are moderately confident about (Kang et al., 2009; Law et al., 2016). The framework, however, fails to explain why people start acquiring information about stimuli they know very little about, which is the initial stage in almost every endeavor. This has led some researchers to hypothesize that learning progress itself generates intrinsic reward (Schmidhuber, 2010; Oudeyer et al., 2007). Thus, individuals would tend to prioritize tasks that are learnable. Several papers in reinforcement learning have also shown that attaching a reward to learning progress could motivate an agent to explore an unknown environment (Oudeyer et al., 2007; Pathak et al., 2017).

Consistent with the idea that people have an inborn affinity for exploration is the fact that people strive for and value the experience of a psychologically rich life (Oishi & Westgate, 2022). Psychologically rich lives are best characterized by a variety of interesting and perspective-changing experiences. Oishi and Westgate (2022) show that many people around the world report that they would choose a psychologically rich life relative to a happy or meaningful life. Furthermore, approximately 30% of the people they survey say that undoing their life's biggest regret would have made their lives psychologically richer.

One important motivation for curiosity and exploration is boredom (Fowler, 1965). Boredom, or the feeling of disinterest and restlessness, is a common human condition that leads people to seek out novel experiences, even when those experiences are unpleasant (Havermans et al., 2015). If curiosity is pulling people toward exploration, boredom is pushing them away from explored territories.

The existence of an innate propensity for exploration raises the question of how PEX relates to some basic personality traits. For example, the Big Five personality traits describe personality along five dimensions derived empirically from the lexical analysis of personality-descriptive texts (McCrae & Costa, 1999). The five fundamental personality traits are:

- **Openness to experience**. It refers to one's willingness to try new things. People who are high in openness are curious about the world, eager to learn new things, and open to new experiences.
- **Conscientiousness**. It refers to one's efficiency and organization. Highly conscientious people tend to be well-organized, mindful of the consequences of their actions, and conscious of deadlines.
- **Extraversion**. It refers to one's willingness to meet new people and socialize. People high in extraversion are outgoing, talkative, and expressive.
- **Agreeableness**. It refers to one's propensity to cooperate and collaborate with others. Agreeable people tend to be more trusting, altruistic, and considerate.
- **Neuroticism**. It refers to one's emotional (in)stability. Individuals who are high in neuroticism tend to be anxious, irritable, and moody.

PEX is a multidimensional concept reflecting one's willingness to engage in various types of exploration (covered in greater detail later in the book). As such, it could be related to all five personality traits listed above. For example, people more open to experience are expected to score high on all types of exploration. Extrovert individuals could find social forms of exploration relatively more attractive than introvert individuals (Chap. 6). More conscientious individuals could be more likely to delegate exploration to others than less conscientious individuals (Chap. 8). Finally, people high in neuroticism could find random exploration more appealing than more structured exploration techniques (Chap. 5).

Cost-Benefit Evaluation

Although unconditional PEX is an important component of exploration-exploitation decisions, it cannot be the only factor guiding exploration. Individual organisms have limited resources. They also navigate harsh and competitive environments. As a result, they must strike the proper balance between exploration and exploitation to survive, i.e., exploring sufficiently to find resources and exploiting sufficiently to harvest them. Thus, living organisms must assess the relative benefits of exploration versus its relative costs (Wilson et al., 2021).

There is evidence that living organisms approach exploration strategically and tend to explore more when the expected benefits of exploration are higher and less when its expected costs increase. The exploration-exploitation dilemma has been well-studied in animal foraging, where species focus on finding a cluster of resources (patch) in the environment (Hills et al., 2015). This research finds that exploration becomes more prevalent when the resources in the currently selected option are depleted and outside options appear more promising (Charnov, 1976; Stephens & Krebs, 1987; Stephens et al., 2008).

One interesting example of the exploration-exploitation dilemma comes from the investigation of risk-sensitivity in animals (Stephens, 1981; Bateson, 2002). Research shows that animals exhibit preferences for variable or unknown outcomes, i.e., preferences for exploration, when they are on a negative energy budget, and preferences for stable and known outcomes, i.e., preferences for exploitation, when they are on a positive energy budget (Giraldeau & Caraco, 2000). Along the same lines, mating aspiration levels increase when the number of available mates increases (Todd & Miller, 1999; Asendorpf et al., 2009).

There is also extensive evidence that living organisms are more prone to exploration earlier in their lives because, in this case, the knowledge that exploration generates could be used multiple times in the future (Wilson et al., 2021; Frankenhuis & Gopnik, 2023). Children are more explorative on explore/exploit tasks than adults (Sumner et al., 2019). Younger children are also more willing to bear the costs of exploration than older children and adults, and this makes them better learners

(Liquin & Gopnik, 2022). Children are also better at learning unusual hypotheses and finding more variable and unique solutions in creative tasks than adults (Gopnik et al., 2017; Hart et al., 2022).

Consistent with a strategic cost-benefit analysis of exploration decisions is also the fact that exploration tends to decrease when the prior knowledge about the environment increases (Gigerenzer & Gaissmaier, 2011). For example, exploration tends to increase with an agent's cognitive ability and confidence level (Mehlhorn et al., 2015). Adding novel options that participants have not seen before also tends to promote exploration (Wittmann et al., 2008; Costa et al., 2019; Wilson et al., 2021).

In sum, there is a consensus in academic research that living organisms are prone to evaluate strategically the costs and benefits of exploration before exploring an option.

The ABC-model of Exploration

This section introduces a stylized model of exploration. We know thus far that the incentive for exploration is fundamentally determined by two factors—an innate propensity for exploration and the perceived benefits and costs of the exploration process. This evidence suggests that the likelihood for exploration increases with respect to both individual PEX as well as the quantity (B—C), where:

B: Is the expected benefit from exploration. This quantity accounts for the number of expected future encounters with the option, the attractiveness of all explored options, and other factors.

C: Is the expected cost of exploration. It includes distance to the option, information acquisition costs, and other factors.

PEX: Is a parameter governing the sensitivity of the exploration decision to the information input. It is genetically inherited, and it is related to personality traits such as curiosity and novelty-seeking.

The parameter PEX is not context-dependent. Data scientists refer to such parameters as hyperparameters. Hyperparameters are external configuration variables controlling a machine learning process. They are set manually before the training of a model rather than being estimated during training. Data scientists could fine-tune the hyper-parameters in a model by retraining (parts of) the model multiple times before they determine their optimal level.

While data scientists can change a hyperparameter and retrain an algorithm, people cannot alter their genetic predispositions and relive their lives. As a result, humans have developed an alternative mechanism for fine-tuning their PEX—the adoption of biased perceptions of the expected benefits and costs of exploration. Thus, one's affinity for exploration contains an inherited and acquired component, which could be expressed as $A = PEX*\beta$. When $\beta > 1$, people would tend to explore more; and when $\beta < 1$, people would tend to explore less.

Considering the above arguments, the probability for engaging in exploration could be modeled with the quantity $P(E) = (PEX*\beta)*(B—C)$, where β is a belief bias parameter. As a result, the following proposition is expected to hold:

Exploration Tuning Hypothesis. Beliefs serve an important purpose of fine-tuning individual PEX. To be an effective tuning mechanism, beliefs need to be biased.

The belief system is a mechanism for fine-tuning one's propensity for exploration. It is an operationally simple approach; it is also flexible because individuals and societies can adjust their beliefs as the environment changes. In this respect, the belief system resembles a pair of glasses. A near-sighted, or myopic, person sees objects clearly at close distances but has difficulty seeing distant objects. This is because their eyes focus light in front of the retina instead of on it. By wearing glasses with concave lenses, such a person can refract the light rays so that they focus on the retina. The glasses distort reality in a way that compensates for the inherited deficiencies of the person. Beliefs carry out a similar purpose.[1] To fulfill this purpose, however, beliefs need to be biased. A great deal of behavioral biases that appear irrational could be rationalized as a mechanism for fine-tuning innate dispositions.

The tuning in this context is analogous to the tuning concept in music. According to Encyclopedia Britannica, "tuning in music is the process of adjusting a sound source, like a voice or string, to produce a desired pitch in relation to a given pitch." Musical instruments generate sounds with different frequencies. Tuning ensures that when any two tones of a musical instrument are sounded together, they produce perfect and pleasant consonance. Since instruments could become 'out of tune' over time, they

[1] Note that beliefs could fulfill other functions as well.

must be readjusted. Our innate traits resemble a musical instrument that is handed to us at birth. It is usually out of tune, and it is up to us and the environment to readjust it.

The ABC-model provides information about the value of exploration. One common way of converting this information into a decision is through the introduction of a threshold. In natural and artificial neural networks, a threshold is a value that determines whether a neuron's output is activated or not based on neuron's input (often a weighted sum of multiple inputs). If the neuron's input exceeds the threshold, the neuron "fires" or is activated, sending a signal to the next layer. If the input is below the threshold, the neuron remains inactive. If we denote the threshold level with *T*, an individual will decide to explore when (PEX*β)*(B—C) > T, and exploit, otherwise. Note that PEX could also be incorporated into the threshold level T. In this case, exploration is activated when β*(B—C) > T/PEX.

While the inherited PEX could be either abnormally high or abnormally low, the latter possibility is far more likely. Exploration is inherently dangerous, and the risks of over-exploration are expected to outweigh the risks of under-exploration. As a result, the forces of natural selection would tend to under-incentivize exploration genetically. In response, under-incentivized individuals could enhance their propensity for exploration through the adoption of beliefs that attach high rewards to unexplored (or under-explored) aspects of the world and low rewards to over-explored aspects of the world. Thus, the following proposition is also expected to hold.

Exploration Deficiency Hypothesis. PEX tends to be under-incentivized genetically. As a result, people are more likely to adopt beliefs encouraging exploration than beliefs discouraging exploration.

The ABC-model is related to a strain of models on optimal foraging in biology, starting with the classical work of Charnov (1976). He studied the optimal foraging behavior of an individual in an environment with discrete patches of resources. Traveling to a new patch is energetically costly. Under these conditions, Charnov derived an optimal foraging strategy for a predator, which is currently known as the marginal value theorem (MVT). The MVT describes the strategy that maximizes gain per unit time in systems where resources decrease with time. In its original form, it states that "[t]he predator should leave the patch it is presently in when the marginal capture rate in the patch drops to the average capture rate for the habitat" (Charnov, 1976).

The MVT assumes that the decision-maker knows well the distribution of the resource across patches as well as its depletion rates. The optimal strategy changes when the uncertainty about the quality of the current resource, the patch boundaries, or the likelihood of finding a better resource changes (Kareiva & Odell, 1987; Hills, 2006). In situations with poorly defined patch boundaries, foragers intensify their search in a local area after encounters with food and explore more as food encounters decline. Such optimization methods of following the best local direction are generally referred to as gradient methods. In a complex environment, however, gradient-following rules may become trapped in an inferior local maximum. In these cases, making occasional large movements independent of recent experience may be beneficial. The precise characterization of such exploratory moves, however, is generally unclear (Ferreira et al., 2012; Hills et al., 2013).

The ABC-model also shares common elements with the more recent literature on curiosity in psychology. For example, Dubey and Griffiths (2020) present a rational analysis of curiosity by factoring in both the probability of occurrence, as well as the amount of knowledge the agent currently has about a stimulus. In their model, the agent faces the problem of what to explore and what to exploit. When exploring, the agent sacrifices immediate reward, but learns more about the environment, so it can obtain higher rewards later. The authors argue that a rational agent should explore stimuli that maximize the usefulness of the acquired knowledge. They also posit that curiosity is a mechanism directing people toward the optimal solution.

The novel approach in this book is that it combines inherited attitudes toward exploration (PEX) and the conditional (cost-benefit) analysis into one unified framework. The framework also identifies beliefs as an important factor for adjusting (upward or downward) one's inherited propensity for exploration.

The ABC-model is related to recent advancements in reinforcement learning algorithms (Sutton & Barto, 1998; Amin et al., 2021; Ladosz et al., 2022). Reinforcement learning is centered around a digital agent who must make a series of decisions in order to achieve a specific outcome. At each step, the agent chooses an action, and the environment subsequently returns a specific state and a corresponding reward. Every time the agent receives a reward, it reinforces the behavior and signals the agent to employ the same tactics again in the future. Every time the agent receives a penalty, it signals the agent to avoid these tactics in the future. Thus, through trial and error, the agent learns what to do (and what not to do). Machine learning algorithms often follow closely the principles of human learning. As a result, machine behavior and human behavior exhibit common elements.

Both machines and humans are designed to accumulate knowledge about the world and use this knowledge to collect as many rewards as possible. The rewards in a reinforcement learning algorithm, however, are externally specified by the data scientist. For example, if the agent is driving a car, its rewards are collected continually depending on whether it follows the traffic rules. If the agent is playing chess, its reward is collected at the end of each game, depending on whether the agent wins or loses the game. Some of these algorithms incentivize exploration by distorting the reward structure of the action space. Such distortions, however, are also specified by the researcher. In life, both the reward system and the belief system emerge naturally as a result of our collective experiences.

The ABC-model of exploration estimates the probability of engaging in exploration. Once individuals decide to explore, they could take two distinct approaches. The first one is direct (trial-and-error) exploration. In this case, the agent engages directly in exploration and learns the corresponding rewards. Direct exploration could be directed or random, depending on whether the agent targets a specific outcome or makes a random selection. The second approach is indirect exploration. In this case, the agent infers the corresponding reward indirectly. There are different ways this could be accomplished. For example, in the case of social exploration, the reward is estimated from the behavior of others. In the case of simulation, the reward is calculated based on a model. All these exploration strategies are analyzed in subsequent chapters of the book.

Concepts

ABC-model of exploration. *The likelihood for the exploration of an option is proportional to the quantity (PEX*β) * (Benefits—Costs), where the four input parameters are defined below.*

Benefits. *Expected benefits of exploration. This parameter accounts for the number of expected future encounters with the option and the expected information gain, among other factors.*

Costs. *Expected costs of exploration. This parameter accounts for the distance to the option, the information acquisition costs, and other factors.*

PEX. *Propensity for Exploration is a genetically inherited parameter governing the sensitivity of the exploration decision to information. It is related to personality traits such as curiosity and novelty-seeking.*

Beliefs (β). *A perception bias parameter magnifying or reducing the perceived benefits and costs of the exploration process.*

Affinity for exploration. *Refers to the quantity* $A = PEX*\beta$.

Hyper-parameter. *Hyper-parameters are external configuration variables that are used to manage machine learning model training. They are manually set before the training of a model.*

Fine-tuning. *An adjustment of hyper-parameters in a model by retraining (parts of) a model many times before they converge to an optimal level.*

Direct exploration. *In this trial-and-error approach, the agent engages directly in exploration and learns the corresponding rewards.*

Indirect exploration. *In this approach, the agent learns the corresponding reward indirectly through observation and inference.*

Exploring Beliefs

Given the importance of beliefs for behavior modification, it is useful to know how beliefs are formed. The literature has identified two main factors driving individual beliefs—information and motivation.

The information aspect of beliefs has been studied extensively in the domains of statistics and economics. Naturally, researchers have focused on beliefs about uncertain outcomes. As an illustration, let's consider the simplest and most basic random phenomena—a binary random variable that can take only two possible values with certain probabilities. Many important outcomes could be modeled with a binary random variable: what is the likelihood that I will pass an exam, somebody else will go on a date with me, or there will be rain tomorrow. Nature continuously sends us information with respect to the likelihood of these binary outcomes. For example, a practice test score could be very informative about future exam performance, non-verbal signals—about whether a person likes us, and today's weather—about the weather tomorrow.

One mechanism of belief revision about the probabilities of possible outcomes is Bayesian updating (or Bayesian inference). It was introduced by Thomas Bayes, an English statistician, philosopher, and Presbyterian minister. Bayes' theorem for updating beliefs based on new evidence was posthumously published by Bayes' friend Richard Price in 1763. Bayesian updating starts with a prior belief about the corresponding probability, which is then updated to a posterior probability in light of new, relevant data (evidence). The probability is updated upward with the occurrence of supporting evidence and downward with the occurrence of contradictory evidence. If we denote the prior probability for the occurrence of an event A with P_0, the new information with I, and the posterior probability conditional on observing I with $P_t(A)$, then this posterior probability could be expressed as $P_t(A) = P_t(A \mid P_0, I)$.

A classic real-world example of Bayesian updating is a medical diagnosis scenario. Imagine a doctor trying to determine if a patient has a rare disease. The doctor starts with the prior probability of the disease being present in the patient population. Afterward, the doctor conducts a test and updates the probability conditional on the outcome of the test. If the test result is positive, then the doctor updates the prior probability upward, while if the test is negative, the doctor updates the prior probability downward.

Even when people use the same information and methodology to update their beliefs, the resulting estimates could be quite different initially because people could hold different prior beliefs. Over time, however, their estimates would tend to converge toward the true probability of the event. When evidence is limited, individual behavior is powerfully determined by their beliefs. This is especially true for exploration, given that people's knowledge about unexplored outcomes is very limited. In a Bayesian world, exploration is guided by (prior) beliefs.

Beliefs could be significantly affected not only by information but also by motivation. Motivated beliefs refer to the tendency for individuals to hold beliefs that align with their desires, needs, and principles. These beliefs are held because people want them to be true, rather than because they are based on evidence. Motivated beliefs are widespread. They are also resistant to contradictory information and include, but are not limited to, phenomena such as wishful thinking, self-deception, and reality denial. Motivated beliefs have been studied extensively in the domain of psychology.

There is plenty of evidence that people tend to hold on to their beliefs even in the case of mounting evidence against them. Self-deception is a widespread phenomenon in the general population (Deweese-Boyd, 2010). In most cases of self-deception, motivationally biased perceptions are relevant not only for the acquisition of the beliefs, but also for their maintenance. People hold on to false beliefs because they keep neglecting some of the relevant evidence, or more precisely, they keep neglecting relevant evidence because they want to hold on to the false beliefs (Mele, 2001).

Delusions form an extreme case of self-deception, as delusional beliefs are rarely challenged or revised (Bortolotti, 2009). Research on delusion formation suggests that most delusions are motivated and tend to fulfill an underlying psychological need (Bortolotti, 2009). Motivated delusions allow the person to avoid negative emotions (McKay et al., 2005). For example, delusions of grandeur could protect a person from low self-esteem. People could also develop a delusion of persecution (everyone hates me) to attribute negative outcomes not to themselves but to others. Yet, it is generally unclear why people from similar environments tend to develop completely different delusions.

I contend that motivated beliefs often serve the important purpose of adjusting or fine-tuning inherited traits toward a more optimal level. A person with abnormally low PEX would be more likely to believe that he has exceptional abilities (delusion of grandeur), while a person with abnormally high PEX would be more likely to believe that he is disadvantaged (somatic delusions) or in constant danger (persecutory delusion). In both cases, motivated beliefs would be biased, yet useful. Consistent with this idea is the fact that motivated beliefs tend to be rewarding (e.g., Bortolotti, 2009). For example, biased beliefs increase confidence and one's chance for success in a variety of tasks (Carrillo & Mariotti, 2000; Bénabou & Tirole, 2004). Belief distortions could also serve as commitment devices in settings where individuals could be steered away from optimal behavior (Epstein, 2008; Dillenberger & Sadowski, 2012). Finally, being convinced of one's abilities could help individuals convince others of their ability to perform (Trivers, 2011; von Hippel & Trivers, 2011).

If we denote the prior probability for the occurrence of an event A with P_0, the information with I, existing motivations with M, and the posterior probability conditional on I and M with P_t (A), then this posterior probability could be expressed as $P_t(A) = P_t(A \mid P_0, I, M)$.

Note that motivation and information are not necessarily highly correlated. As a result, they could push behavior in different directions. Motivated beliefs are often shaped by culture and existing social norms. Many important world views are instilled early in the life of a child by their parents, teachers, and the environment. Once a person matures and accumulates knowledge about the world, they could revise their beliefs.

Exploration Culture

Every social group inevitably develops a set of values, beliefs, and customs that govern its behavior. They are commonly referred to as culture. People acquire their cultural attitudes from other members of society through teaching, imitation, and other forms of social transmission (Richerson & Boyd, 2005).

Social research has identified numerous important cultural dimensions. For example, based on survey results conducted among IBM employees of different foreign subsidiaries, Hofstede classified national cultures along four dimensions: power distance (PD), individualism (IDV), masculinity (MAS), and uncertainty avoidance (UA) (Hofstede, 1980). Power distance refers to the degree of inequality that exists, and is accepted, among people within a country. Individualism refers to the strength of ties among people in the community. Masculinity refers to how much a society values traditional male and female roles. Finally, uncertainty avoidance reflects the degree of anxiety society members feel in uncertain or unknown environments.

Beliefs about exploration are an important component of every culture. For example, attitudes toward entrepreneurial activity and innovation exhibit a significant cultural dimension. Baumol (1990) argues that entrepreneurial activity at a given time and place depends heavily on the prevailing reward structure in society. When people celebrate and encourage entrepreneurship, entrepreneurial activity flourishes. In contrast, when society discourages social change, entrepreneurial activities contract. In light of this, it is interesting to note that the meaning of the word "innovation" has been evolving dramatically over time. As pointed out by Morck & Yeung (2002), a quick look at the Oxford English Dictionary reveals that the use of the word "innovation" in English had strongly negative connotations from the sixteenth to the nineteenth centuries. Innovation was synonymous with rebellious, troublesome, and opportunistic behavior. The dictionary attributes the first use of the word innovation as a useful and creative change to the economist Josef Schumpeter (Schumpeter, 1947).

Societies could use various mechanisms to instill and transmit cultural attitudes toward exploration. One important vehicle for the transmission of cultural norms is narratives. For example, proverbs provide knowledge about the world handed down from generation to generation. According to Miguel de Cervantes, "proverbs are short sentences drawn from long experience" (Cervantes, 1992). While some proverbs encourage exploration—e.g., "Fortune favors the bold," "Strike while the iron is hot," "Better late than never"; others tend to discourage it—e.g., "Curiosity killed the cat," "The grass is always greener on the other side of the fence," "Better safe than sorry." Individuals and societies could (de)emphasize either one of these views, depending on the perceived benefits of exploration.

The Exploration-Exploitation Tradeoff

The exploration-exploitation decision always takes the form of a tradeoff, whereas commitment to one of the two actions is always at the expense of the other. When exploring, a person sacrifices immediate rewards, but learns more about the environment, so that (s)he can obtain higher rewards later. When exploiting, a person sacrifices the knowledge that s(he) could have obtained from exploration to take advantage of current opportunities. The exploration-exploitation optimization problem arises because people are endowed with limited physical and cognitive resources (Sutton & Barto, 1998).

As an illustration, suppose that you are endowed with 10 units of a resource, which could be used either for the exploration or the exploitation of an option. Let's consider the following two scenarios:

1. Explore only one option and exploit this option nine times. If this option generates a reward R_1, your total reward or utility will be: $U_1 = 9*R_1$.
2. Explore five options, pick up the best one, and exploit this option five times. In this case, you receive a total reward of: $U_5 = 5*\max\{R_1, \ldots, R_5\}$.

It is not clear *ex ante* which one of the two options is better. The more you explore, the less you exploit in terms of consumption units, but the quality of the consumption improves. If the quality of all options is similar, then exploration does not pay off. If the options are very heterogeneous, however, exploration could be worthwhile. If you can direct your exploration toward high-reward options, then exploration would be even more worthwhile. Directed exploration, however, always incurs some additional costs. It is evident that, even in this simple setting, the optimal solution to the exploration-exploitation dilemma is very nuanced.

Considering these challenges, it is not surprising that the neural mechanisms underlying the exploration-exploitation decisions in humans are complex and still not well understood. A host of neural circuits initiate and control exploration decisions based on available information and motivations, factoring in their expected net benefits as well as their uncertainty (Fuster, 2008). The circuits interact with numerous other brain structures associated with the control of attention, action evaluation, and outcome prediction (Hills et al., 2015). These interactions are further influenced by numerous neuromodulators, such as dopamine, that modulate reward-seeking behavior (Hills, 2006; Barron et al., 2010).

Exploration and Choice

Individual choice is guided by our innate preferences, synthesizing the experience of millions of individuals through numerous generations. The choices that these preferences entail, however, are embedded in a more fundamental choice of when and what to explore. If we denote the set of explored options from an action space with *E*, then the choices we make are a function of both our primary preferences *P* and the set of explored options *E*. Thus, choice has the following functional form: CHOICE = C (P, E).

The above observation leads to two important conclusions. The first one is that the explored set of options could be too small or too large. If it is too small, it could constrain individual choice to a very limited set of options. This creates incentives for people to explore more. However, exploration is not free. As a result, an individual could over-explore if they dedicate resources for exploration that bring small benefits.

The second observation is that, because our primary preferences are exogenously determined, once exploration is completed, the actual choices we make are largely predetermined by these preferences. It seems that freedom of choice resides in the action space of exploration. But because affinity for exploration takes the form A = PEX*Beliefs, and PEX is also inherited, our freedom to choose is effectively reduced to our freedom to form (different) beliefs. I elaborate more on this topic in Chap. 13.

Conclusion

This chapter looks closely at the exploration-exploitation decision. This decision is important because it creates strong path-dependence in life accentuating early life experiences. Building on recent scientific evidence, the chapter introduces the ABC-model of exploration. It states that the likelihood for the exploration of an option increases with the quantity $(PEX*\beta)*(B - C)$, where B is the expected benefit of exploration, C is the expected cost of exploration, PEX is one's inherited propensity for exploration, and β is a belief bias parameter about the expected net benefits of exploration.

The analysis suggests that beliefs are an important factor governing exploration decisions in life. Joseph Campbell's quote suggests that the exploring human needs to enter the forest "at the darkest point, where there is no path." Information exhibits a limited impact on this decision. Once a person identifies the darkest area of the forest, all it takes to step into it is courage. If a person is more optimistic or positive about an outcome, they would be more likely to explore it. If a person is more pessimistic or negative, they would be less likely to explore it. The next section argues that one reason positive illusions have been so prevalent is that they could be used to motivate exploration.

References

Amin, S., Gomrokchi, M., Satija, H., Van Hoof,, H., & Precup, D. (2021). A survey of exploration methods in reinforcement learning. arXiv preprint arXiv:2109.00157.

Asendorpf, J., Beckage, N., Penke, L., & Todd, P. (2009). Testing sequential patterns in human mate choice using speed-dating. In *Proceedings of the Annual Meeting of the Cognitive Science Society* (Vol. 31, No. 31).

Baranes, A., & Oudeyer, P. Y. (2013). Active learning of inverse models with intrinsically motivated goal exploration in robots. *Robotics and Autonomous Systems*, *61*(1), 49–73.

Baranes, A., Oudeyer, P.-Y., & Gottlieb, J. (2014). The effects of task difficulty, novelty and the size of the search space on intrinsically motivated exploration. *Frontiers in Neuroscience, 8*, 1–9.

Barron, A. B., Søvik, E., & Cornish, J. L. (2010). The roles of dopamine and related compounds in reward-seeking behavior across animal phyla. *Frontiers in Behavioral Neuroscience, 4*, 1–9.

Bateson, M. (2002). Recent advances in our understanding of risk-sensitive foraging preferences. *Proceedings of the Nutrition Society, 61*(04), 509–516.

Baumol, W. J. (1990). Entrepreneurship: Productive, Unproductive, and Destructive, *Journal of Political Economy*, University of Chicago Press, vol. *98* (5), 893–921

Bénabou, R., & Tirole, J. (2004). Willpower and personal rules. *Journal of Political Economy, 112*(4), 848–887.

Berlyne, D. E. (1950). Novelty and curiosity as determinants of exploratory behaviour. *British Journal of Psychology. General Section, 41*(1–2), 68–80.

Blanchard, T. C., Hayden, B. Y., & Bromberg-Martin, E. S. (2015). Orbitofrontal cortex uses distinct codes for different choice attributes in decisions motivated by curiosity. *Neuron, 85*, 602–614.

Bortolotti, L. (2009). *Delusions and other irrational beliefs*. Oxford University Press.

Bromberg-Martin, E. S., & Hikosaka, O. (2009). Midbrain dopamine neurons signal preference for advance information about upcoming rewards. *Neuron, 63*, 119–126.

Campbell, J. (1949). *The hero with a thousand faces*. Princeton UP.

Carrillo, J. D., & Mariotti, T. (2000). Strategic ignorance as a self-disciplining device. *Review of Economic Studies, 67*(3), 529–544.

Charnov, E. L. (1976). Optimal foraging, the marginal value theorem. *Theoretical Population Biology, 9*(2), 129–136.

Costa, V. D., Mitz, A. R., & Averbeck, B. B. (2019). Subcortical substrates of explore-exploit decisions in primates. *Neuron, 103*(3), 533–545.

De Cervantes, M (1992). *Don Quixote* (P. A. Motteaux, Trans.). Wordsworth Editions.

Deweese-Boyd, I. (2010). Self-deception. In E. N. Zalta (Ed.), *Stanford Encyclopedia of Philosophy* (Fall 2010 Edition). http://plato.stanford.edu/archives/fall2010/entries/self-deception/

Dillenberger, D., & Sadowski, P. (2012). Ashamed to be selfish. *Theoretical Economics, 7*(1), 99–124.

Dubey, R., & Griffiths, T. L. (2020). Reconciling novelty and complexity through a rational analysis of curiosity. *Psychological Review, 127*(3), 455.

Düzel, E., Bunzeck, N., Guitart-Masip, M., & Düzel, S. (2010). NOvelty-related motivation of anticipation and exploration by dopamine (NOMAD): Implications for healthy aging. *Neuroscience & Biobehavioral Reviews, 34*(5), 660–669.

Eliaz, K., & Schotter, A. (2007). Experimental testing of intrinsic preferences for noninstrumental information. *American Economic Review, 97*(2), 166–169.

Epstein, L. G. (2008). Living with risk. *Review of Economic Studies, 75*(4), 1121–1141.

Ferreira, A. S., Raposo, E. P., Viswanathan, G. M., & Da Luz, M. G. E. (2012). The influence of the environment on Lévy random search efficiency: Fractality and memory effects. *Physica A: Statistical Mechanics and Its Applications, 391*(11), 3234–3246.

Fowler, H. (1965). *Curiosity and exploratory behavior.* Macmillan.

Frankenhuis, W. E., & Gopnik, A. (2023). Early adversity and the development of explore–exploit tradeoffs. *Trends in Cognitive Sciences, 27*(7), 616–630.

Fuster, J. M. (2008). Prefrontal cortex. In *Comparative neuroscience and neurobiology* (pp. 107–109). Birkhäuser Boston.

Gigerenzer, G., & Gaissmaier, W. (2011). Heuristic decision making. *Annual Review of Psychology, 62*(1), 451–482.

Giraldeau, L.-A., & Caraco, T. (2000). *Social foraging theory.* Princeton University Press.

Gopnik, A., O'Grady, S., Lucas, C. G., Griffiths, T. L., Wente, A., Bridgers, S., Aboody, R., Fung, H., & Dahl, R. E. (2017). Changes in cognitive flexibility and hypothesis search across human life history from childhood to adolescence to adulthood. *Proceedings of the National Academy of Sciences*, 114(30), 7892–7899.

Gottlieb, J., & Oudeyer, P. Y. (2018). Towards a neuroscience of active sampling and curiosity. *Nature Reviews Neuroscience, 19*(12), 758–770.

Hart, Y., Kosoy, E., Liquin, E. G., Leonard, J. A., Mackey, A. P., & Gopnik, A. (2022). The development of creative search strategies. *Cognition, 225*, 105102.

Havermans, R. C., Vancleef, L., Kalamatianos, A., & Nederkoorn, C. (2015). Eating and inflicting pain out of boredom. *Appetite, 85*, 52–57.

Hills, T. T. (2006). Animal foraging and the evolution of goal-directed cognition. *Cognitive Science, 30*(1), 3–41.

Hills, T. T., Kalff, C., & Wiener, J. M. (2013). Adaptive Lévy processes and area-restricted search in human foraging. *PLoS One, 8*(4), e60488.

Hills, T. T., Todd, P. M., Lazer, D., Redish, A. D., & Couzin, I. D. (2015). Exploration versus exploitation in space, mind, and society. *Trends in Cognitive Sciences, 19*(1), 46–54.

Hofstede, G. (1980). *Culture's consequences: International differences in work-related values.* Sage.

Kang, M. J., Hsu, M., Krajbich, I. M., Loewenstein, G., McClure, S. M., Wang, J. T. Y., & Camerer, C. F. (2009). The wick in the candle oflearning: Epistemic curiosity activates reward circuitry and enhances memory. *Psychological Science, 20*(8), 963–973.

Kareiva, P., & Odell, G. (1987). Swarms of predators exhibit "preytaxis" if individual predators use area-restricted search. *The American Naturalist, 130*(2), 233–270.

Ladosz, P., Weng, L., Kim, M., & Oh, H. (2022). Exploration in deep reinforcement learning: A survey. *Information Fusion, 85*, 1–22.

Law, E., Yin, M., Goh, J., Chen, K., Terry, M. A., & Gajos, K. Z. (2016, May). Curiosity killed the cat, but makes crowdwork better. In Proceedings of the 2016 CHI Conference on Human Factors in Computing Systems (pp. 4098–4110).

Lehman, J., & Stanley, K. O. (2011). Abandoning objectives: Evolution through the search for novelty alone. *Evolutionary Computation, 19*(2), 189–223.

Liquin, E. G., & Gopnik, A. (2022). Children are more exploratory and learn more than adults in an approach-avoid task. *Cognition, 218*, 104940.

Loewenstein, G. (1994). The psychology of curiosity: A review and reinterpretation. *Psychological Bulletin, 116*, 75–98.

McCrae, R. R., & Costa, P. T., Jr. (1999). A five-factor theory of personality. Handbook of personality: Theory and research (2nd ed., pp. 139–153).

McKay, R., Langdon, R., & Coltheart, M. (2005). "Sleights of mind": Delusions, defences, and self-deception. *Cognitive Neuropsychiatry, 10*(4), 305–326.

Mehlhorn, K., Newell, B. R., Todd, P. M., Lee, M. D., Morgan, K., Braithwaite, V. A., Hausmann, D., Fiedler, K., & Gonzalez, C. (2015). Unpacking the exploration–exploitation tradeoff: A synthesis of human and animal literatures. *Decision, 2*(3), 191.

Mele, A. (2001). *Self-Deception Unmasked*. Princeton University Press.

Morck, R., & Yeung, B. (2002). The economic determinants of innovation. In S. Rao & A. Sharpe (Eds.), *Productivity issues in Canada* (pp. 361–418). University of Calgary Press, Industry Canada, and Public Works and Government Services Canada.

Oishi, S., & Westgate, E. C. (2022). A psychologically rich life: Beyond happiness and meaning. *Psychological Review, 129*(4), 1–22.

Oudeyer, P. Y., Kaplan, F., & Hafner, V. V. (2007). Intrinsic motivation systems for autonomous mental development. *IEEE Transactions on Evolutionary Computation, 11*(2), 265–286.

Pathak, D., Agrawal, P., Efros, A. A., & Darrell, T. (2017, July). Curiosity-driven exploration by self-supervised prediction. In *Proceedings of the international conference on machine learning* (pp. 2778–2787). PMLR.

Ranganath, C., & Rainer, G. (2003). Neural mechanisms for detecting and remembering novel events. *Nature Reviews Neuroscience, 4*(3), 193–202.

Richerson, P. J., & Boyd, R. (2005). *Not by genes alone: How culture transformed human evolution*. University of Chicago Press.

Schmidhuber, J. (2010). Formal theory of creativity, fun, and intrinsic motivation (1990–2010). *IEEE Transactions on Autonomous Mental Development, 2*(3), 230–247.

Schumpeter, J. (1947). The creative response in economic history. *Journal of Economic History, 7*, 149–159.

Stephens, D. W. (1981). The logic of risk-sensitive foraging preferences. *Animal Behaviour, 29*(2), 628–629.

Stephens, D. W., Brown, J. S., & Ydenberg, R. C. (Eds.). (2008). *Foraging: Behavior and ecology*. University of Chicago Press.

Stephens, D. W., & Krebs, J. R. (1987). *Foraging theory*. Princeton University Press.

Sumner, E., Steyvers, M., Sarnecka, B. W. (2019). It's not the treasure, it's the hunt: Children are more explorative on an explore/exploit task than adults. In A. K. Goel et al. (Eds.), *Proceedings of the annual meeting of the cognitive science society* (Vol. 41, pp. 2891–2897).

Sutton, R. S., & Barto, A. G. (1998). *Reinforcement learning: An introduction*. MIT Press.

Todd, P. M., & Miller, G. F. (1999). From pride and prejudice to persuasion: Satisficing in mate search. In G. Gigerenzer, P. M. Todd & The ABC Research Group, *Simple heuristics that make us smart* (pp. 287–308). Oxford University Press.

Trivers, R. (2011). *The folly of fools: The logic of deceit and self-deception in human life*. Basic Books (AZ).

Vasconcelos, M., Monteiro, T., & Kacelnik, A. (2015). Irrational choice and the value of information. *Scientific Reports, 5*(1), 13874.

von Hippel, W., & Trivers, R. (2011). The evolution and psychology of self-deception. *Behavioral and Brain Sciences, 34*(1), 1–56.

Wilson, R. C., Bonawitz, E., Costa, V. D., & Ebitz, R. B. (2021). Balancing exploration and exploitation with information and randomization. *Current Opinion in Behavioral Sciences, 38*, 49–56.

Wittmann, B. C., Daw, N. D., Seymour, B., & Dolan, R. J. (2008). Striatal activity underlies novelty-based choice in humans. *Neuron, 58*(6), 967–973.

CHAPTER 4

Positive Illusions

'What is optimism?' asked Cacambo.
'It's the passion for maintaining that all is right when all goes wrong with us,' replied Candide.

—Voltaire

Source: Voltaire, 1694–1778. (1947). Candide. Translated by John Butt. London: Penguin Classics. (**p. 86**)

Contents

C. A. Pirinsky, *A Theory of Dynamic Preferences*,
https://doi.org/10.1007/978-3-032-13334-2_4

Introduction

It is a long-wondered question: If God is all-powerful and merciful, then why there is so much evil, injustice, and suffering in the world? To resolve the so-called "problem of evil," the German philosopher Gottfried Leibniz (1646–1716) coined the concept of "the best of all possible worlds." According to his doctrine, despite the imperfections of the current world, God would still be regarded as merciful if any other possible world would have been worse than the current one (Leibniz, 1969).

Leibniz's philosophical optimism incurred considerable criticism from Enlightenment philosophers, most notably, Voltaire. In his novel *Candide*, Voltaire ridicules Leibniz's views by contrasting them with the cruel realities of life. The novel follows the adventures of a young man, Candide, indoctrinated in the "best possible world" ideas by his tutor Pangloss. Throughout his life, Candide endures countless hardships and disasters such as wars, earthquakes, and shipwrecks. His journey takes him to distant places—from Constantinople to the golden streets of El Dorado in South America. In all these places, however, Candide encounters pain, suffering, and misfortune. By tirelessly putting his character in harm's way, Voltaire is trying to "cure" him of his hopeless optimism. But did he succeed?

Everyone who has read *Candide* knows that the novel ends on a very positive note. At the end of the novel, Candide and his companions settle in Turkey, where they meet an old farmer. The farmer invites them to feast with him and his family. During the quiet evening, he shares with his guests that the purpose of his life has always been to abstain from politics and to cultivate the fruits in his garden for the market. All the characters are enchanted with their meal and the peacefulness of the situation. Then, reflecting on their life paths, Pangaloss comments:

> There is a concatenation of all events in the best of possible worlds; for, in short, had you not been kicked out of a fine castle for the love of Miss Cunegund; had you not been put into the Inquisition; had you not traveled over America on foot; had you not run the Baron through the body; and had you not lost all your sheep, which you brought from the good country of El Dorado, you would not have been here to eat preserved citrons and pistachio nuts.

The book concludes with Candide's response: "Excellently observed … but let us cultivate our garden."

The ending of Candide has been one of the most analyzed lines in literature. Yet, the focus of the analysis has been predominantly on the very last statement, "let us cultivate our garden." Critics have suggested various interpretations of this statement, such as that we should: devote more time to ourselves, live in moderation, not become overly engaged in politics, or accept the world as it is. It has also been observed that the "garden" is a recurring motif in the novel that has its own symbolism going back to the Garden of Eden. Nevertheless, it is unclear what Candide actually meant when he said these words. Was he indeed giving up on the idea that "everything happens for the best"?

The garden reference, however, is a response to Pangaloss' statement with which Candide unequivocally agrees. Independent of its metaphysical interpretation, optimism is practically useful. Candide's optimism was the force pushing him forward toward what happened to be, an extremely rich and fulfilling life. He falls in love, fights wars and battles, and meets kings and dignitaries. His journey takes him to all corners of the world where he encounters interesting people and cultures. At the end, wiser and transformed, Candide is far from cynical about life.

Some of the most consequential choices in life are into the unknown. Yet, motivating exploration is difficult. Positive illusions, or our tendency to hold unrealistically favorable beliefs, are an effective mechanism for incentivizing exploration in life. Even if they are not factually correct, these beliefs are useful because they serve an important purpose. Not surprisingly, positive illusions are widespread and persistent. In Candite's own words, optimism is "the madness of maintaining that everything is right when it is wrong."

This chapter reviews four well-documented psychological biases within the positive illusions category—optimism, overconfidence, illusion of control, and planning fallacy. It also argues that some aspects of religious faith and many superstitions could be utilized to cultivate positive attitudes in life.

Optimism Bias

Optimism bias is a cognitive condition that causes people to believe that they are more likely to experience positive events and less likely to experience negative events in life than they actually are. For example, people consistently underestimate their chances of getting divorced, being in a car accident, or getting sick. People also expect to outlive their actuarial age, overestimate their employment prospects, and believe that their children are more talented than they actually are.

The optimism bias is widely considered one of the most prevalent and robust cognitive biases observed in psychology and behavioral economics. It transcends gender, ethnicity, and nationality (O'Sullivan, 2015). Eliminating the optimism bias has been nearly impossible, as efforts to reduce the bias make it even stronger (Weinstein & Klein, 1995). Optimism biases are even reported in animals (Sharot, 2011). For example, in an experiment with birds, Matheson et al. (2008) taught European starlings to press a red lever whenever they heard a short (2-s) signal in order to receive an immediate reward and a green lever when they heard a long (10-s) signal in order to receive a delayed reward. The birds were primed to press the correct lever because if they made a mistake, they would not receive a reward at all. The researchers then tested the bird's reaction by presenting them with a medium-length signal. They found that a large percentage of birds pressed the lever associated with the immediate reward, suggesting that the birds expected a positive outcome, although there was no objective reason to do so. Comparable results have been reported in mice by Harding et al. (2004).

Why do people (and animals) remain overly optimistic despite a lifetime of experience with reality? A quick answer would be that positive beliefs make us happier. Yet, this is not correct. Low expectations seem a better recipe for happiness because overly optimistic individuals are more likely to experience disappointments in life. Optimistic beliefs are a form of self-deception, and the people holding these beliefs are also more likely to set up unrealistic goals and make costly mistakes. As a result, optimists could be at a disadvantage in competitive interactions with people holding accurate beliefs. Thus, it is unclear why optimism has been favored in natural selection (McKay & Dennett, 2009).

I argue that optimistic beliefs are an effective tool for the promotion of exploration. If you feel better about a trip, you would be more likely to undertake it. You might be disappointed on many of your journeys, but you would not be disappointed on all of them. Indeed, occasionally you will discover a place, a culture, or people you really like.

Optimism has also been widely used to promote exploration in machine learning context. Reinforcement learning is centered around the learning of a digital agent. Through trial and error, the agent learns what to do and what not to do by being rewarded and punished accordingly. Because the agent has incomplete knowledge about the environment, it needs to explore which actions earn higher rewards. One common way of incentivizing the agent to explore an option is to artificially inflate the reward associated with this option. In this case, the agent is "tricked" to explore the option even when it was not initially inclined to do that (Sutton & Barto, 1998).

Optimism is costly for humans, animals, and machines alike. But this is the price we have to pay to acquire knowledge about the world and our place in it. Using the garden-metaphor from Candide, before deciding to cultivate our garden, we need to decide on where to settle, what plants to grow, and how to cultivate them. We also need to find a marketplace and customers for our produce. Gardening requires a substantial exploration. Optimistic people would be more likely to engage in these explorations and, in the process, become better gardeners.

Consistent with the idea that optimism is evolutionarily advantageous is the fact that excessive optimism tends to be a sign of good mental health (Taylor & Brown, 1988; Leary, 2007). Indeed, only (mildly) depressed individuals tend to exhibit correct perceptions of reality (Strunk et al., 2006). In contrast, overly optimistic people feel hopeful even in the face of adversity (Janoff-Bulman & Brickman, 1982; Schulz et al., 1996).

The optimism bias also displays patterns that are consistent with exploration. For example, the bias is stronger for negative events, i.e. people are more likely to underestimate the likelihood of negative events than to overestimate the likelihood of positive events (Gouveia & Clarke, 2001; Gold & Martyn, 2016). While the overestimation of positive events could improve one's self-esteem, the underestimation of negative events can encourage novelty-seeking and risk-taking behavior when they are needed the most (Shepperd et al., 2002). Thus, the asymmetry of the optimism bias supports the idea that it promotes exploration.

If optimism biases have evolved to encourage exploration, then they must be more prevalent when people have more control in a situation. There is extensive evidence that this is the case (Weinstein, 1980; Harris, 1996; Klein & Helweg-Larsen, 2002). For example, people are more likely to think that they will not be harmed in a car accident if they are driving the vehicle (Harris, 1996). Along these lines, academic research also shows that while optimistic people are more likely to divorce, they are also more likely to remarry (Puri & Robinson, 2007).

Overconfidence

Do you think that you are a better driver than the average person? If the answer is yes, then you are in a big company. A study from the 1980s shows that 88% of American drivers think that their driving abilities are better than average (Svenson, 1981). Numerous subsequent studies have confirmed that most people believe themselves to be better than average across a wide range of activities, or to be overconfident (Buehler et al., 1994; Presson & Benassi, 1996; Kruger & Dunning, 1999).

The evolutionary benefits of overconfidence are unclear. Many have argued that since overconfident individuals are prone to mistakes, they could incur losses to themselves and others. Social psychologist Scott Plous comments that "[n]o problem in judgment and decision making is more prevalent and more potentially catastrophic than overconfidence" (Plous, 1993). Indeed, overconfidence has been often blamed for disasters, poor executive decisions, and stock market bubbles.

For example, the Deepwater Horizon oil spill, the largest marine oil spill in history, was attributed to executive overconfidence. The disaster happened on April 20, 2010 and was caused by an explosion on the Deepwater Horizon oil rig leased by the oil company BP. The rig was situated in the Gulf of Mexico, around 40 miles off the coast of Louisiana. The oil spill released more than 130 million gallons of oil into the ocean, creating a surface oil slick about the size of the state of Virginia.[1] In September of 2010, BP released findings from its own internal investigation. The report concluded that human judgment and ignored warnings about potential problems by team leaders overseeing the project contributed to the disaster.

Overconfidence could also account for bad corporate acquisitions (Hayward & Hambrick, 1997; Malmendier & Tate, 2005). Companies often make bids to acquire other companies. Upon the public announcement of the bid, however, the stock price of the bidding firm usually reacts negatively. Given that the average acquisition destroys value for the shareholders of the acquiring company, it is unclear why managers keep overpaying for assets that do not benefit their enterprise. Inflated self-confidence of chief executive officers (or hubris) seems a plausible explanation. In this context, the famed investor Warren Buffett once compared corporate mergers to the princess from the fairy tale *The Frog Prince* by the Brothers Grimm. Buffett said that many corporate acquirers think of themselves as beautiful princesses, sure that their kisses can turn toads into handsome princes. The acquirers pay substantial premiums over market value, believing that they can turn a failing company into a successful one and "release

[1] See https://www.britannica.com/event/Deepwater-Horizon-oil-spill.

the imprisoned prince." But, as Buffett comments, thus far "[w]e've observed many kisses but very few miracles" (1981 Berkshire Hathaway Annual Report).

Excessive confidence could also account for the high trading volume in capital markets (Odean, 1998; Statman et al., 2006) and the formation of financial bubbles (Daniel et al., 1998; Scheinkman & Xiong, 2003). According to Scheinkman and Xiong, overconfidence, or the belief of an investor that his or her information is more accurate than it is, generates disagreement in the market about the value of a stock. The disagreement encourages people to pay prices that exceed their own stock valuations because they believe that in the future, they will find a buyer willing to pay even more. This leads to stock market bubbles, or extremely high valuations that are difficult to sustain. Such high valuations are inevitably followed by stock market crashes.

While overconfidence usually has a bad connotation in economics, there is overwhelming evidence that it correlates positively with exploration. Let's take entrepreneurship as an example. Most new ventures are destined to fail. For example, Dunne et al. (1988) estimate that more than 60% of all entrants exit within 5 years, and most of these exits are failures. Moskowitz and Vissing-Jorgensen (2002) also find that the returns on private equity are not higher than the returns on public equity, even though private equity investors are poorly diversified. In the harsh reality of entrepreneurship, overconfidence could be the main factor sustaining entrepreneurial activity. Consistent with this idea, Camerer & Lovallo (1999) show that overconfidence is related to the persistently high rates of entrepreneurial entry. Koellinger et al. (2007) also find that entrepreneurial activity is related to the entrepreneur's belief that (s)he possesses sufficient skills, knowledge, and ability to start a business.

Confidence is also positively related to individual willingness to take risks and participate in competitive interactions, and extreme confidence intensifies these effects. Overconfident people are also more likely to participate in voluntary organizations, political parties, and the signing of petitions (Pirinsky, 2013). These findings are particularly interesting considering the theories on human cooperation. Rational economic models suggest that self-interested people would under-participate in cooperative interactions even when it is socially beneficial due to a free-rider problem (Axelrod, 1997). This idea is well illustrated in the paradox of voting first introduced by Downs (1957). The paradox states that since in a general election the probability that a single vote can affect the outcome is small, citizens would have no rational reason to vote. The fact that overconfident citizens are more likely to vote suggests that they could overestimate their ability to influence the political process. Thus, overconfidence could also explain some of the human propensity for cooperation.

Illusion of Control

The illusion of control refers to the tendency of people to overestimate their ability to control events. Even when something is a matter of chance, people tend to believe that they can influence its outcome (Thompson et al., 1998).

The term "illusion of control" was introduced by Langer (1975). In her original paper, she conducted a series of experiments on the subject. In each experiment, participants had to participate in games governed by chance, such as card games and lotteries. Langer found that people's confidence in their chances of winning was influenced by their degree of involvement in the game, even if the involvement had no impact on the probability of success. For example, people became more confident in their odds of winning a lottery if they had more time to think about it. Numerous subsequent laboratory experiments and observed behaviors have confirmed this effect (Plous, 1993; Presson & Benassi, 1996).

The illusion of control bias also exhibits patterns consistent with the idea that it promotes exploration. For example, being in a position of power strengthens the illusion of control (Fast et al., 2009). Being in a position of power, however, inevitably puts more responsibility on people to explore (and exploit) their environment. Along similar lines, existing evidence also suggests that people are more likely to develop an illusion of control if they are personally affected by the random outcome (Yarritu et al., 2014).

The illusion of control exhibits an interesting asymmetry. Although people are likely to overestimate their control when they don't have it, they also tend to underestimate their control when they have it (Gino et al., 2011). People are more likely to have more control over explored aspects of their lives. For example, you would feel more in control of your dinner choice if you were in a familiar restaurant versus a restaurant that you have never visited before. By downplaying control in explored and familiar situations, people are effectively making unexplored and unfamiliar situations look relatively more attractive.

Sometimes people attempt to gain control by transferring responsibility to more capable or "luckier" others, even when it comes to events of pure chance (or gamble). This phenomenon is called illusion of control by proxy, and it is also difficult to reconcile with rational behavior (Wohl & Enzle, 2009). Illusion of control by proxy, however, encourages people to explore the environment by engaging in random actions (see Chap. 5).

Planning Fallacy

The Sydney Opera House is one of the world's most distinctive buildings and widely regarded as a masterpiece of twentieth-century architecture. Interestingly, its construction is also regarded as one of the greatest management failures in history. The building was initially planned on an AUD 7 million budget for a 4-year completion period. It ended up costing more than AUD 102 million, and it took more than 14 years to complete. The project was completed 10 years late and 1.357% over budget (Jones, 2006). One of the greatest achievements of modern architecture was also one of the greatest mismanagements in modern history. Perhaps this is not a coincidence!?

In 1957, the Australian government organized a contest to select an architect for its future "National Opera House." The competition was won by Danish architect Jorn Utzon. He proposed a dramatic design envisioning the building as a collection of interlocking white "shells" overlooking the Sydney Harbor. The implementation of the original design required a brand-new approach to construction, and none of the parties involved had a clear idea about the construction process at the time. Even Utzon himself was surprised to learn that he had won the competition.

Utzon delivered beautiful designs for both the external and internal spaces, and the team started working on their implementation. The construction, however, did not go as smoothly as planned. The project launched with no finalized execution strategy. Shortly after that, the government officials of New South Wales decided that the building needed to contain four theaters instead of the originally planned two. This created tension between the government officials and the design team, which exacerbated over time. Emerging technical engineering issues resulted in a series of delays and setbacks. After Robert Askin, a vocal critic of the project, became the new Premier of New South Wales in 1965, things got worse.[2] The escalating conflicts led to the resignation of Utzon on February 28, 1966. Although he was appointed later as a design consultant, his departure likely slowed the project even further.[3] The Sydney Opera House was finally completed on October 20, 1973.

The Sydney Opera House experience is not unusual. It represents another type of positive illusion in which people underestimate the time and resources needed to complete a future task. It is called planning fallacy (Kahneman & Tversky, 1979). There is also significant experimental evidence on planning fallacies. For example, Buehler et al. (2002) conducted an experiment with college students asking them to estimate how long it would take them to finish their senior theses. The average estimate was 33.9 days, while the average actual completion time was 55.5 days, with only 30% of the students completing their thesis in the amount of time they predicted.

In line with other positive illusions, the planning fallacy also encourages exploration because an individual who is planning optimistically would consider taking on more projects than an individual who is planning realistically. Indeed, this might be the main reason the planning fallacy exists. Consistent with this interpretation is the fact that the bias only affects predictions about one's own tasks. When outside observers predict task completion times, they tend to exhibit pessimistic bias and overestimate the time needed (Buehler et al., 1995). This asymmetry suggests that planning fallacies do not reflect cognitive limitations and could be, at least in part, strategically motivated.

If the Sydney Opera project had been assessed correctly, very likely it would not have been selected because it would have been considered too risky and expensive. The design competition received 233 entries, representing architects from 32 countries. Without planning fallacy, perhaps a more conventional and reasonably priced project would have been selected. Indeed, the website of the Opera House states "The Sydney Opera House exists because a few brave people dared to think differently. From conception to completion, the building tested the limits of engineering, construction and design."

[2] *See* Farrelly, Elizabeth (30 November 2008). "High noon at Bennelong Point." Archived from the original on 7 August 2015. Retrieved 3 December 2014.

[3] *See* Murray, Peter (2004). The Saga of the Sydney Opera House. London: Spon Press.

The Sydney Opera House is not simply an interesting building. It profoundly transformed modern architecture by opening the way for complex geometric forms, computer-aided design, and reinforced concrete structures.[4] In June 2007, the Sydney Opera House was included on the UNESCO World Heritage List as one of the most outstanding places on Earth. Without positive illusions, the Sydney skyline, and possibly the world, would have been far less exciting.

Concepts

Positive illusions and exploration. *Positive illusions are unrealistically favorable beliefs about one's circumstances or abilities. It is hypothesized that they are an effective way for incentivizing exploration in life. There are four well-documented psychological biases within the positive illusions category: optimism bias, overconfidence, illusion of control, and planning fallacy.*

Optimism bias. *A cognitive condition that causes people to believe that they are more likely to experience positive events and less likely to experience negative events in life than they actually are.*

Overconfidence. *Excessive confidence in one's abilities or judgment.*

Illusion of control. *The tendency of people to overestimate their ability to control events. The concept "illusion of control by proxy" refers to allowing another person to make decisions (or gamble) on one's behalf simply because they are perceived as luckier.*

Planning fallacy. *A cognitive bias that causes people to underestimate the time and resources they would need to complete a task.*

Superstitions. *Widely held beliefs that are considered to be irrational or supernatural. Many of them are effective tools for the creation of positive illusions—for example, by offering protection and good luck.*

[4] Geddes, Robert (2013). Watson, Anne (ed.). Building a Masterpiece: The Sydney Opera House. Sydney: Powerhouse Press. p. 56.

Religion and Exploration

Religion is a complex phenomenon dating back to the origin of human civilization. It encompasses a wide set of values, beliefs, and worldviews shared by most members of a group. Religious experiences tend to enhance life satisfaction and personal happiness. Research has identified numerous beneficial aspects of religiosity, such as enhanced social integration and support, the encouragement of mindfulness and self-reflection, and the provision of structure and purpose in one's life (Ellison, 1991). I argue that another important benefit of religiosity is that it promotes exploration in life.

The cross-sectional and time-series patterns in religiosity support the idea that it facilitates explanatory activities. Indeed, individuals who are less prone to exploration are more likely to be religious. For example, Miller and Hoffmann (1995) report a negative correlation between religiosity (measured by church attendance and a subjective rating of religion's importance in one's life) and self-reported attitudes toward risk-taking behavior. Osoba (2003) finds that risk avoidance and church attendance are positively correlated, while Dehejia et al. (2005) show that religious participants have less volatile income streams. There is also evidence that religious individuals tend to be more politically conservative (Davis, 2018).

Hilary and Hui (2009) use archival data from the European Social Survey and find that respondent religiosity correlates *positively* with their perceived importance of "living in safe and secure surroundings" and *negatively* with their perceived importance of "thinking about new ideas" and "trying new and different things in life." The authors also find that the positive link between individual religiosity and risk avoidance influences organizational behavior. Specifically, firms located in counties with higher levels of religiosity display lower degrees of risk exposure than firms located in counties with lower levels of religiosity.

Religious faith also tends to intensify during times of adversity and extreme uncertainty. For example, people regularly turn to the supernatural or the spiritual after experiencing major events that are beyond their control (Aten et al., 2019). Furthermore, religiosity intensifies following adversities, such as earthquakes (Bentzen, 2019), war-related violence (Henrich et al., 2019), and mass shootings (Roman et al., 2019). Frijters et al. (2024) cite Pargament (1997), who in his book The Psychology of Religion and Coping, states that "[t]here may be no better laboratory for studying and learning about religion in its most palpable forms than times of crisis and coping." It is also exactly during these times of crisis when exploration is needed the most.

Superstition

If positive illusions are beneficial, then mechanisms would emerge to supply them. Here, I argue that some superstitious beliefs could be such mechanisms.

Superstition is a multi-faceted phenomenon that includes a wide range of activities and practices. The Merriam Webster dictionary defines superstition as "a belief or practice resulting from ignorance, fear of the unknown, trust in magic or chance, or a false conception of causation." A subset of these beliefs promotes a more optimistic approach to life.

All cultures around the world have their own symbols and rituals for good luck. For example, the gesture of *crossing one's fingers* for luck or protection against misfortune is deeply ingrained in numerous cultures. While the gesture resembles the Cross of Christ, many believe that it originated during pre-Christian times in Western Europe (Marolt, 2006). *Knocking on wood* is another superstition for attracting good luck and/or for protection against the evil. In the West, people could ward off evil by *tossing salt* over their shoulders. Most cultures also believe that certain numbers have special meaning or significance. For example, the number 7 is considered a lucky symbol in Christian-influenced cultures, while the number 8 is considered lucky in Chinese-influenced cultures.

Another way of promoting good luck is through the possession of objects believed to confer protection upon their possessor. Such objects are commonly known as amulets, good luck charms, or phylactery. Amulets are widely used in most cultures and religions traditions, and include objects such as coins, plant or animal parts, and written words (Gonzalez-Wippler, 1991).

There is evidence that people who believe in good luck are more optimistic and satisfied with their lives, while people who believe that they are unlucky are less satisfied and less likely to take advantage of opportunities (Maltby et al., 2008). As advocated earlier, optimism encourages people to explore their environment. Thus, seemingly irrational superstitions could be beneficial, and this might be the reason they have survived the test of time.

Negative Illusions

While the inherited PEX is expected to be below optimal levels, there are situations where it could become abnormally high. Such situations are more likely to occur following long periods of abundance and prosperity. The available resources and the low-risk environment would naturally prompt people to explore more (a la Charnov, 1976). When opportunities shrink and uncertainty increases, however, people will realize that their inherited PEX is abnormally high. In such cases, people are expected to develop negative illusions and beliefs discouraging exploration.

The above conjecture is supported by the US experience during the Great Depression. The economy in the years leading up to the Great Depression was characterized by significant growth and numerous technological innovations (e.g., electricity and the telephone). Since the returns to exploration during this period were high, people became accustomed to it; their propensity for exploration increased. There is extensive evidence, however, that the Great Depression created a long-lasting shift toward more conservative economic behavior (Friedman & Schwartz, 1963). For example, Malmendier et al. (2011) show that CEOs who grew up during the Great Depression are reluctant to borrow and rely excessively on internal finance. Along similar lines, Malmendier and Nagel (2011) also find that individuals who have experienced low stock market returns are less likely to participate in the stock market and are more pessimistic about future stock returns. The pessimistic beliefs that emerged during the Great Depression served as a correction to the legacy of economic optimism. The emerging pessimism was fine-tuning individual propensity for exploration toward more optimal levels.

Conclusion

Exploration is inherently dangerous, and the risks of over-exploration are expected to outweigh the risks of under-exploration. As a result, the forces of natural selection would under-incentivize exploration genetically. In response, people are expected to develop alternative ways of motivating exploration. One effective mechanism for incentivizing exploration is the adoption of an unrealistically positive outlook on the outcomes of the exploration process (positive illusions). Positive illusions encompass a wide range of behavioral biases such as excessive optimism, overconfidence, the illusion of control, and others.

This chapter presents evidence that positive illusions incentivize exploration. By being unrealistically positive about the unknown, optimistic individuals are more likely to make costly mistakes. However, one important advantage of these biases is that they allow people to explore aspects of the environment they know very little about. Numerous well-documented patterns of these biases support this interpretation. Any belief structure that allows people to maintain a more positive outlook in life would have the same benefits. The chapter argues that, by offering a sense of meaning, purpose, and security, religious faith and some superstitious beliefs could also promote exploration.

References

Aten, J. D., Smith, W. R., Davis, E. B., Van Tongeren, D. R., Hook, J. N., Davis, D. E., Shannonhouse, L., DeBlaere, C., Ranter, J., O'Grady, K., & Hill, P. C. (2019). The psychological study of religion and spirituality in a disaster context: A systematic review. *Psychological Trauma: Theory, Research, Practice, and Policy*, *11*(6), 597–613.

Axelrod, R. (1997). *The complexity of cooperation*. Princeton University Press.

Bentzen, J. (2019). Acts of god? Religiosity and natural disasters across subnational world districts. *Economic Journal*, *129*(622), 2295–2321.

Buehler, R., Griffin, D., & Ross, M. (1994). Exploring the "planning fallacy": Why people underestimate their task completion times. *Journal of Personality and Social Psychology*, *67*, 366–381.

Buehler, R., Griffin, D., & Ross, M. (1995). It's about time: Optimistic predictions in work and love. *European Review of Social Psychology*, *6*(1), 1–32.

Buehler, R., Griffin, D., & Ross, M. (2002). Inside the planning fallacy: The causes and consequences of optimistic time predictions. *Heuristics and Biases: The Psychology of Intuitive Judgment*, 250–270.

Camerer, C., & Lovallo, D. (1999). Overconfidence and excess entry: An experimental approach. *American Economic Review*, *89*, 306–318.

Charnov, E. L. (1976). Optimal foraging, the marginal value theorem. *Theoretical Population Biology*, *9*(2), 129–136.

Daniel, K., Hirshleifer, D., & Subrahmanyam, A. (1998). Investor psychology and security market under-and overreactions. *Journal of Finance*, *53*(6), 1839–1885.

Davis, N. T. (2018). Religion and partisan-ideological sorting, 1984–2016. *Social Science Quarterly*, *99*(4), 1446–1466.

Dehejia, R., DeLeire, T., & Luttmer, E. (2005). Insuring consumption and happiness through religious organizations. NBER Working Paper no. 11576.

Downs, A. (1957). *An economic theory of democracy*. Harper and Row.

Dunne, T., Roberts, M., & Samuelson, L. (1988). Patterns of firm entry and exit in US manufacturing industries. *Rand Journal of Economics, 19*, 495–515.

Ellison, C. G. (1991). Religious involvement and subjective well-being. *Journal of Health and Social Behavior*, 80–99.

Fast, N. J., Gruenfeld, D. H., Sivanathan, N., & Galinsky, A. D. (2009). Illusory control: A generative force behind power's far-reaching effects. *Psychological Science, 20*(4), 502–508.

Friedman, M., & Schwartz, A. J. (1963). *A Monetary History of the United States, 1867–1960.* Princeton: Princeton University Press.

Frijters, P., Johnston, D. W., Knott, R. J., & Torgler, B. (2024). Importance of religion after adversity. *Journal for the Scientific Study of Religion, 63*(1), 62–75.

Gino, F., Sharek, Z., & Moore, D. A. (2011). Keeping the illusion of control under control: Ceilings, floors, and imperfect calibration. *Organizational Behavior and Human Decision Processes, 114*(2), 104–114.

Gold, R. S., & Martyn, K. (2016). Event valence and unrealistic optimism. *Psychological Reports, 92*(3_suppl), 1105–1109. https://doi.org/10.2466/pr0.2003.92.3c.1105

Gonzalez-Wippler, M. (1991). Complete book of Amulets and Talismans. *Sourcebook Series St.*. Lewellyn Publications. ISBN 978-0-87542-287-9

Gouveia, S. O., & Clarke, V. (2001). Optimistic bias for negative and positive events. *Health Education, 101*(5), 228–234. https://doi.org/10.1108/09654280110402080

Harding, E. J., Paul, E. S., & Mendl, M. (2004). Cognitive bias and affective state. *Nature, 427*, 312.

Harris, P. (1996). Sufficient grounds for optimism? The relationship between perceived controllability and optimistic bias. *Journal of Social and Clinical Psychology, 15*(1), 9–52. https://doi.org/10.1521/jscp.1996.15.1.9

Hayward, M. L., & Hambrick, D. C. (1997). Explaining the premiums paid for large acquisitions: Evidence of CEO hubris. *Administrative Science Quarterly, 42*, 103–127.

Hilary, G., & Hui, K. W. (2009). Does religion matter in corporate decision making in America? *Journal of Financial Economics, 93*(3), 455–473.

Janoff-Bulman, R., & Brickman, P. (1982). Expectations and what people learn from failure. In N. T. Feather (Ed.), *Expectations and action: Expectancy-value models in psychology* (pp. 207–272). Erlbaum.

Jones, P. (2006). *Ove Arup: Masterbuilder of the twentieth century.* Yale University Press.

Joseph, H., Bauer, M., Cassar, A., Chytilová, J., & Purzycki, B. G. (2019). War increases religiosity. *Nature Human Behaviour, 3*(2), 129–135.

Kahneman, D., & Tversky, A. (1979). Intuitive prediction: Biases and corrective procedures. *Management Science, 12*, 313–327.

Klein, C. T., & Helweg-Larsen, M. (2002). Perceived control and the optimistic bias: A meta-analytic review. *Psychology and Health, 17*(4), 437–446.

Koellinger, P., Minniti, M., & Schade, C. (2007). I think I can, I think I can: Overconfidence and entrepreneurial behavior. *Journal of Economic Psychology, 28*, 502–527.

Kruger, J., & Dunning, D. (1999). Unskilled and unaware of it: How difficulties in recognizing one's own incompetence lead to inflated self-assessments. *Journal of Personality and Social Psychology, 77*(6), 1121.

Langer, E. J. (1975). The illusion of control. *Journal of Personality and Social Psychology, 32*(2), 311.

Leary, M. R. (2007). Motivational and emotional aspects of the self. *Annual Review of Psychology, 58*, 317–344. https://doi.org/10.1146/annurev.psych.58.110405.085658

Leibniz, G. W. (1969). The monadology, 1714. In *Gottfried Wilhelm Leibniz: Philosophical papers and letters*.

Malmendier, U., & Nagel, S. (2011). Depression babies: Do macroeconomic experiences affect risk taking? *The Quarterly Journal of Economics, 126*(1), 373–416.

Malmendier, U., & Tate, G. (2005). CEO overconfidence and corporate investment. *Journal of Finance, 60*, 2661–2700.

Malmendier, U., Tate, G., & Yan, J. (2011). Overconfidence and early-life experiences: The effect of managerial traits on corporate financial policies. *Journal of Finance, 66*(5), 1687–1733.

Maltby, J., Day, L., Gill, P., Colley, A., & Wood, A. M. (2008). Beliefs around luck: Confirming the empirical conceptualization of beliefs around luck and the development of the Darke and Freedman beliefs around luck scale. *Personality and Individual Differences, 45*(7), 655–660.

Marolt, R. (2006). *FYI-Bean counters have sexy ideas too: Histories and mysteries of words used in the office* (Vol. 1). 3-Winged Creations.

Matheson, S. M., Asher, L., & Bateson, M. (2008). Larger, enriched cages are associated with 'optimistic' response biases in captive European starlings (Sturnus vulgaris). *Applied Animal Behaviour Science, 109*(2–4), 374–383.

McKay, R. T., & Dennett, D. C. (2009). The evolution of misbelief (PDF). *Behavioral and Brain Sciences, 32*(6), 493–561. https://doi.org/10.1017/S0140525X09990975

Miller, A., & Hoffmann, J. (1995). Risk and religion: An explanation of gender differences in religiosity. *Journal for the Scientific Study of Religion, 34*, 63–75.

Moskowitz, T. J., & Vissing-Jørgensen, A. (2002). The returns to entrepreneurial investment: A private equity premium puzzle? *American Economic Review, 92*(4), 745–778.

O'Sullivan, O. P. (2015). The neural basis of always looking on the bright side. *Dialogues in Philosophy, Mental and Neuro Sciences, 8*(1), 11–15.

Odean, T. (1998). Volume, volatility, price, and profit when all traders are above average. *Journal of Finance, 53*, 1887–1934.

Osoba, B. (2003). Risk preferences and the practice of religion: Evidence from panel data. Unpublished Working Paper, West Virginia University.

Pargament, K. I. (1997). *The psychology of religion and coping: Theory, research, practice*. Guilford Press.

Pirinsky, C. (2013). Confidence and economic attitudes. *Journal of Economic Behavior and Organization, 91*, 139–158.

Plous, S. (1993). *The psychology of judgment and decision making*. S&P Global.

Presson, P. K., & Benassi, V. A. (1996). Illusion of control: A meta-analytic review. *Journal of Social Behavior and Personality, 11*, 493–510.

Puri, M., & Robinson, D. T. (2007). Optimism and economic choice. *Journal of Financial Economics, 86*(1), 71–99.

Roman, S., Luis, D. K. M., Hook, J. N., Captari, L. E., Aten, J. D., Davis, E. B., & Campbell, C. D. (2019). Religious support buffers the indirect negative psychological effects of mass shooting in church-affiliated individuals. *Psychological Trauma: Theory, Research, Practice, and Policy, 11*(6), 571–577.

Scheinkman, J., & Xiong, W. (2003). Overconfidence and speculative bubbles. *Journal of Political Economy, 111*, 1183–1219.

Schulz, R., Bookwala, J., Knapp, J., Scheier, M., & Williamson, G. (1996). Pessimism, age and cancer mortality. *Psychology and Ageing, 11*, 304–309.

Sharot, T. (2011). The optimism bias. *Current Biology, 21*(23), R941–R945.

Shepperd, J. A., Carroll, P., Grace, J., & Terry, M. (2002). Exploring the causes of comparative optimism. *Psychologica Belgica, 42*(1-2), 65–98.

Statman, M., Thorley, S., & Vorkink, K. (2006). Investor overconfidence and trading volume. *The Review of Financial Studies, 19*, 1531–1565.

Strunk, D. R., Lopez, H., & DeRubeis, R. J. (2006). Depressive symptoms are associated with unrealistic negative predictions of future life events. *Behaviour Research and Therapy, 44*(6), 861–882.

Sutton, R. S., & Barto, A. G. (1998). *Reinforcement learning: An introduction*. MIT Press.

Svenson, O. (1981). Are we all less risky and more skillful than our fellow drivers? *Acta Psychologica, 47*(2), 143–148.

Taylor, S. E., & Brown, J. D. (1988). Illusion and well-being: A social psychological perspective on mental health. *Psychological Bulletin, 103*(2), 193–210.

Thompson, S. C., Armstrong, W., & Thomas, C. (1998). Illusions of control, underestimations, and accuracy: A control heuristic explanation. *Psychological Bulletin, 123*(2), 143–161.

Weinstein, N. D. (1980). Unrealistic optimism about future life events. *Journal of Personality and Social Psychology, 39*(5), 806–820.

Weinstein, N. D., & Klei, W. M. (1995). Resistance of personal risk perceptions to debiasing interventions. *Health Psychology, 14*(2), 132–140. https://doi.org/10.1037/0278-6133.14.2.132

Wohl, M. J., & Enzle, M. E. (2009). Illusion of control by proxy: Placing one's fate in the hands of another. *British Journal of Social Psychology, 48*(1), 183–200.

Yarritu, I., Matute, H., & Vadillo, M. A. (2014). Illusion of control: The role of personal involvement. *Experimental Psychology, 61*(1), 38–47. https://doi.org/10.1027/1618-3169/a000225

CHAPTER 5

Randomization

So much of life, it seems to me, is determined by pure randomness.

—Sidney Poitier

Source: *The Washington Post, December 2, 1995*

Contents

Introduction

Most card games, regardless of their rules and objectives, share one common element—the shuffling of the card deck. Over the course of play, cards are often arranged in a predictable manner. Some players could further manipulate the deck to increase their winning odds.

C. A. Pirinsky, *A Theory of Dynamic Preferences*,
https://doi.org/10.1007/978-3-032-13334-2_5

These developments unfairly advantage some players at the expense of others. By destroying the emerging order in the deck, shuffling brings randomness and unpredictability to the game. This in turn reinforces the players' trust in the fairness of the game and their willingness to play.

Life has similar elements to a game of cards. It is a sequence of events that are social, competitive, and guided by specific rules. In the game of life, sometimes we win and sometimes we lose. The sequencing of events also creates structured and predictable behavioral patterns governed by habits, routines, and conventions. These patterns often skew our odds—sometimes in our favor, sometimes against us. Similarly to the shuffling of the card deck, randomization in life could even the playing field by breaking old behavioral patterns and creating new ones.

This section introduces randomization, or the act of selecting actions in a random way, as an exploration mechanism. It is contrasted with directed exploration, or the act of selecting actions based on their perceived net benefits. Although directed exploration seems superior to randomization, it has some inherent limitations. First, evaluating and comparing unexplored options is difficult and cognitively costly. Second, directed exploration is always influenced by some outside forces. Habits, conventions, and social pressures could direct choices not in the best interest of the individual making these choices. In all these cases, randomization could be a superior exploration mechanism.

The problem of exploration resembles closely the problem of sampling in statistics. It is well established that a random selection of a sample, where each member of the population has the same chance of being selected, achieves the highest degree of representativeness. Such representativeness is critical for scientific inference because it allows all sample-based conclusions to be generalized to the whole population (Harrison & List, 2004; Morgan & Winship, 2014). In the case of exploration, randomization also guarantees that explored outcomes comprise a representative subset of all available alternatives.

Operationalizing randomization, however, is challenging. Traditional randomization mechanisms, such as flipping a coin or tossing a dice, cannot be effectively employed in everyday situations. This chapter argues that people have developed alternative randomization mechanisms that could promote exploration by introducing random elements into individual choices. The chapter analyzes three such mechanisms: context-dependent choice, self-sabotaging behavior, and divination.

Directed Vs. Random Exploration

There are two general strategies for direct exploration: a directed strategy in which choices are biased toward options with greater net benefits, and a random strategy in which choices are delegated to chance (Dayan & Berridge, 2014; Otto et al., 2014; Hills et al., 2015). The ABC-model can inform an individual about when and what to explore by evaluating the relative attractiveness of new courses of action.

By factoring in the expected benefits and costs of various options, directed exploration can lead to greater long-term rewards. Directed exploration, however, has some inherent limitations. A defining characteristic of unexplored states is that we know very little about them. The scarcity of information could make the analysis and comparison of these states very difficult. Indeed, there is evidence that directed exploration is cognitively costly. For example, neuroscientists have found that directed exploration, but not random exploration, is associated with active brain activity of several prefrontal structures and systems (Zajkowski et al., 2017; Wilson et al., 2021). Directed exploration has also been linked to prefrontal dopamine, a neurotransmitter that plays a crucial role in the operation of the brain (Costa et al., 2014; Chakroun et al., 2020).

Directed exploration is always skewed by external forces. The choices of children are heavily influenced by their parents, teachers, and peers. Individual choices are also directed by habits, norms, and conventions. These influences imply that directed exploration often exhibits limited ability to generate new information. In all these cases, randomization could be a superior exploration mechanism. This is the main reason it has been used actively in machine learning. For example, in reinforcement learning, an agent could be programmed to explore by randomly sampling less-rewarding options instead of choosing the best one (greedy action). Another common technique used in stochastic optimization is to "change the temperature" of the search, using a "hotter," more random search initially to ensure exploration and gradually "cooling off" the search (Kirkpatrick et al., 1983; Cohen et al., 2007; Schulz & Gershman, 2019).

Human exploration resembles closely the search process in stochastic optimization problems. Stochastic optimization algorithms attempt to identify the maximum or minimum value of a function by trial and error (Ruder, 2016). They usually start from an arbitrary point and move in the direction of the steepest ascent or descent of the function (the gradient) around that point. The algorithm makes steps until an optimal position is reached. Gradient descent algorithms, however, can become trapped in a local minimum, a point where the function's value is lower than the values in its surroundings, yet it is not the lowest possible value (the global minimum). Similarly, gradient ascent algorithms can become trapped in a local maximum, a point where the function's value is higher than the values in its surroundings, but it is not a global maximum. Randomization is a common way of "escaping" these local traps. For example, running the optimization process multiple times with different random initializations can increase the chances of finding the global optimum.

Random exploration is expected to be more valuable when the environment is more complex and/or when the person has limited information about the outside world. For example, randomization would be more beneficial early in life. Consistent with this conjecture is the fact that children tend to engage more in random exploration than adults (Meder et al., 2021; Bonawitz et al., 2014).

It is also important to note that every exploration has elements of both directed and random exploration. On the one hand, the information used in directed exploration is imperfect, which inevitably introduces an element of noise to directed exploration. Columbus sailed away from Spain with the firm conviction that he will discover a new route to the East Indies. Instead, he encountered a whole new world. On the other hand, randomization, as simple as it seems, requires the use of a randomization mechanism. As most randomization mechanisms are imperfect, they inevitably introduce an element of direction into exploration decisions. Perhaps for these reasons, living organisms tend to use both directed and random strategies to solve the exploration–exploitation dilemma (Wilson et al., 2014).

Creating Randomness

Since the dawn of civilization, people have been interested in random phenomena. In ancient Athenian democracy, the traditional and primary method for appointing political officials was through a random allocation (sortition) (Hansen, 1999). To generate random numbers, Athenians used a special device called *kleroterion*. The practice of sortition is also widely used today: for example, for selection of the jury members in a jury trial.

Randomness is an essential element in sampling. In statistics, quality control, and survey design is important to select a representative subset of the population to estimate characteristics of the whole population. Sampling has lower costs and shorter data collection times compared to recording data from the entire population. In many cases, collecting information about the whole population is even impossible. The US Census usually uses a 5% sample interviewing 1 in 20 Americans. To be effective, however, the sample needs to be representative, and random selection may be the best way to achieve such representativeness.

Using random sampling, the French mathematician Pierre-Simon Laplace was able to estimate the population of France in 1783. He proposed a simple capture–recapture method for the estimation of the size of any population when it is impossible to count every individual (e.g., counting the number of fish in a pond). The method is based on a statistical technique utilizing two independent random samples. At the first stage, a subsample of the population is captured, marked, and released. At the second stage, another subsample of the population is captured and the number of marked individuals within the sample is counted. Since the number of marked individuals within the second sample is expected to be proportional to the number of marked individuals in the whole population, one can estimate the whole population based on the observed quantities. For example, if the size of the total population is p, the size of the first sample is m, the size of the second sample is M, and the number of marked individuals in the second sample is R, then $R/M = m/p$. From here, the total population can be estimated as $p = M * m/R$.

Laplace used the same method to estimate the total population of France (see Amorós, 2014). Instead of physically "capturing" people, he used existing lists from public registers. At that time, every community in France recorded the number of newborn children each year. This was his first sample—newborn babies. A few communities also recorded their total population, including the number of newborn babies. This was his second sample. Based on this information, he was able to calculate that the population of France at the time was 25.29 million. In addition to the point estimate, Laplace also developed a method to estimate the accuracy of the estimate, which was a major contribution to statistics.

The accuracy of the capture-recapture method depends crucially on the randomness of the two samples. If the second subsample over- or under-weighs the number of market individuals R, then the formula would under-

or over-estimate the size of the total population. Random selection eliminates such biases and results in an unbiased estimation of the population.

Another illustration of the importance of random sampling is Gallup's success in predicting that Franklin Roosevelt will defeat Alfred Landon in the 1936 US presidential election. The company was founded one year earlier in 1935 by George Gallup. Gallup was able to successfully predict the outcome in the upcoming presidential election, in direct contradiction to the widely respected magazine *The Literary Digest*. The reason for Gallup's success was that it used a smaller but more representative sample of voters compared to The *Literary Digest's* sample. The magazine relied on a sample drawn largely from telephone directories and car registrations, which disproportionately represented wealthier voters, who were also more likely to vote Republican.

Through history, the demand for randomness has led to the development of different methods for generating random outcomes (random number generators or RNGs). RNGs are capable of generating a sequence of numbers or symbols that cannot be predicted better than by random chance. There are two approaches for generating random data—direct and indirect. The direct method generates a random outcome. Examples of direct RNGs are coin flipping, the rolling of a dice, and roulette wheels. These RNGs are still used today, mainly in games and gambling, as they tend to be too slow for most scientific applications that utilize large amounts of random data. To save time, people used to tabulate the random outcomes of these experiments in books.

The indirect generators of random numbers rely on some naturally occurring external data-generating mechanism. Many natural phenomena generate random "noise" signals. Most of them are based on some random atomic or subatomic physical phenomena whose unpredictability can be traced to the laws of quantum mechanics. Examples of such naturally occurring RNGs are the photoelectric effect, radio noise, and nuclear decay (Sunar, 2009). In all these cases, nature "flips a coin" and the observer records the outcome.

Computer applications also often rely on pseudo-random number generators. These mechanisms use computational algorithms that can produce long sequences of data. These data are, in fact, completely determined by an initial value, known as a seed value or a key. As a result, the entire seemingly random sequence can be reproduced if the seed value is known. This type of generator typically does not rely on sources of naturally occurring randomness.

How do people (and other living organisms) randomize? We cannot flip a coin or roll a dice any time we would like to engage in a random action. Human brain activity is governed by quantum laws that are inherently random. As such, it is potentially capable of generating random impulses in a controlled manner. To the best of my knowledge, existing research has not explored this possibility yet. There is evidence, however, that living organisms could utilize indirect forms of randomization that rely on some externally generated random sources. The remainder of this chapter reviews some mechanisms that could effectively incorporate random elements into individual choices.

Concepts

Random variable. *A variable whose values are numerical realizations of a random phenomenon. The likelihood of the outcomes is guided by a probability distribution, where more probable outcomes are more likely to be realized than less probable outcomes. Random variables could be either discrete or continuous, depending on whether they take discrete or continuous values.*

Randomization. *The process of choosing an option based on a random criterion.*

Directed exploration. *An exploration strategy evaluating the costs and benefits of various exploration options and directing the exploration toward the best option.*

Random exploration. *An exploration strategy that makes a random choice among various exploration options.*

Context-dependent choice. *A choice guided by preferences where the attractiveness (reward) of a particular option may change depending on what other options are available, or the "context."*

Self-sabotaging behavior. *A behavior where someone acts not in their best interest. Self-sabotaging decisions can be either conscious or subconscious.*

Divination. *The practice of seeking knowledge of the future or the unknown by supernatural means.*

Context-Dependent Choice

A body of work spanning neuroscience, economics, and psychology suggests that decision-making is context-dependent, which means that the perceived value of an option depends on the other options in the choice set, or the "context" (Otto et al., 2022). As an illustration, an individual could prefer A to B, when an option C is added to the mix; but B to A, when an option D is added to the mix. This generates inconsistent behavior, which is often interpreted as irrational. Context-dependent choice, however, could effectively promote exploration by introducing a random element to everyday choices. Below, I analyze two well-documented context-effects: the decoy effect and the framing effect.

The decoy effect is a cognitive bias that occurs when the addition of a dominated alternative to the opportunity set strictly increases the choice probability of superior alternatives (Dhar & Glazer, 1996; Pettibone & Wedell, 2000). For example, a person might prefer buying a medium coffee for \$1.80 instead of a large coffee for \$2.00. However, when a small coffee is added to the list for the price of \$1.00, the person could decide to buy the large coffee instead. The reason is that the third option makes the price differential between the first two options look smaller. As a result, people feel that they are making a logical choice by choosing the more expensive of the original two options. There is also evidence that the addition of a more valuable "distractor" item tends to decrease individuals' propensity to choose the highest-valued item (Louie et al., 2013; Chau et al. 2020). The reason is that the best option does not look as attractive in the company of other good options as it does in the company of more inferior options.

One interesting examination of the decoy effect in a non-experimental setting is provided by Otto et al. (2022). They look at restaurant ratings on Yelp, a web-based application for crowd-sourced reviews of local businesses. The authors observe that the likelihood that a user chooses the highest-rated option among similar restaurants in an area increases as a function of the difference between the highest-rated option and the second-highest-rated option. This means that people take ratings into consideration when choosing a restaurant. However, the authors also find that users make fewer ratings-maximizing choices in choice sets with more high-rated options. In other words, more valuable "distractor" items make the highest-valued items less attractive. This is the decoy effect.

Context-dependent choice is widespread in the animal kingdom as well (Li & Yu, 2018). The decoy effect has been documented in animal experiments involving hummingbirds, honeybees, gray jays, starlings, and even plasmodial slime molds (Hurly & Oseen, 1999; Shafir et al., 2002; Bateson, 2002; Latty & Beekman, 2011). Animal choice experiments typically present an animal with a set of mutually exclusive food options and record its consumption choice. For example, in the mold experiment, unicellular, slime mold *Physarum polycephalum* was offered a choice between food options that varied in food quality and light exposure (the mold is photophobic). Researchers observed that *Physarum polycephalum*'s preference for a focal alternative increased when a third, inferior quality option was added to the choice set, i.e., the mold decision exhibited a decoy effect.

The discovery of contextual effects in phylogenetically distant species suggests that this behavior is likely to serve a common purpose. Exploration could be one such purpose. More valuable alternatives (distractor-items) make exploration less costly and living organisms— more likely to explore these options. The choice among the distractor items, however, is generally affected by arbitrary random factors. Thus, context-dependent choice promotes random exploration. In contrast, if the alternatives are relatively poor, they would make the best option (and exploitation) relatively more attractive. Indeed, there is evidence that context-dependent choice promotes exploration in the context of animal foraging (Hurly & Oseen, 1999; Bateson, 2002; Li & Yu, 2018).

The next example of context-dependent choice is framing. It is about choosing among risky alternatives. Every choice has uncertainty embedded into it. Since the options we consider and our circumstances are never the same, the rewards associated with our choices are always uncertain. Uncertain quantities are generally modeled with random variables specifying the possible outcomes and their corresponding probabilities. Based on this information, one could form an expectation about the corresponding quantity and how uncertain or risky this expectation is.

Let's consider a random outcome that could take both positive and negative values with certain probabilities. For example, if you make an investment, it could generate either a profit or a loss. The framing-effect states that people avoid risk when the outcome of a decision is framed as a gain but prefer risk when the outcome of the decisions is framed as a loss. The problem was originally demonstrated by Tversky & Kahneman (1981) in an experiment where participants were asked to "imagine that the U.S. is preparing for the outbreak of an unusual Asian disease, which is expected to kill 600 people." Two alternative programs to combat the disease have been proposed. The first group of participants was presented with a choice between programs A and B, as follows:

Program A: "200 people will be saved"
Program B: "there is a 1/3 probability that 600 people will be saved, and a 2/3 probability that no people will be saved"

In this experiment, 72% of participants preferred program A (the remainder, 28%, opting for program B). The second group of participants was presented with the choice between programs C and D as follows:

Program C: "400 people will die"
Program D: "there is a 1/3 probability that nobody will die, and a 2/3 probability that 600 people will die"

In this decision frame, 78% preferred program D, with the remaining 22% opting for program C.

Programs A and C are identical, as are programs B and D. People generally preferred the certain outcome when it was positively framed, thus offering an assurance of gains. People were more likely to gamble when the certain outcome was negatively framed, thus offering an assurance of a loss. As a result, this type of behavior is often described as loss aversion.

The framing effect has also been documented among animals. For example, Marsh & Kacelnik (2002) tested an analogous scenario with starlings. They found that, like humans, the birds preferred the risky option in the loss condition and therefore exhibited an effect of framing. Chen et al. (2006) found similar results with capuchin monkeys (Cebus apella).

Exploration also provides a useful lens to look at the framing effect. The effect states that when an alternative is framed positively (in terms of a gain or benefit), people would be less likely to take risks. Conversely, when an alternative is framed negatively (in terms of a loss or danger), people would be more likely to take risks. Most frames in life are not strategically manipulated by a scientist and occur naturally. Since bad outcomes would tend to frame our circumstances more negatively, the framing effect suggests that people are more likely to take risks and explore uncertain outcomes when confronted with bad outcomes. The value of exploration is also expected to be more valuable in these circumstances. So, while the framing effect would appear irrational in a carefully designed experiment, it could be an optimal response in the natural course of events because it promotes exploration.

Self-Sabotaging Behavior

People often engage in self-sabotaging behavior, or actions that undermine their long-term goals and aspirations. This section argues that self-sabotaging decisions also could facilitate exploration in life. Indeed, every act of exploring the unknown, instead of choosing the best available alternative, is a self-sabotaging act. Below, I elaborate on one popular case of self-sabotaging behaviors—procrastination.

Procrastination refers to the act of voluntarily delaying something even when there are negative consequences for doing so. The term originates from the Latin verb "procrastinare," which means "to put off or postpone until another day" (Wilson & Nguyen, 2012). The evidence of procrastination is abundant. Most college students engage in procrastination, and almost 50% procrastinate consistently (Schouwenburg, 2004; Day et al., 2000). The problem extends far beyond the college classroom, however, as procrastination chronically affects 20–25% of adults (e.g., Wilson & Nguyen, 2012).

The causes and consequences of procrastination are not well understood. Some authors have emphasized the negative side of procrastination. For example, research has established a significant negative correlation between self-reported procrastination and health (Klingsieck, 2013). People themselves often characterize procrastination as harmful (Steel, 2007).

There is evidence, however, that procrastination exhibits a series of beneficial effects. First, procrastination could boost creativity (Shin & Grant, 2021). The reason is that procrastination allows the brain to explore the task and creatively recombine different approaches. Second, procrastination could allow the decision maker to accumulate more relevant information (Chen & Qu, 2017). There is also evidence that moderate stress levels are productive. Given that procrastination can intensify stress, it could enhance productivity (Demeter & Davis, 2013; Corbett, 2015). A simple self-reflection also suggests that when we are time constrained, we tend to engage more cognitive resources to complete a task.

When we are presented with a task, we could start working on it right away and exploit existing knowledge. This is an exploitative approach to the problem. Instead of doing that, however, a person could dedicate time to the exploration of alternative ideas. This process could be subconscious. Thus, by procrastinating, people free up time for explorative ideas. Procrastination could promote exploration.

There is also interesting evidence that sabotaging behavior within groups can enhance group creativity. For example, by delaying collective decisions, dissent can increase the number of exploratory options considered in a group (Nemeth & Wachtler, 1983). The presence of uninformed individuals in a group could also inhibit the ability of a powerful minority to manipulate the group (Couzin et al., 2011). In the latter case, uniformed individuals naturally randomize the decision of the group, which in turn promotes exploration.

Divination

Throughout history, people have been relying on signs, prophecies, and omens to direct the course of their lives. These activities are commonly referred to as divination. More formally, the Meriam-Webster Dictionary defines divination as "the art or practice that seeks to foresee or foretell future events or discover hidden knowledge usually by the interpretation of omens or by the aid of supernatural powers."

Divination has been an extremely common practice throughout history (Flad, 2008; Boyer, 2020). Farmers have used divination to decide where and when to plant their crops (Fiskesjö, 2017). Kings, presidents, and celebrities have long used divination to guide their decisions (Chou, 1979). Even today, many people continue to seek guidance in life from horoscopes, card readings, and other divination practices.

Divination is often dedicated to people (diviners), which are generally perceived as "skilled" in the craft. People also carefully discriminate among diviners according to perceived skill, ability, or success (Hong & Henrich, 2021). For example, Princess Diana frequently sought advice from the fortune teller Sally Morgan. The American president Ronald Reagan used an astrologer named Joanne Quigley to advise him on important policy decisions. The actor Brad Pitt has been regularly consulting the psychic Ron Bard to gain insight into his life and relationships.

Divination does not always rely on a diviner. It takes many forms, including inferring meaning from yarrow sticks (I-Ching), inquiring about one's fate through the position of the stars and planets at the time of one's birth (astrology), or deciphering gods' messages from the flight patterns of birds (augury). Divination could also affect individual behavior through widely followed social norms. For example, in many cultures, horoscopes provide insights into a person's life based on seemingly random inputs such as their birth year or birthday.

From a conventional perspective, divination practices appear striking because they do not seem to generate accurate information or forecasts based on our understanding of the causal structure of reality. Some explanations proposed in the literature are that divination could be a way to claim political legitimacy and power (Flad, 2008), reduce anxiety (Kracke, 1992), resolve disputes (Burkert, 1985), or express intuitions (Struck, 2016). Many of these effects, however, make sense only if people place some faith in the validity of the divination practice. Yet, divination often appears completely random.

The mere purpose of divination, however, could be to incorporate randomness into individual decisions. Some recurrent features of divination suggest that it could be used to promote exploration through randomization. For example, divination is called upon in major life choices when conventional actions do not seem promising. Our decisions are ultimately constrained by what we know, and what we can do. Often, this might not be enough to direct us toward a promising alternative. In all these cases, it might be beneficial to delegate some decisions to chance and divination accomplishes exactly that.

Randomness and Fairness

Through history, randomness has been fundamentally linked to fairness. For example, in Athenian democracy, the traditional and primary method for appointing political officials was through a random allocation (sortition). The Athenians believed that since elections tend to favor candidates with greater status or popularity, they contradict the principle of equal rights for all citizens (Hansen, 1999). The random allotment of positions also served as a deterrent to vote-buying and corruption, as it made it impossible to predict who would be elected. For all these reasons, Athenians viewed random allocations to public office as fairer and more democratic than elections.

It is not surprising that sortition spread through history, and it is widely used even today. The selection of the members of a jury during a jury trial uses randomization. Courts compile a representative list of potential jurors from various public records. This jury pool is commonly referred to as the *venire*. Afterward, potential jurors are randomly selected from the venire and notified to appear in court on a specific date. Public charter schools also commonly use lotteries to select their students when they are oversubscribed. This randomness provides researchers a tool for evaluating the effectiveness of charter schools by comparing the performance of randomly admitted with randomly not-admitted students (Chabrier et al., 2016).

The fairness embedded in random selection highlights an important advantage of randomization as an exploration mechanism—it is unbiased and immune to influence. Directed exploration could be skewed by existing circumstances. It is also vulnerable to influences from outside forces. Manipulation involves influencing another person's actions or thoughts for personal gain. Some manipulations are direct. For example, a person could use guilt, emotional blackmail, or false promises to get someone to do something they wouldn't otherwise choose to do. Other manipulations are more subtle and could exploit certain psychological vulnerabilities. For example, highlighting certain features of a product or service while downplaying others could influence consumers' choice (Thaler & Sunstein, 2009). Thus, an exploration decision guided by an advertiser might not be as useful as an exploration decision guided by chance.

In a recent study, Hakimov et al. (2021) analyze the effectiveness of various non-price-based allocation mechanisms. For example, authorities introduce online booking systems that allow appointment seekers to book in advance and avoid queues. Typically, these online booking systems are based on first-come-first-served rules. Such rules, however, are often abused by scalpers, or firms booking slots in advance and selling them to appointment seekers. The emerging black market for appointment slots defies the objective of providing equal access to the public service. The authors of the article argue that random allocation in online booking systems could effectively eliminate speculative booking practices. They propose an alternative batch system that collects applications for slots over a certain time period and then randomly allocates slots to applicants. The batch system is not vulnerable to scalping because a seeker faces the same probability of getting a slot when buying from the scalper as when applying directly, which makes the scalper intermediation useless.

Random exploration could also be an important factor for human cooperation. When people exhibit preferences to behave fairly, these preferences would prompt them to sacrifice valuable resources. Thus, it is unclear how "fair" individuals could survive in competition with self-interested individuals who keep everything for themselves. Rand et al. (2013) provide an interesting solution to this puzzle: selfish individuals are compelled to behave "fairly" when they face some (albeit completely random) chance for retaliation (see also Fowler & Christakis, 2013). This penalty does not need to come from the enforcers of the law or existing social norms. A completely random reaction of an arbitrary person would be enough to sustain cooperation in society.

Conclusion

There are two ways people can explore their environment directly. First, they could evaluate critically all available options and reach out for the best. Alternatively, they could make a random selection from a set of alternatives. Randomization has important advantages compared to directed exploration. It takes less time and effort; it is also less vulnerable to influence.

One could even make the case that randomness is a distinguishing feature of any exploration. Exploitation is predetermined by one's preferences. As such, it leaves no room for randomness. If a person knows well how they value a set of options, they will quickly identify the best alternative. Exploration is about choosing among largely unfamiliar outcomes. The lack of information makes it difficult to rank all unexplored options and choose among them. The ranking of unexplored options is also likely to be noisy. Thus, exploration always has an element of uncertainty embedded into it.

References

Amorós, J. (2014). Recapturing Laplace. *Significance, 11*(3), 38–39.

Bateson, M. (2002). Context-dependent foraging choices in risk-sensitive starlings. *Animal Behaviour, 64*(2), 251–260.

Bonawitz, E., Denison, S., Griffiths, T. L., & Gopnik, A. (2014). Probabilistic models, learning algorithms, and response variability: Sampling in cognitive development. *Trends in Cognitive Sciences, 18*(10), 497–500.

Boyer, P. (2020). Why divination? Evolved psychology and strategic interaction in the production of truth. *Current Anthropology*, *61*(1), 100–123.

Burkert, W. (1985). *Greek Religion*. Harvard University Press.

Chabrier, J., Cohodes, S., & Oreopoulos, P. (2016). What can we learn from charter school lotteries? *Journal of Economic Perspectives*, *30*(3), 57–84.

Chakroun, K., Mathar, D., Wiehler, A., Ganzer, F., & Peters, J. (2020). Dopaminergic modulation of the exploration/exploitation trade-off in human decision-making. *Elife*, *9*, e51260.

Chau, B. K., Law, C. K., Lopez-Persem, A., Klein-Flügge, M. C., & Rushworth, M. F. (2020). Consistent patterns of distractor effects during decision making. *Elife*, *9*, e53850.

Chen, B. B., & Qu, W. (2017). Life history strategies and procrastination: The role of environmental unpredictability. *Personality and Individual Differences*, *117*, 23–29.

Chen, M. K., Lakshminarayanan, V., & Santos, L. R. (2006). How basic are behavioral biases? Evidence from capuchin monkey trading behavior. *Journal of Political Economy*, *114*, 517–537.

Chou, H. H. (1979). Chinese oracle bones. *Scientific American*, *240*(4), 134–149.

Cohen, J. D., McClure, S. M., & Yu, A. J. (2007). Should I stay or should I go? How the human brain manages the trade-off between exploitation and exploration. *Philosophical Transactions of the Royal Society B: Biological Sciences*, *362* (1481), 933–942.

Corbett, M. (2015). From law to folklore: Work stress and the Yerkes-Dodson Law. *Journal of Managerial Psychology*, *30*(6), 741–752.

Costa, V. D., Tran, V. L., Turchi, J., & Averbeck, B. B. (2014). Dopamine modulates novelty seeking behavior during decision making. *Behavioral Neuroscience*, *128*(5), 556–566.

Couzin, I. D., Ioannou, C. C., Demirel, G., Gross, T., Torney, C. J., Hartnett, A., Conradt, L., Levin, S. A., & Leonard, N. E. (2011). Uninformed individuals promote democratic consensus in animal groups. *Science*, *334*(6062), 1578–1580.

Day, V., Mensink, D., & O'Sullivan, M. (2000). Patterns of academic procrastination. *Journal of College Reading and Learning*, *30*, 120–134.

Dayan, P., & Berridge, K. C. (2014). Model-based and model-free Pavlovian reward learning: Revaluation, revision, and revelation. *Cognitive, Affective, and Behavioral Neuroscience*, *14*(2), 473–492.

Demeter, D. V., & Davis, S. E. (2013). Procrastination as a tool: Exploring unconventional components of academic success. *Creative Education*, *4*(7), 144–149.

Dhar, R., & Glazer, R. (1996). Similarity in context: Cognitive representation and violation of preference and perceptual invariance in consumer choice. *Organizational Behavior and Human Decision Processes*, *67*(3), 280–293.

Fiskesjö, M. (2017). People first: The WA world of spirits and other enemies. *Anthropological Forum*, *27*, 340–364. 4

Flad, R. K. (2008). Divination and power: A multiregional view of the development of oracle bone divination in early China. *Current Anthropology*, *49*(3), 403–437.

Fowler, J. H., & Christakis, N. A. (2013). A random world is a fair world. *Proceedings of the National Academy of Sciences*, *110*(7), 2440–2441.

Hakimov, R., Heller, C. P., Kübler, D., & Kurino, M. (2021). How to avoid black markets for appointments with online booking systems. *American Economic Review*, *111*(7), 2127–2151.

Hansen, M. H. (1999). *The Athenian democracy in the age of demosthenes: Structure, principles, and ideology*. University of Oklahoma Press.

Harrison, G. W., & List, J. A. (2004). Field experiments. *Journal of Economic Literature*, *42*(4), 1009–1055.

Hills, T. T., Todd, P. M., Lazer, D., Redish, A. D., & Couzin, I. D. (2015). Exploration versus exploitation in space, mind, and society. *Trends in Cognitive Sciences*, *19*(1), 46–54.

Hong, Z., & Henrich, J. (2021). The cultural evolution of epistemic practices: The case of divination. *Human Nature*, *32*(3), 622–651.

Hurly, T. A., & Oseen, M. D. (1999). Context-dependent, risk-sensitive foraging preferences in wild rufous hummingbirds. *Animal Behaviour*, *58*(1), 59–66.

Kirkpatrick, S., Gelatt Jr, C. D., & Vecchi, M. P. (1983). Optimization by simulated annealing. *Science*, *220*(4598), 671–680.

Klingsieck, K. B. (2013). Procrastination: When good things don't come to those who wait. *European Psychologist*, *18*, 24–34. https://doi.org/10.1027/1016-9040/a000138

Kracke, W. (1992). Cultural aspects of dreaming. In *Encyclopedia of dreams*. International Institute for Dream Research.Available online at https://www.dreamresearch.ca/pdf/cultural.pdf

Latty, T., & Beekman, M. (2011). Irrational decision-making in an amoeboid organism: Transitivity and context-dependent preferences. *Proceedings of the Royal Society B: Biological Sciences*, *278*(1703), 307–312.

Li, S., & Yu, N. N. (2018). Context-dependent choice as explained by foraging theory. *Journal of Economic Theory*, *175*, 159–177.

Louie, K., Khaw, M. W., & Glimcher, P. W. (2013). Normalization is a general neural mechanism for context-dependent decision making. *Proceedings of the National Academy of Sciences*, *110*(15), 6139–6144.

Marsh, B., & Kacelnik, A. (2002). Framing effects and risky decisions in starlings. *Proceedings of the National Academy of Sciences*, *99*, 3352–3355.

Meder, B., Wu, C. M., Schulz, E., & Ruggeri, A. (2021). Development of directed and random exploration in children. *Developmental Science*, *24*(4). https://doi.org/10.1111/desc.13095 (Article e13095).

Morgan, S. L., & Winship, C. (2014). *Counterfactuals and causal inference: Methods and principles for social research*. Cambridge University Press.

Nemeth, C. J., & Wachtler, J. (1983). Creative problem solving as a result of majority vs. minority influence. *European Journal of Social Psychology, 13*(1), 45–55.

Otto, A. R., Devine, S., Schulz, E., Bornstein, A. M., & Louie, K. (2022). Context-dependent choice and evaluation in real-world consumer behavior. *Scientific Reports, 12*(1), 17744.

Otto, A. R., Knox, W. B., Markman, A. B., & Love, B. C. (2014). Physiological and behavioral signatures of reflective exploratory choice. *Cognitive, Affective, and Behavioral Neuroscience, 14*(4), 1167–1183.

Pettibone, J. C., & Wedell, D. H. (2000). Examining models of nondominated decoy effects across judgment and choice. *Organizational Behavior and Human Decision Processes, 81*(2), 300–328.

Rand, D. G., Tarnita, C. E., Ohtsuki, H., & Nowak, M. A. (2013). Evolution of fairness in the one-shot anonymous ultimatum game. *Proceedings of the National Academy of Sciences, 110*(7), 2581–2586.

Richards, D. (1995). To sir with honors. Sidney Poitier, sharing the credits. *Washington Post*, December 2, 1995.

Ruder, S. (2016). An overview of gradient descent optimization algorithms. preprint arXiv:1609.04747.

Schouwenburg, H. C. (2004). Procrastination in academic settings: General introduction. In H. C. Schouwenburg, C. H. Lay, T. A. Pychyl, & J. R. Ferrari (Eds.), *Counseling the procrastinator in academic settings* (pp. 3–17). American Psychological Association. https://doi.org/10.1037/10808-001

Schulz, E., & Gershman, S. J. (2019). The algorithmic architecture of exploration in the human brain. *Current Opinion in Neurobiology, 55*, 7–14.

Shafir, S., Waite, T. A., & Smith, B. H. (2002). Context-dependent violations of rational choice in honeybees (Apis mellifera) and gray jays (Perisoreus canadensis). *Behavioral Ecology and Sociobiology, 51*(2), 180–187.

Shin, J., & Grant, A. M. (2021). When putting work off pays off: The curvilinear relationship between procrastination and creativity. *Academy of Management Journal, 64*(3), 772–798.

Steel, P. (2007). The nature of procrastination: A meta-analytic and theoretical review of quintessential self-regulatory failure. *Psychological Bulletin, 133*(1), 65–94. https://doi.org/10.1037/0033-2909.133.1.65

Struck, P. T. (2016). *Divination and human nature: A cognitive history of intuition in classical antiquity*. Princeton University Press.

Sunar, B. (2009). True random number generators for cryptography. In *Cryptographic engineering* (pp. 55–73). Springer US.

Thaler, R. H., & Sunstein, C. R. (2009). *Nudge: Improving decisions about health, wealth, and happiness*. Penguin.

Tversky, A., & Kahneman, D. (1981). The framing of decisions and the psychology of choice. *Science*, *211*(4481), 453–458.

Wilson, B. A., & Nguyen, T. D. (2012). Belonging to tomorrow: An overview of procrastination. *International Journal of Psychological Studies*, *4*(1), 211–217.

Wilson, R. C., Bonawitz, E., Costa, V. D., & Ebitz, R. B. (2021). Balancing exploration and exploitation with information and randomization. *Current Opinion in Behavioral Sciences*, *38*, 49–56.

Wilson, R. C., Geana, A., White, J. M., Ludvig, E. A., & Cohen, J. D. (2014). Humans use directed and random exploration to solve the explore–exploit dilemma. *Journal of Experimental Psychology: General*, *143*(6), 2074–2081.

Zajkowski, W. K., Kossut, M., & Wilson, R. C. (2017). A causal role for right frontopolar cortex in directed, but not random, exploration. *Elife*, *6*, e27430.

CHAPTER 6

Social Exploration

By three methods we may learn wisdom: first, by reflection, which is the noblest; second, by imitation, which is easiest; and third, by experience, which is the bitterest.

—Unknown

Source: The quote is commonly attributed to the ancient philosopher Confucius, although the exact wording does not appear in old Chinese texts.

Contents

C. A. Pirinsky, *A Theory of Dynamic Preferences*, https://doi.org/10.1007/978-3-032-13334-2_6

Introduction

Everybody's life journey is unique, which inevitably fragments the explored area in society into small and relatively isolated personal spaces. In aggregate, however, these spaces cover a large territory. During their lifetime, even a highly traveled individual can explore only a small part of the world. But if we aggregate the experiences of all people, we will see that humans have been in places as diverse as Mount Everest, Antarctica, and the Faroe Islands. This creates incentives for people to learn from the experience of others. I refer to this learning process as social exploration. This chapter explores the properties and implications of social exploration.

Social exploration is a form of indirect exploration because it does not require interaction with the object of exploration. Social exploration has several advantages over direct exploration. First, it is often less costly to implement. Second, it could generate information faster than direct exploration. Social exploration, however, could be imprecise. People exhibit different characteristics, and what is optimal or desirable for some, might not be optimal or desirable for others. Social information could also be mis-interpreted or manipulated. For all these reasons, individuals need to assess the relative advantages and disadvantages of social exploration versus direct exploration.

Social comparisons theory (SCT) in psychology suggests that individuals that are more similar to a person are expected to generate more relevant social information because they are more likely to have similar preferences. More similar individuals, however, are also more likely to have similar experiences. As a result, albeit more relevant, the information these individuals generate would also be less useful. This suggests that the value of social information exhibits an inverted U-shape relationship with respect to similarity, and it is maximized for social comparison targets that exhibit a moderate level of similarity to the observer.

The value of social exploration is also expected to exhibit a non-linear relationship with respect to group connectivity. Greater connectivity lowers the cost of information acquisition, which favors social exploration. Connectivity, however, could de-incentivize people to engage in direct exploration because they could free-ride on the information produced by others. This, in turn, would lower the quality of social information in the pool. Thus, the value of social information in a group would also exhibit an inverted-U relationship with respect to network connectivity.

The chapter also analyzes how emerging conformism in social exploration could result in the mass-adoption of suboptimal behavior. People could make a poor decision because they mistakenly believe that it is informative. Reputation concerns could also make it more costly for people to deviate from the prevailing norms of behavior. These negative externalities of social exploration create incentives for people to develop non-conformist tendencies. The chapter discusses two such tendencies—the propensity for rebellion and differentiation.

Given the inherent costs and risks of exploration, social groups have an incentive to record and pass on the acquired knowledge through various mechanisms such as cultural norms and narratives. The chapter also discusses how the tendencies of market-oriented economies to provide people with information they like could limit their incentives for exploration.

I would like to note that the term social exploration has different meanings across disciplines. In biology, it refers to the collective exploration efforts of a group, e.g., an ant colony (Hills, 2015). In psychology, it refers to expanding one's social network (Tsang et al., 2025). The concept of social exploration in this book is about inferring information from the behavior of others. As such, it is closely related to the concept of social learning in psychology and education, emphasizing the importance of social interactions for individual development. The primary focus of this book, however, is on the evolution of individual preferences.

Signals and Cues

Social exploration refers to the act of learning about the rewards associated with particular actions from the experience of others. It can be based either on signals or cues provided inadvertently by individuals engaged in their activities (Danchin et al., 2004).

Signals are traits and behaviors specifically designed to convey information that benefits both the sender and the receiver. Signaling systems are shaped by mutual interest. For example, signals are commonly used in courtship displays. The choosing sex achieves the highest fitness by choosing the partner of the highest (genetic) quality. Given that this quality cannot be observed directly, the advertising sex can evolve signals about its quality in the form of dances, songs, and other activities (Andersson, 1994). When a potential prey detects a stalking predator, it usually emits a warning call. This signal is useful not only to other potential prey but also to the predator, which could quit wasting its time stalking this particular prey (Bergstrom & Lachmann, 2001; Getty, 2002).

Social exploration can also be based on cues provided involuntarily by individuals engaged in the performance of their activities. The gathering of a large group of individuals in a location may indicate the presence of favorable living resources. Although this information is not intentionally produced, it could be highly valuable. The fact that cues are generally observed from a distance also makes them a nonlocal exploration resource. Unlike signals, however, cues generally do not benefit the individual providing the cue. This makes them effectively a "free" source of information. For example, birds and herding mammals often observe their mates' probing success to decide when to leave a patch in search of another (Smith et al., 1999). Animals also tend to select their breeding places close to successful pairs to benefit from the same favorable conditions (Templeton & Giraldeau, 1995). Habitat copying is also observed in experimental settings (Doligez et al., 2004).

Social exploration is widely used in breeding decisions. The survival likelihood of an offspring depends significantly on the genetic quality of the parents. As a result, species try to assess more effectively the quality of potential mates by observing their social interactions. For example, female birds "eavesdrop" on neighboring song competitions between males and then seek extra-pair fertilizations from the winning singer (Mennill et al., 2002). There is also evidence that female fish species mate preferentially with winners of male-male contests (Johnstone, 2001; Oliveira et al., 2001). The presence of a female audience also increases the fighting rates of males (Doutrelant et al., 2001).

Humans use information from both signals and cues to explore their surroundings. The person's voice, facial expressions, gestures, posture, and appearance provide important information about their experiences. For example, the way a person looks at a potential partner could provide information about whether they are interested in them. This is a mutually beneficial signal, which could encourage or discourage further exploration of a romantic relationship. Observing a person across the room smiling provides information that this person is in a good company. This is a cue because the person emitting the information does not benefit directly from it. Social information is not always visual, and it could be transmitted through various channels, such as social networks, internet platforms, and the media.

The need for social information could also prompt people to extend their social networks. In a recent article, Tsang et al. (2025) point out that social networks themselves are subject to an exploitation-exploration tradeoff. People often face a decision between exploring new relationships versus deepening existing ones. The authors argue that people would tend to extend their social networks when they find it more rewarding and less costly, and when the environment offers many opportunities to do so.

Records

Exploration is beneficial but costly and often dangerous. Given the inherent risks of exploration, social groups have an incentive to record and pass on the knowledge accumulated in exploratory activities. For example, humans have valued mushrooms for their nutritional and medicinal properties for centuries (Valverde et al., 2015). Understanding the properties of different mushroom species, however, is difficult. There are more than 14,000 species of mushrooms, most of which look very similar, and many of which are highly toxic. As a result, through history, people have been exploring the properties of various mushroom species and passing on the accumulated knowledge to the next generation. Thanks to this knowledge, we do not need to risk our lives any time we would like to eat a mushroom.

Societies transmit accumulated knowledge through various channels, which could be broadly classified into oral and written traditions. The oral tradition, or oral lore, is a form of human communication in which knowledge, ideas, and culture are transmitted orally from one generation to another in the form of tales and stories. The written tradition passes on accumulated wisdom in written text. Most major religions have relied on both the oral and the written traditions to transmit their canonical scriptures, and so have the sciences, arts, and crafts (Goody, 1987; Mouralis, 2022). Recent technological developments have also enabled societies to record their experience in non-textual forms, such as pictures and film.

One important vehicle for the transmission of exploration knowledge is narratives. Stories have been an essential part of human experience. There is evidence that people respond strongly to narratives in fields as diverse as marketing (Escalas, 2007); journalism (Machill et al., 2007); education (McQuiggan et al., 2008); and health interventions (Slater et al., 2003) (see Shiller, 2017 for a review). Every story offers unique opportunities for individuals to feel a shared identity with someone else and internalize their experience (Chatman, 1980; MacIntyre, 1981). Thus, stories allow people to learn about life situations different from their own.

The knowledge generated through human exploration is also commonly recorded in monographs, handbooks, and guides. Such resources provide systematic information about places, subjects, and activities of interest to the public. The Peterson Field Guides (PFG) were a popular and influential series of books intended to assist people in the identification of birds, plants, and other natural phenomena. The guides were created and edited by renowned American ornithologist Roger Peterson (1908–1996). Universities and other research institutions further generate information about the environment and summarize this information in articles and research monographs. All these records facilitate social exploration across space and time.

Social exploration could be adversely affected by a free-rider problem. The free-rider problem refers to the tendency of people to under-produce or overuse public goods when property rights over these goods are not well defined. In this light, the public nature of social information could de-incentivize people from engaging in costly trial-and-error exploration and waiting for others to do the exploration for them. When all people stop exploring, however, the amount of social information will decrease. To incentivize people to explore, connected societies could develop social norms promoting exploration. For example, they could hold entrepreneurs and risk-takers in high regard and recognize their achievements.

Social Exploration and Social Proximity

Compared to direct exploration, social exploration has two major advantages. First, it could provide useful information at a relatively low cost compared to trial-and-error learning (Doligez et al., 2003). You do not need to watch (the first 30 minutes of) every film to decide whether you like it or not. Instead, you could form an opinion based on the recommendations of film critics and reviewers. Second, social exploration typically generates information faster than direct exploration where rewards could be delayed over long periods of time. It could take years to learn the quality of your family doctor or financial advisor. Here, again, the recommendations of others could be very useful.

The main cost of social exploration is that it provides a noisy signal about the attractiveness of an option. The message could be misinterpreted. The information gathered in social exploration might also not automatically apply to the person receiving the information. While public information is the same for different observers, the observers are not the same. People might not share the same tastes or preferences. For example, peanuts are generally regarded as nutritious and delicious. This information, however, could be misleading for a person who is allergic to peanuts.

One way people could address the relevance problem is to utilize social information only from people who are similar to them. Social comparison theory (SCT) contends that people tend to behave that way (Festinger, 1954). SCT posits that there are two critical factors in determining whether someone will choose a person as a target for social comparisons. The first factor is relevance of the domain to the self. For example, an academic is likely to compare themselves with other academics or scholars, but less so with tennis players or company executives. The second factor is similarity—both in terms of personal characteristics (e.g., gender, race, occupation) or performance (e.g., a pro-league athlete vs. an amateur-league athlete).

When it comes to social exploration, target similarity carries an internal tension. On the one hand, more similar individuals are expected to generate social information that is more relevant for a person. On the other hand, however, more similar individuals are also more likely to have similar experiences. As a result, the information they generate would be less useful. It seems that the value of social information exhibits an inverted U-shape relationship with respect to similarity, and it is maximized for targets who exhibit a moderate level of similarity to the observer (see Fig. 6.1).

Social Exploration and Connectivity

How does the level of connectivity in a group affect social exploration? People exhibit different patterns of sociability. Some interact with a relatively small number of individuals, usually reduced to relatives and close friends. Such connections are commonly referred to as strong ties. Other people are more sociable and connected. Since people exhibit limited social resources, the interactions of more sociable individuals need to be less frequent or more superficial. Such connections are commonly referred to as weak ties.

Network theorists have proposed several metrics to measure connectivity in a network. Some of them are local and measure the connections of a particular member of the network (node).

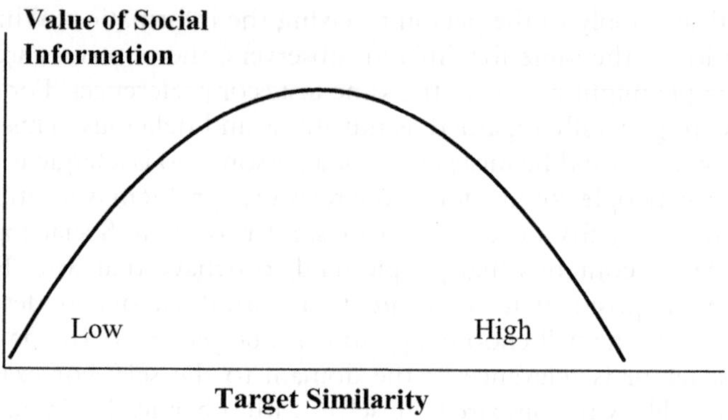

Fig. 6.1 Target similarity and the value of social information. The figure plots the value of social information as a function of the similarity between the source (target) and the receiver of social information

For example, *centrality* measures the importance of a person within a network in terms of connections and ability to influence the flow of information. Other measures are global and describe properties of the whole network. For example, network density is a global measure of connectivity, calculating the proportion of actual connections to possible connections in a network. Another global measure is the clustering coefficient, measuring the degree to which nodes in the network tend to cluster together.

The relationship between social exploration and connectivity could be analyzed locally, from the perspective of a single individual, or globally—from the perspective of the whole group. The local implications of connectivity were first explored by Granovetter (1973) in his article "The Strength of Weak Ties." In his original article, Granovetter conducted a survey of how people in the United States of America got their jobs. He found that people with a larger number of casual acquaintances (weak ties) had better performance in the labor market than people with a smaller number of connections (strong ties). This is because weak ties provide access to a larger and more diverse pool of information than strong ties. Subsequent research on the diffusion of innovation in networks also confirms that better-connected individuals tend to obtain better information and adopt earlier innovations than less-connected individuals (Rogers, 2003). Locally, connectivity seems to favor social exploration.

The relationship between global connectivity in a network and social exploration is more complex. On the one hand, by providing more access to social information, greater connectivity would incentivize people to acquire information from others (*a la* Granovetter). This, however, would disincentivize direct trial-and-error exploration in the group. As a result, the amount of information produced in well-connected groups will decline. As the quality of information in the network declines, so would the value of social information. Thus, the value of social information in a network would exhibit an inverted-U relationship with respect to global network connectivity (see Fig. 6.2).

Some studies on network structure and performance have suggested a non-linear relationship between network connectivity and information production. For example, Lazer & Friedman (2007) present an agent-based computer simulation model of information sharing in which the less successful emulate the more successful. They show that, while network efficiency could enhance the short-run performance of the system, it could lower its long-run performance. This is because an inefficient network maintains diversity and is thus better tuned for exploration than an efficient network.

The nonlinear relationship between connectivity and the value of social exploration also suggests that a society could try to identify the optimal amount of social exploration given its level of connectivity.

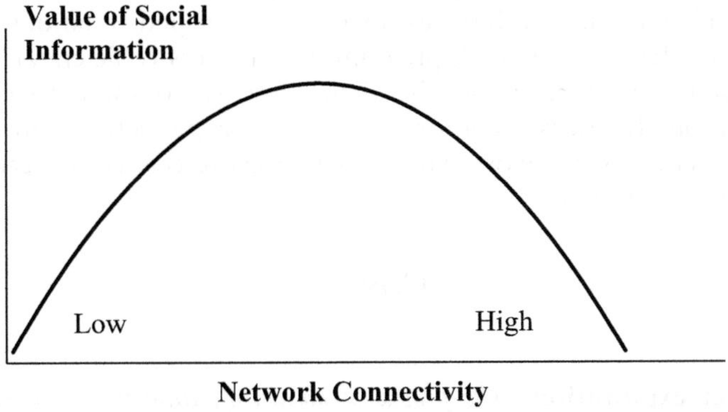

Fig. 6.2 Network connectivity and the value of social information. The figure plots the value of social information as a function of the level of connectivity among people in a network

Communities with more interpersonal trust and larger social networks would tend to rely more on social exploration. Such communities, however, are also expected to develop social norms encouraging direct exploration and information production. For example, a culture of individualism would encourage people to be more self-reliant and not to over-use social information. Consistent with this idea is the fact that societies high in interpersonal trust, such as the Nordic countries, also tend to score high on individualism (Gatchev et al., 2025).

One interesting case of social exploration is the stock markets. Investors approach capital markets with some private information about firms, and they trade according to this information. The more positive (negative) and certain they feel about a company's prospects, the more likely they are to place a buy (sell) order of its stock. Capital markets aggregate this order flow and set up stock prices in accordance with it. The emerging stock prices aggregate information from millions of investors and communicate this information among them.

The efficient market hypothesis (EMH) states that security prices fully reflect all available information. Grossman and Stiglitz present a critique of the EMH (Grossman & Stiglitz, 1980). They argue that if prices reflect all available information, then investors would have no incentive to collect costly information because they would not be able to profit from it. But if no one gathers information, then stock prices will become inefficient. A perfectly efficient market is therefore impossible. Grossman & Stiglitz's paper also suggests that the value of investment information exhibits an inverted-U shaped relationship with respect to the level of stock price informativeness (efficiency). If prices incorporate information poorly, then there is no value to collecting information. If prices incorporate information perfectly, then information collection is not worthwhile either because one could learn everything from the price.

Concepts

Direct exploration. *The process of obtaining information about the attractiveness and properties of an object from direct interactions with it.*

Indirect exploration. *The process of obtaining information about the attractiveness and properties of an object without direct interactions with it.*

Social exploration. *The process of obtaining information about the attractiveness and properties of an object from the behavior and choices of others.*

Social signals. *Traits and behaviors specifically designed to convey information that tend to benefit both the sender and the receiver.*

Social cues. *The information that living organisms send inadvertently through their body language and expressions.*

Filter bubbles. *The information set of individuals that is manipulated by personalization algorithms to include only information and opinions that conform to and reinforce their own beliefs, attitudes, and revealed preferences.*

Emerging Conformism

Social exploration inevitably leads to the replication of behavioral patterns across the population. This emerging conformism could be suboptimal for two reasons. First, people could make a poor choice. Second, when the degree of adoption increases, the quality of the choice could deteriorate. For example, Christakis & Fowler (2007) show that obesity spreads through social networks. Even life satisfaction is significantly affected by the life satisfaction of individuals with up to three degrees of separation, i.e., the friends of one's friends' friends (Fowler & Christakis, 2008).

In an original study, Bikhchandani et al. (1992) model situations of sequential decision making where agents could derive information from both their own sources as well as the actions of others. The authors show that when people consider the behavior of other agents to be as informative as their personal information, they tend to repeat the choice of the first few agents regardless of the information they possess themselves. The authors call this phenomenon an "informational cascade" and suggest that it could cause fads, fashion, and other cultural phenomena.

Informational cascades lead to conformity where people mechanically copy the behavior of others, even when this behavior is suboptimal.

Conformity could also arise from reputational considerations. When people are concerned about their professional reputation, they could be reluctant to deviate from the behavior of their peers. For example, to avoid being seen as an outlier, a fund manager could choose to invest in a popular asset (say, crypto currency) even if their own analysis suggests otherwise. Keynes famously said that "it is better for reputation to fail conventionally than to succeed unconventionally" (Keynes, 1936). Similarly to informational cascades, reputation-induced herding leads to inefficient aggregation of information because people choose to ignore their private information and follow the crowd.

When the number of people adopting certain behavior increases, the benefits of this behavior could decrease. This intuition is reflected in the efficient market discussion at the end of the previous section. When more people start learning from prices, the quality of the information contained in prices deteriorates. When every individual explores the same opportunity, the aggregate exploration in a group also declines. Indeed, there is evidence that people are aware of the diminishing marginal benefits of social exploration. For example, Winet et al. (2022) find that when the amount of social exploration in a group increases, the propensity of its group members to engage in direct (trial-and-error) exploration also increases.

Emerging Non-Conformism

If social learning leads to suboptimal conformism, then people are expected to develop an affinity for non-conformist behavior. Extensive research in sociology suggests that this is indeed the case. For example, from a very young age, most people exhibit the tendency for rebellion. Forbidding children from doing something often sparks their curiosity. Indeed, the urge to rebel is so strong that caregivers and parents of children are often using it to motivate children to do something. Reverse psychology refers to the idea of trying to make someone do what you want by asking them to do the opposite and expecting them to disagree with you.

People are not only affected by social influence but also exhibit a remarkable tendency to resist it. To explain individual non-conformism, Jack W. Brehm developed the reactance theory (Brehm, 1966). According to this theory, people experience unpleasant feelings when they are restricted from behaving freely. Thus, the urge to rebel and do the opposite of what we are told could be an effort to regain a sense of control in a situation. Building on these ideas, Brewer (1991) introduced the optimal distinctiveness theory. According to this theory, individuals have two fundamental and competing human needs—the need for inclusion and the need for differentiation. These needs could be balanced in moderately inclusive (optimally distinct) groups.

Societies also exhibit robust tendencies to build countercultures. A counterculture is a culture whose values and norms of behavior differ substantially from those of mainstream society. John Milton Yinger coined the term "contraculture" in his 1960 article in the American Sociological Review. When it reaches a critical mass, a counter-culture can trigger dramatic cultural changes and establish itself as a mainstream culture. In this respect, counter-cultures are a form of social exploration. Prominent examples of countercultures are Bohemianism and the Hippy movement. Bohemianism was a social movement following non-traditional lifestyles, especially by artists in major European cities during the second half of the nineteenth century. The term originates from the French *bohème* and spread to the English-speaking world. Hippies became the largest and most visible countercultural group in the United States during the late 1960s.

Filter Bubbles

As noted at the beginning of this chapter, everybody's life experience is unique, which creates an incentive for people to expand their perspectives. Social exploration could be an effective tool for achieving this objective. The attractiveness of exploration, however, depends on the relative availability of exploitation options. When the available options are good and plentiful, people would be tempted to select one of them instead of settling for something uncertain.

Businesses have been relying increasingly on machine learning algorithms to predict individual tastes based on information about their past choices and other personal data. On the surface, recommendation systems appear very efficient because they can directly cater to individual preferences. By isolating people from products, views, and options that appear different, however, recommendation systems could also hurt exploration. It is commonly referred to this state of artificial isolation as filter bubbles.

The term filter bubble was coined by internet activist Eli Pariser (2011). In his book with the same name, he predicted that individualized personalization by algorithmic filtering could lead to isolation and social fragmentation. Is this really happening? The evidence appears mixed. Some research has suggested that filter bubbles could indeed lead to isolation (Poell et al., 2021; Sharma et al., 2024). Other research has contended that filter bubbles are less widespread than commonly assumed, and their effect could be even positive (Ross Arguedas et al. 2022; Guess et al., 2023). A better understanding of filter bubbles could help us design better recommendation systems, promoting exploration rather than restricting it.

Conclusion

Exploration can be either direct, using trial-and-error tactics to interact with the environment, or indirect—inferring information about opportunities without interacting with them. This chapter analyzes one common form of indirect exploration—learning from the experiences of others, or social exploration.

Social exploration has two major advantages over direct exploration. First, it is often less costly to implement. Second, the rewards in social exploration typically occur faster than in direct exploration. Social exploration, however, could be imprecise. People also exhibit different characteristics, and what is optimal or desirable for some might not be optimal or desirable for others. For all these reasons, individuals need to assess the relative advantages and disadvantages of social exploration versus direct exploration.

The chapter argues that the value of social exploration tends to decrease with respect to its prevalence in a group. This is because high levels of social exploration make direct exploration less popular. When the level of direct exploration decreases, however, so does the quality of social information. In response, individuals and societies are expected to adopt contrarian behaviors, discouraging the use of social information. The chapter reviews some contrarian behaviors, such as one's tendency for rebellion, preference for distinctiveness, and counter-cultural phenomena.

References

Andersson, M. (1994). *Sexual Selection*. Princeton University Press.

Bergstrom, C. T., & Lachmann, M. (2001). Alarm calls as costly signals of antipredator vigilance: The watchful babbler game. *Animal Behaviour*, *61*(3), 535–543.

Bikhchandani, S., Hirshleifer, D., & Welch, I. (1992). A theory of fads, fashion, custom, and cultural change as informational cascades. *Journal of Political Economy, 100*(5), 992–1026.

Brehm, J. W. (1966). *A theory of psychological reactance*. Academic Press.

Brewer, M. B. (1991). The social self: On being the same and different at the same time. *Personality and Social Psychology Bulletin, 17*, 475–482.

Chatman, S. (1980). *Story and discourse: Narrative structure in fiction and film*. Cornell University Press.

Christakis, N. A., & Fowler, J. H. (2007). The spread of obesity in a large social network over 32 years. *New England Journal of Medicine, 357*(4), 370–379.

Danchin, E., Giraldeau, L. A., Valone, T. J., & Wagner, R. H. (2004). Public information: From nosy neighbors to cultural evolution. *Science, 305*(5683), 487–491.

Doligez, B., Pärt, T., Danchin, E., Clobert, J., & Gustafsson, L. (2004). Availability and use of public information and conspecific density for settlement decisions in the collared flycatcher. *Journal of Animal Ecology, 73*(1), 75–87.

Doutrelant, C., McGregor, P. K., & Oliveira, R. F. (2001). The effect of an audience on intrasexual communication in male Siamese fighting fish, Betta splendens. *Behavioral Ecology, 12*(3), 283–286.

Escalas, J. E. (2007). Self-referencing and persuasion: Narrative transportation versus analytical elaboration. *Journal of Consumer Research, 16*, 421–429.

Festinger, L. (1954). A theory of social comparison processes. *Human Relations, 7*, 117–140.

Fowler, J. H., & Christakis, N. A. (2008). Dynamic spread of happiness in a large social network: Longitudinal analysis over 20 years in the Framingham Heart Study. *British Medical Journal, 337*, a2338.

Gatchev, V., Pirinsky, C., & Wang, Q. (2025). Short selling and cultural arbitrage in financial markets. Working paper.

Getty, T. (2002). The discriminating babbler meets the optimal diet hawk. *Animal Behaviour, 63*(2), 397–402.

Goody, J. (1987). *The interface between the written and the oral*. Cambridge University Press.

Granovetter, M. S. (1973). The strength of weak ties. *American Journal of Sociology, 78*(6), 1360–1380.

Grossman, S. J., & Stiglitz, J. E. (1980). On the impossibility of informationally efficient markets. *The American Economic Review, 70*(3), 393–408.

Guess, A. M., Malhotra, N., Pan, J., Barberá, P., Allcott, H., Brown, T., Crespo-Tenorio, A., Dimmery, D., Freelon, D., Gentzkow, M., & González-Bailón, S. (2023). How do social media feed algorithms affect attitudes and behavior in an election campaign? *Science, 381*(6656), 398–404.

Hills, T. T., Todd, P. M., Lazer, D., Redish, A. D., & Couzin, I. D. (2015). Exploration versus exploitation in space, mind, and society. *Trends in Cognitive Sciences, 19*(1), 46–54.

Johnstone, R. A. (2001). Eavesdropping and animal conflict. *Proceedings of the National Academy of Sciences*, 98(16), 9177–9180.

Keynes, J. M. (1936). *The general theory of employment, interest and money*. Reprint 1997 Prometheus.

Lazer, D., & Friedman, A. (2007). The network structure of exploration and exploitation. *Administrative Science Quarterly, 52*(4), 667–694.

Machill, M., Köhler, S., & Waldhauser, M. (2007). The use of narrative structures in television news. *European Journal of Communication, 22*(2), 185–205.

MacIntyre, A. (1981). The nature of the virtues. *Hastings Center Report, 11*, 27–34.

McQuiggan, S. W., Rowe, J. P., Lee, S., & Lester, J. C. (2008). Story-based learning: The impact of narrative on learning experiences and outcomes. In B. P. Woolf, E. Aïmeur, R. Nkambou, & S. Lajoie (Eds.), *Intelligent tutoring systems* (pp. 530–539). Springer.

Mennill, D. J., Ratcliffe, L. M., & Boag, P. T. (2002). Female eavesdropping on male song contests in songbirds. *Science, 296*(5569), 873–873.

Mouralis, B. (2022). *Orality. Encyclopedia of African religions and philosophy* (pp. 537–539). Springer.

Oliveira, R. F., Lopes, M., Carneiro, L. A., & Canário, A. V. (2001). Watching fights raises fish hormone levels. *Nature, 409*(6819), 475–475.

Pariser, E. (2011). *The filter bubble: How the new personalized web is changing what we read and how we think*. Penguin.

Poell, T., Nieborg, D. B., & Duffy, B. E. (2021). *Platforms and cultural production*. John Wiley & Sons.

Rogers, E. M. (2003). *Diffusion of innovations*. Free Press.

Ross Arguedas, A., Robertson, C., Fletcher, R., & Nielsen, R. (2022). Echo chambers, filter bubbles, and polarisation: a literature review. *Reuters Institute for the Study of Journalism*. Available at: https://ora.ox.ac.uk/objects/uuid:6e357e97-7b16-450a-a827-a92c93729a08 (accessed 10 March 2024).

Sharma, N., Liao, Q. V., & Xiao, Z. (2024). Generative echo chamber? Effect of llm-powered search systems on diverse information seeking. In Proceedings of the 2024 CHI Conference on Human Factors in Computing Systems (pp. 1–17).

Shiller, R. J. (2017). Narrative economics. *American Economic Review, 107*(4), 967–1004.

Slater, M. D., Bueller, D. B., Waters, E., Archibeque, M., & LeBlanc, M. (2003). A test of conversational and testimonial messages versus didactic presentations of nutrition information. *Journal of Nutrition Education and Behavior, 35*(5), 255–259.

Smith, J. W., Benkman, C. W., & Coffey, K. (1999). The use and misuse of public information by foraging red crossbills. *Behavioral Ecology, 10*(1), 54–62.

Templeton, J. J., & Giraldeau, L. A. (1995). Patch assessment in foraging flocks of European starlings: Evidence for the use of public information. *Behavioral Ecology, 6*(1), 65–72.

Tsang, S., Barrentine, K., Chadha, S., Oishi, S., & Wood, A. (2025). Social exploration: How and why people seek new connections. *Psychological Review, 132*(3), 656–679.

Valverde, M. E., Hernández-Pérez, T., & Paredes-López, O. (2015). Edible mushrooms: Improving human health and promoting quality life. *International Journal of Microbiology, 2015*, 376387.

Winet, Y. K., Tu, Y., Choshen-Hillel, S., & Fishbach, A. (2022). Social exploration: When people deviate from options explored by others. *Journal of Personality and Social Psychology, 122*(3), 427–442. https://doi.org/10.1037/pspi0000350

Wood, R. J. (2019). Dictionary of quotations from ancient and modern, English and foreign Sources: A treasury of wisdom and inspiration. *Good Press*. https://www.gutenberg.org/files/48105/48105-h/48105-h.htm

CHAPTER 7

Exploration Through Simulation

Contents

Introduction

The *Treachery of Images* (French: La Trahison des Images) is a 1929 painting by Belgian surrealist painter René Magritte. The painting (below) shows an image of a pipe. Below it, Magritte wrote "This is not a pipe" (French: "Ceci n'est pas une pipe"). The apparent contradiction has stirred numerous discussions. The image is clear, and the simplicity of the painting automatically rules out any camouflaged images or hidden meanings. Why is this not a pipe? (Fig. 7.1).

C. A. Pirinsky, *A Theory of Dynamic Preferences*,
https://doi.org/10.1007/978-3-032-13334-2_7

Fig. 7.1 René Magritte, *The Treachery of Images, 1929*[1]

The painting is not a pipe but a representation of a pipe. It captures important properties of the object, such as its shape and color. The image could be useful. For example, to teach a person who has never seen a pipe what it is. It could also carry an esthetic or sentimental value for some people. This is how the artist comments himself "[C]ould you stuff my pipe? No, it's just a representation, is it not? So, if I had written on my picture 'This is a pipe', I'd have been lying!" The painting is a good example of a simulation—an imitative representation of a process or a system.

Simulations are ubiquitous. Physical simulations surround us. Our minds are constantly simulating possible situations and circumstances, often subconsciously. This chapter provides a formal definition of simulations and analyzes their use as a tool for exploration. Direct exploration is often costly and time consuming. In many of these cases, simulations could provide valuable information about an object or situation at relatively low cost. Simulations, however, are not exact representations of reality. As such, simulation-based exploration is subject to errors.

Suppose that you are considering relocating to Hawaii. You have never visited the island before, and you do not know how you would like living there. Unfortunately, it is impossible to experience living in

[1] CREDIT: © 2025 C. Herscovici / Artists Rights Society (ARS), New York and © 2025 Phototheque R. Magritte / ADAGP / DACS Images.

another state in its entirety before you move. However, you could simulate the experience to gain an insight into the experience of living in another state. First, you could simulate the experience physically by taking a trip to the island and staying there for a few days. Second, you could watch some relevant films or talk to people who have already lived there. Third, you could recall memories from visits to places resembling Hawaii (e.g., Japan or California). In total, these simulations provide some useful, albeit imperfect, information about living in Hawaii.

Simulations allow an individual to estimate the expected reward of an action based on past experiences. The more experienced a person is, the more "material" he or she has for such mental explorations. Thus, the value of simulations generally increases with the number of past experiences.

The chapter also argues that people could often manipulate their social environment to learn about the people participating in it. For example, couples go through an extensive dating process before committing to a relationship. Dating is an act of social simulation. It follows strict social norms, most of which are designed to facilitate learning about the other party. People could even strategically instigate conflicts before entering binding long-term contracts to learn how the other party would behave in challenging circumstances.

Simulations also provide an insight into art and other creative endeavors. Art has been an integral part of human societies since the dawn of civilization. As a simulation, art could facilitate exploration for both the creator and the people experiencing the art. Indeed, there are numerous accounts of the therapeutical and transformational power of art.

At the end, this chapter discusses the increasing importance of computer simulations as a tool for scientific discovery. The traditional scientific method is based on experiments aimed at validating or refuting certain theoretical predictions. The experimental method, however, has limitations. For example, designing controlled experiments is often difficult. Current theories also demand increasingly complex equipment for the design of a reliable experiment. Computer simulations could effectively circumvent some of these limitations.

Simulations

A simulation is a stylized representation of a process, system, or condition that maintains certain properties of an architype. Simulations have numerous practical applications. For one, they can be used to evaluate the real effects of alternative conditions and factors on an object. Simulations are also used when the real system cannot be engaged directly because it may not be accessible, or it may be dangerous or impossible to engage. In this sense, a simulation is often referred to as a model. Models could be simulated in three different environments: the physical world, computers, and the mind.

Physical simulation refers to a simulation in which the archetype is substituted with a physical object. The physical objects are often chosen because they are smaller or cheaper than the actual object or system. One example of physical simulation is the wind tunnel. It is a mechanism that produces a controlled stream of air for examining how a building or a vehicle behaves under strong wind conditions. Because it is difficult to directly observe the air movement, multiple air flow visualization methods have been developed for testing in a wind tunnel.

Computer simulations model complex real-life or hypothetical situations on a computer. Computer-generated images were introduced to the film industry in the 1970s. In 1995, the film Toy Story became the first film to use only computer-generated images, and, shortly after that, computer-generated graphics became the leading choice for special effects in films. Simulation games have become also very popular among people of all ages. They use computer-generated images to model realistically various game environments. Examples of popular simulation games include SimCity and Tiger Woods PGA Tour.

Computer simulations have been also used to study the behavior of complex systems such as financial markets. For example, a stress test is a simulation designed to determine the ability of a given financial instrument or financial institution to deal with an economic crisis (Geithner, 2015). A company or its regulators may perform stress testing by simulating shocks to basic economic variables, such as the unemployment rate, GDP growth, oil prices, interest rates, and others. Large international banks began using internal stress tests in the early 1990s. In 1996, the Basel Capital Accord was amended to require banks and investment firms to conduct stress tests to determine their ability to respond to market events. Financial stress testing has been also applied to various payment and settlement systems.

Physical and computer simulations have been also extensively used for education and training purposes. Sometimes, it is prohibitively expensive or too dangerous to allow trainees to use real equipment. In such situations, they could learn valuable lessons in a "safe" virtual environment. For example, a flight simulator artificially re-creates aircraft flight and the environment in which it flies, which could be used for pilot training. Driving simulators are often used for training as well as entertainment. Driving simulators also allow researchers to study drivers' behavior under conditions in which it would be illegal and/or unethical to place drivers. Clinical healthcare simulators have been used for training on a wide range of procedures, ranging from blood draw to laparoscopic surgery.

Finally, mental simulations recreate objects and situations in one's mind. When faced with a complex and difficult choice, people often deliberate over different possibilities by constructing imagined future scenarios and evaluating how these possibilities compare across these scenarios (Buckner & Carroll, 2007; Hills et al., 2015; Redish, 2013). The ability to imagine what might happen in the future upon taking specific actions helps people plan and solve problems. In effect, these simulations generate experiences, which are effectivley explorations.

Exploration Through Simulation

Suppose that you would like to explore how a particular wing shape would affect the speed, maneuverability, and lift force of a commercial aircraft. Building a real plane with the corresponding wing shape for the sake of experimentation would be very costly. One possible solution is to approach the problem analytically and derive an exact model describing the dynamics of the plane as a function of input variables. For example, the lift force F generated by a plane could be expressed as a function of certain characteristics of the plane, such as the shape and size of its wings, the angle at which the wings meet the oncoming air (angle of attack), the length and weight of its body (the fuselage), and others. If we denote all these characteristics with S_n, for $n = 1, \ldots, N$, then the lift force could be expressed as a function of these characteristics $F = F(S_1, S_2, \ldots, S_N)$. Using the laws of aerodynamics, one could find the exact form of this functional relationship, enter the characteristics of the wings, and derive theoretically the lift force they generate.

The laws of fluid mechanics, however, are very complex. Most of the existing relationships are highly non-linear and difficult to formulate. Small alterations of the initial conditions could also result in large divergences of the dynamics of the fluid. For all these reasons, deriving a precise model describing the behavior of a plane is extremely difficult.

Simulations provide an alternative solution to this complex exploration problem. One can build an exact (smaller) replica of the plane and position it in a wind tunnel that could generate a stream of air with various speeds and directions. This simulated environment is a distorted representation of the real flying situation. If we denote the element of distortion for a particular simulation *i* with e_i, the resulting lift force generated by a simulation could be expressed as Fi = F $(S_1, S_2, \ldots, S_N)$ + ei = F + e_i. The wind tunnel, however, allows us to run multiple simulations by changing the characteristics of the airflow. If the distortions of the simulator are unbiased, i.e., the expected distortion of a simulation is equal to 0, then when the number of simulations increases, the average distortion from all simulations would converge to 0. The latter follows from the Law of Large Numbers (LLN).

The LLN in probability theory states that given a sample of independent and identically distributed random variables, the sample mean converges to the true mean of these variables when the sample size increases. With respect to the simulations, this implies that the average simulated lift force will converge to the true force, when the number of simulations K increases. This is summarized in (Eq. 7.1) below:

$$\frac{F_1 + F_2 + \ldots + F_K}{K} = F + \frac{e_1 + e_2 + \ldots + e_K}{K} \underset{K \to \infty}{\to} F \tag{7.1}$$

Exploring the rewards associated with a particular choice is even more challenging than the above example. Given that social dynamics are far more complex than fluid dynamics, deriving a functional representation for the value of a particular career, friendship, or lifestyle is nearly impossible. In all these cases, simulations could be very helpful.

If you would like to know whether you would like the *Game of Thrones* show, direct exploration would require you to purchase and watch all 73 episodes. This trial-and-error approach takes substantial resources. Watching a film also brings very little future benefits because the utility of watching it for a second or a third time is substantially lower than the utility of watching it for the first time. Assessing analytically how rewarding a particular film would be is also very difficult. Although one can identify certain characteristics predicting the appeal of a film, such as its genre, director, and lead actors, incorporating these characteristics into an analytical model is not trivial. The laws governing human preferences are not as well defined as the laws of physics. However, one could simulate the experience of watching the TV show by watching its trailer, a random episode, or a commentary about it. Indeed, this is the main reason trailers and film critics exist.

Let's consider in greater detail the act of choosing a career. This is an important, yet very complex, decision most people face early in their lives. Would you like to work for somebody else or start your own business? What type of industry would you like to position yourself in? Do you want to be a pastry chef, an accountant, or a doctor? If you would like to go into the medical field, you need to narrow down one out of several hundred medical specialties and subspecialties. You also need to decide on the medical school you would like to attend. What makes the decision even more difficult is that people live in an information bubble where their information sources are confined to the experiences of their immediate family and close friends.

Every job incurs numerous responsibilities. The rewards are also complex and include not only monetary compensation but also non-pecuniary considerations, such as the feelings of being useful and connected to others. In such complex decisions, simulations could be an important tool for exploration that enables people to "place" themselves in various circumstances and evaluate alternatives as closely as possible to reality.

To help children navigate the complexities of career choice, schools organize career days—events where professionals visit the school to share information about their jobs, including the skills and education it requires. Parents also introduce their children to various career opportunities, often unintentionally. For example, a child could consider the medical field simply because his or her parents are doctors.

Children could also take specific steps to learn about employment opportunities. For example, a person considering a medical career could meet doctors, nurses, or other healthcare professionals to ask questions about their experiences and learn about the different aspects of their jobs. Gaining hands-on experience through volunteering in hospitals or clinics could also provide information about different medical professions. Watching news stories, documentaries, or television shows, such as ER, Scrubs, and House MD, could provide additional insights into the lifestyle of medical professionals.

In all the above cases, however, the information obtained is incomplete and fragmented. As such, it does not always present a realistic picture of any career. To gain a more complete understanding, people need to put this information together in a real context. Mental simulations allow them to do that. By simulating numerous life situations within the context of a particular profession, people can learn how they would like or dislike the corresponding lifestyle. Mental simulations provide a sophisticated tool for the exploration of complex choices.

Note that every act of mental simulation also changes the person engaging in it. This implies that simulating multiple times the same situation could be worthwhile because the person is evolving with every iteration. Paraphrasing Heraclitus, stepping multiple times in the same mental simulation is impossible because the person behind the simulation would never be the same person. This artifact could explain why our minds are constantly working and tirelessly playing out seemingly similar scenarios.

The Value of Simulations

Mental simulations approximate new experiences with old ones. We can think about simulations as a projection of an experience onto an abstract space of past experiences. Sometimes the new experience is approximated well with old experiences, and sometimes it is approximated poorly. The quality of the projection depends on how similar the new experience is to the set of past experiences. For example, a person who knows the tastes of peanuts and chocolate could use this information to approximate the taste of a *Reese's* peanut butter cup. Of course, such a simulation is not perfect as the value of the combination could either under-state or over-state the value of its ingredients.

By adding new experiences to their lives, people increase the dimensionality of the projection space and its ability to approximate the rewards of various activities. Thus, the value of simulations is expected to increase with the amount of direct exploration conducted in the past. Simulated experiences, albeit informative about a particular activity, do not expand the projection space because they are comprised of old experiences. Thus, the following proposition is expected to hold.

Proposition. The value of simulations increases with the number of direct explorations and decreases with the number of simulated explorations in the past.

The above proposition suggests that the value of simulations increases over the lifetime as people accumulate more experiences. As a result, as people grow older, they are expected to substitute direct forms of exploration with indirect forms of exploration, such as social exploration and simulation.

Living organisms are more prone to exploration earlier in their lives because the knowledge that early exploration generates could be used multiple times in the future. This idea is intuitive, and it could be traced to the works of the Swiss psychologist Jean Piaget (Piaget, 1954). Numerous studies have confirmed empirically that children are more explorative than adults. For example, Gopnik et al. (2017) find that children and adolescents are more likely to adopt unusual hypotheses to explain behavioral patterns than adults. Sumner et al. (2019) and Liquin and Gopnik (2022) also find that children explore more than adults and learn the true structure of the environment better. Hart et al. (2022) focus on creativity and show that, when compared to adults, children allocate their attention to more unusual spaces and can produce more unique products.

Declining propensity for exploration is also embedded in many machine learning models (Frankenhuis & Gopnik, 2023). A common approach in these models is to begin with more exploration and gradually substitute exploration with exploitation. For example, simulated annealing uses random search techniques to find the global optimum of a given function. The algorithm begins with a random (higher-temperature) search and gradually cools off to a more localized search. Similarly, reinforcement learning algorithms start with noisier, less data-driven, actions and gradually increase their sensitivity to the data.

Although exploration declines over the lifetime, not all forms of exploration are expected to behave the same way. Direct (trial-and-error) exploration is expected to be relatively more important early in life when almost every choice is exploratory. Over time, as people expand their social circles, the value of social exploration is expected to increase. The accumulated experience also makes mental simulations more effective. Thus, we expect that delegated and direct exploration will be the dominant forms of exploration early in life. Over time, these forms of exploration are gradually substituted with social exploration and simulations. This is reflected in Fig. 7.2.

Existing empirical evidence supports the tradeoff outlined above. For example, Hart et al. (2022) compare the exploration of creative tasks across children and adults. They find that compared to adults, children spend more time on exploration and produce more unique creative products. As children grow up, however, their creative products become more similar. The convergence suggests that as children develop, they would be more likely to substitute random exploration with more structured exploration techniques.

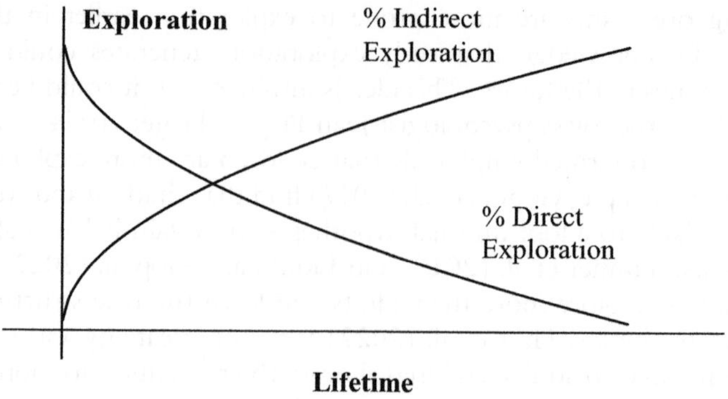

Fig. 7.2 Exploration during the life cycle. The figure plots the relative importance of various types of exploration over the lifetime: direct (trial-and-error) exploration and indirect (social and simulated) exploration

Concepts

Simulation. *A stylized representation of a process, system, or condition that maintains certain properties of an architype. Simulation is often used interchangeably with a model.*

Physical simulation. *A simulation in which the archetype is substituted with a physical object. The physical objects are often chosen because they are smaller or cheaper than the actual object or system.*

Computer simulation. *A simulation in which the archetype is substituted with a computer model.*

Mental simulation. *A simulation in which the archetype is substituted with a mental model or a representation.*

Exploration through simulation. *The use of mental models and other simulations to explore circumstances that would be dangerous and often impossible to explore with other means.*

Art as an Exploration

As René Magritte's piece suggests, art is a simulation. As such, it carries important information about reality. This might be the main reason we seek and consume creative expressions all the time. However, art as a phenomenon cannot be understood well only from the demand side. To be sustained, creative expressions need to benefit the creator as well. While markets allow creative people to monetize some of their efforts, the monetary compensation for these activities seems very small. Why do artists engage in creation?

Exploration provides a feasible explanation. Creative expressions could be beneficial for the artist because they provide different perspectives on their own lives. Art works originate in the domain of the subconscious. As such, they usually have a prototype—an object, an emotion, or other mental condition. The process of creation could help the artist understand better these underlying conditions. From this perspective, art resembles a therapy that could transform both its creator and the people experiencing it.

There are numerous examples that artists are evolving together with their works. Vincent van Gogh used vibrant colors and dynamic brushstrokes to express his personal experiences and struggles. He also often felt a deep emotional connection to his creations. His paintings "The Starry Night" and "Wheatfield with Crows" are well-known expressions of his emotional turmoil. It is not surprising that his work heavily influenced the twentieth century art movement of expressionism that prioritized the representation of subjective emotional states rather than objective reality. Every work of art, however, has an expressionist element in it, as it is impossible to separate the work from its creator.

The famous Russian novelist Leo Tolstoy was also deeply affected by the characters in his works. While writing "Anna Karenina," a novel about love, desire, and betrayal in contemporary Russia, Tolstoy expressed a plethora of mixed emotions about the main character. Some of his feelings were reflected in the novelist's diary. There are even accounts that Tolstoy was deeply emotionally distressed by the tragic suicide of his character.

The emerging complex relationships between artists and their creations suggest that art transforms the artist. Art is exploration through simulation. Voltaire started writing Candide to satirize the hypocrisy of religion and its philosophical optimism (see Chap. 4). Throughout the novel, the author was trying to change Candide's views by confronting the character with numerous unfortunate events and injustices. Yet, he did not succeed. It is interesting to know why Voltaire did not change Candide. But perhaps an even more interesting question is whether Candide changed Voltaire. The answer might be Yes. Despite his criticism of religion, Voltaire was not an atheist. Indeed, one of his favorite sayings was: "If God did not exist, it would be necessary to invent Him" ("Si Dieu n'existait pas, il faudrait l'inventer"). Voltaire first published these words in "Letter to the Author of The Three Impostors" in 1770. Note that this happened 11 years after he published Candide. Did Candide change his mind?

Manipulating the Environment

Similarly to the way the operator of a wind tunnel manipulates its air flow, a person could strategically alter a social situation to gain an insight into the people involved in it. Learning about other people is particularly valuable before entering long-term contracts. To facilitate this learning process, people engage in a series of interactions. These interactions are simulations that provide information about how the other party would behave in a real situation. The simulations often take place in different environments. For example, it is common for business people to negotiate while having dinner, attending public events, or playing a round of golf. These settings provide information about a person and their character.

Learning about a potential partner before entering a romantic relationship is also very valuable because relationships are difficult to break. Most of the existing social norms of dating, such as going to different places and engaging in various activities, are designed to facilitate social learning. For example, a woman might not know what kind of father a potential mate would be, but she can learn something about it from his interactions with children.

Interpersonal conflicts could be also analyzed from the perspective of exploration. Disagreements often emerge because people have different interests, values, and opinions. Yet, the level of disagreement among people seems to greatly exceed their differences. I contend that many conflicts in relationships could be strategically instigated because they provide information on how a (prospective) partner behaves in challenging situations. Some of the disagreements and conflicts in the world could be explorations through argumentation.

The New Scientific Method

The traditional scientific method is an empirical method for acquiring knowledge. It generally involves making conjectures (hypotheses), predicting certain outcomes, and carrying out experiments or empirical observations aimed at validating or refuting these predictions. Some hypotheses are formulated quantitatively; others are formulated qualitatively—for example, by stating that some phenomenon exhibits certain characteristics. It is also common for some hypotheses to be probabilistic in nature. All hypotheses, however, must be falsifiable, implying that it is possible to identify a possible outcome of an experiment or observation that contradicts the predictions of the hypothesis.

Once predictions are made, a hypothesis can be tested by experiments. If a test contradicts the predictions, the theoretical arguments are called into question. If the experimental results confirm the predictions, the theoretical arguments are considered more likely to be correct. The validity of an experiment, however, could be also questioned because the experiment design could be flawed or the outcome of the experiment could be distorted. For example, in 2011, scientists from CERN observed in an experiment that neutrinos could move faster than the speed of light. Neutrinos are subatomic particles that belong to the lepton family. They are known for being nearly massless and traveling near the speed of light. Faster-than-light neutrinos, however, would have contradicted the fundamental principles of the special theory of relativity. In 2012, the research team discovered that the experiment's clocks were out of sync, which overstated the speed of the neutrinos in the experiment.

Controlled experiments try to minimize distortions by creating an environment where only one factor is intentionally changed, while all other factors are kept the same. This is possible in areas such as healthcare, and more difficult in other areas. For example, implementing an economic policy as an experiment would be extremely risky. Designing experiments in astrophysics is technically impossible. In all these cases, researchers rely on natural experiments. Since these naturally occurring situations resemble the environment of controlled experiments, they could provide important insights about the laws of nature.

Natural experiments are widely used in astronomy because of our inherent inability to manipulate celestial bodies. In 1933, while investigating the great Coma cluster of galaxies, the Swiss astrophysicist Fritz Zwicky stumbled upon a major contradiction. Since the average speed of galaxies within a cluster depends on the total mass of the cluster, from the observed speeds of galaxies within the Coma cluster, Zwicky was able to calculate the total mass of the cluster. He then calculated the mass of luminous stars in the cluster based on the light from the galaxies in the cluster. To his surprise, the calculated mass of the cluster based on the speed of its galaxies was about ten times greater than the mass of the cluster calculated based on its total light output. Zwicky concluded that the Coma cluster must contain an enormous quantity of unseen matter. This was effectively the discovery of *dark matter*.

As important as it has been historically, the experimental method is reaching its limitations. Some of them are technical, as experiments are reaching the limits of their ability to distinguish between possible outcomes in a reasonable timeframe. The Large Hadron Collider (LHC) is the world's largest particle accelerator, designed to study the fundamental building blocks of the universe by colliding particles at near-light speeds. The LHC, while groundbreaking, faces technical limitations concerning the strength of its magnets, their cryogenic cooling, and its ability to achieve higher energies. This limits the ability of scientists to test the latest theories about the laws governing the quantum world.

Some of the limits to experimentation are also fundamental in nature. Fundamental limits are built into the laws of physics and are impossible to circumvent with any technology. An example of a fundamental limit is the Heisenberg Uncertainty Principle. The uncertainty principle states that we cannot know both the position and the speed of a particle, such as a photon or electron, with perfect accuracy. This is because the more accurate the measurement of one of these quantities is, the less accurate the measurement of the other quantity would be. This is not a deficiency of the measurement tool, but a fundamental limitation imposed by the wave nature of matter.

Computer simulations are gradually emerging as a new scientific method for understanding the fundamental laws of nature. While the traditional methods use complicated analytical models and a relatively small number of experiments, simulations use relatively simple models but a large number of (simulated) experiments. Simulations could be particularly useful for understanding the underlying principles of complex systems. Analyzing the properties of these systems analytically is nearly impossible. Simulations can provide an insight into these systems quickly and at a relatively low cost.

Conclusion

The human mind is constantly working—recalling memories, playing out scenarios, and engaging in random thought processes. Active brain activity often triggers substantial emotional responses that could lead to restlessness, stress, and sleep problems. Yet, calming the mind is difficult. It seems that mental activity is a defining characteristic of the human condition.

This chapter argues that a significant amount of brain activity could be linked to simulations. Generating scenarios is an effective way for our minds to explore different possibilities. Replaying past situations could lead to an understanding of our failures and how to avoid them in the future. Imagining hypothetical scenarios can also help us prepare for future events. While often stressful, mental activities are also highly beneficial because they allow an individual to estimate the expected rewards of possible actions based on past experiences.

References

Buckner, R. L., & Carroll, D. C. (2007). Self-projection and the brain. *Trends in Cognitive Sciences, 11*(2), 49–57.

Frankenhuis, W. E., & Gopnik, A. (2023). Early adversity and the development of explore–exploit tradeoffs. *Trends in Cognitive Sciences, 27*(7), 616–630.

Geithner, T. F. (2015). *Stress test: Reflections on financial crises.* Crown.

Gopnik, A., O'Grady, S., Lucas, C. G., Griffiths, T. L., Wente, A., Bridgers, S., Aboody, R., Fung, H., & Dahl, R. E. (2017). Changes in cognitive flexibility and hypothesis search across human life history from childhood to adolescence to adulthood. *Proceedings of the National Academy of Sciences*, 114(30), 7892–7899.

Hart, Y., Kosoy, E., Liquin, E. G., Leonard, J. A., Mackey, A. P., & Gopnik, A. (2022). The development of creative search strategies. *Cognition, 225*, 105102.

Hills, T. T., Todd, P. M., Lazer, D., Redish, A. D., & Couzin, I. D. (2015). Exploration versus exploitation in space, mind, and society. *Trends in Cognitive Sciences, 19*(1), 46–54.

Liquin, E. G., & Gopnik, A. (2022). Children are more exploratory and learn more than adults in an approach-avoid task. *Cognition, 218*, 104940.

Piaget, J. (1954). *The construction of reality in the child* (M. Cook, trans.) New York: Ballantine Books.

Redish, A. D. (2013). *The mind within the brain: How we make decisions and how those decisions go wrong*. Oxford University Press.

Sumner, E., Li, A. X., Perfors, A., Hayes, B., Navarro, D., & Sarnecka, B. W. (2019). *The exploration advantage: Children's instinct to explore allows them to find information that adults miss*. PsyArXiv. https://doi.org/10.31234/osf.io/h437v

CHAPTER 8

Exploration Through Delegation

A man only learns in two ways, one by reading, and the other by association with smarter people.

—Will Rogers

Source: It appears in one of Will Rogers's syndicated newspaper Weekly Articles, #147, dated October 5, 1925

Contents

Introduction

Life is an endless process of self-discovery. As discussed in Chap. 3, this process is reflected in the hero-myth common across most world mythologies. At the beginning of the hero narrative, the protagonist lives an ordinary

C. A. Pirinsky, *A Theory of Dynamic Preferences*,
https://doi.org/10.1007/978-3-032-13334-2_8

life and receives a call to go on an adventure. A critical element in most myths is an encounter with a mentor who helps the protagonist overcome hesitation and embark on their journey. The mentor provides the wisdom, knowledge, and confidence the hero needs to accomplish his mission.

This chapter develops the idea that delegation is an important factor facilitating exploration. Mentors often fulfill this role. Early life exploration is largely delegated to family, educational institutions, and other social structures. Later in life, people start utilizing other direct and indirect forms of exploration. People could also delegate responsibilities to others by accepting their recommendations or advice. Indeed, exploration could account for the growth and popularity of the advisory industry both at the personal and the business level.

One advantage of delegation is that it could be directed toward a more qualified person. Delegation, however, could be beneficial even when delegating to non-experts. The action space consists of three areas: explored states (E), known unexplored states (U), and unknown unexplored states (U2). Direct exploration is usually confined to U, or the options a person knows about. By transferring responsibilities to others, people can explore states of the world they do not know exist.

But how much responsibility should a person delegate to others? Delegation requires trust and people low in trust could under-delegate. In this case, valuable resources would remain untapped. Too much trust, however, could result in over-delegation. Delegation is costly, and using it when its benefits are small could be sub-optimal. The delegating person could also be expropriated, especially when their institutional protection is weak. Thus, the right amount of delegation strikes a delicate balance.

Exploration Through Delegation

Delegation is the process of entrusting responsibilities to someone else—an organization, an expert, or an acquaintance. Delegation is widely regarded as an essential element of effective management. The distribution of work and responsibilities to subordinate workers enables employees to gain experience and develop valuable skills that can improve the organization (Banford et al., 2014). Delegation also builds trust and self-confidence in employees (Treher et al., 2011). The benefits of delegation, however, extend beyond the organization.

The main advantage of delegation, as compared to alternative forms of exploration, is that it could be directed toward a more qualified person. By delegating exploration to others, people could also explore a wide set of opportunities and free up resources to focus on activities they are better at. There are various reasons why some people and organizations could be better at exploration than others. For one, they could be more prone to exploration than the person delegating responsibilities to them. Some people could also have greater access to opportunities and information.

Delegation could be beneficial even when delegating to non-experts. Most forms of direct exploration are local and tend to be biased toward familiar outcomes. If you decide to try a new restaurant, you would tend to choose among the restaurants you know about. Yet, there could be plenty of options you are not familiar with. Randomization often has the same flaw because we tend to randomize among the options we know about. While the toss of a die generates six outcomes, the world offers a far greater number of possibilities. Social exploration is also constrained by the network of a person, which usually consists of people who are similar to them.

The action space could be generally divided into three areas: explored states (E), known unexplored states (U), and unknown unexplored states (U2). While direct exploration is confined to U, delegated exploration allows for the exploration of U2 because what is unknown to some could be familiar to others. By transferring responsibilities to others, people can explore states of the world that they are not even aware exist (see Fig. 8.1).

Delegation also has its costs. First of all, it is not free. It takes time and resources to delegate, as well as to incentivize people to explore on one's

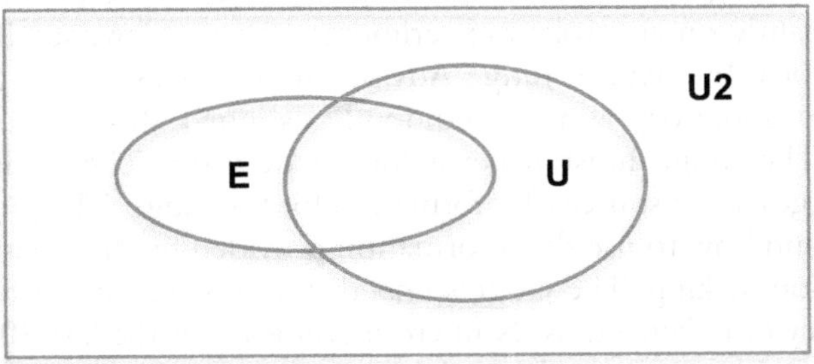

Fig. 8.1 Exploration and the unexplored. The figure presents the set of explored options (E), the set of unexplored options a person is aware of (U), and the set of unexplored options a person is unaware of (U2). The intersection of E and U refers to partially-explored states

behalf. Second, as in social exploration, delegation could be noisy. People value different things, and what is good and valuable for some might not be good and valuable for others. Third, successful delegation also depends on a person's ability to identify expertise. It requires meta-exploration, where a person needs to identify the best entity to delegate to.

Exploration and Advice

People could delegate responsibilities to others by accepting their advice. Advice refers to the guidance or recommendation extended from one person, group, or organization to another. Giving and receiving advice has been an essential component of decision-making.

Most important choices in life are rarely made in isolation. Presidents rely on advisors to guide their policy decisions. Firm CEOs may talk to numerous employees, consulting firms, and peers before making a major corporate decision. University deans often have advisory boards. A college applicant is likely to consult his or her parents and friends about which college to select. Upon graduation, they are also likely to consult with others about which job offer to accept.

Advice-taking and advice-giving have been studied in numerous disciplines, such as psychology, economics, and organizational behavior. In economics, mentorship is recognized as a vital resource for entrepreneurs providing them guidance and support. The willingness of entrepreneurs to take advice from investors and other partners has also been regarded as an important factor for success in the venture capital industry (Timmons & Bygrave, 1986).

In psychology, research on advice-giving and advice-taking has relied predominantly on controlled experiments (for a review, see Bonaccio & Dalal, 2006). In a typical Judge-Advisor System (JAS) study, participants enter the laboratory and are randomly assigned the role of *judge* or *advisor*. The judge must make a formal decision. The advisor, as the name suggests, is a source of information for the judge. The judge decides whether and how to use the information provided by the advisor in his or her decision making. The judge's final decision is then evaluated in terms of accuracy or effectiveness. Numerous studies over the last 30 years have explored various aspects of the advising process in this setting.

The findings in JAS studies are generally consistent with the idea that judges consider advisors an important source of information. There is also evidence that the benefits of the advice increase with the number of advisors and their degree of independence (Johnson et al., 2001; Soll, 1999; Yaniv, 2004). Further, expert advice is considered to be more helpful than novice advice (Goldsmith & Fitch, 1997). Recommendations given by more confident advisors are also more likely to be followed than recommendations given by less confident advisors (Van Swol & Sniezek, 2005).

The popularity of advisory services has been increasing rapidly in recent years. Investment advisors, personal trainers, and life coaches are used by an increasingly large number of individuals. Companies are often utilizing external consultants with strategic industry knowledge. Part of this growth is fueled by the increased need of individuals and organizations to explore an increasingly complex world.

Delegation and Social Connections

People with smaller social networks are expected to benefit more from delegation because they have a limited number of opportunities for social exploration. Imagine that you have two close friends: A and B. Your social exploration is bound by their experiences. Imagine also that Person A has 20 friends. By delegating exploration to A, you would be able to increase your social resource 10-fold. Of course, for this to happen 1) you need to be willing to entrust exploration to A and 2) A needs to be motivated to explore on your behalf.

One important concept in network theory is degrees of separation. It describes how connected people are to each other through acquaintances. In the example above, A has 20 friends. Assuming that you and B are two of them, this leaves 18 people that A knows and you don't know directly. All these people have one degree of separation from you. The friends of their friends have two degrees of separation from you, while their friends—three degrees of separation, and so on.

The "six degrees of separation" hypothesis states that all people are six or fewer social connections away from each other. As a result, a chain of "friend of a friend" can be made to connect any two people in a maximum of six steps. Although the number six is a speculation, it is true that people have been becoming more connected over time. As of now, the degree of separation in the world could have become even lower than six. The idea of "six degrees of separation" was popularized throughout the 1990s by a parlor game where players challenge each other to find the shortest path from an actor to the actor Kevin Bacon, where two actors are considered connected if they appear in the same film.[1]

[1] See https://www.sixdegrees.org/.

Interesting is the interpretation of the six degree-hypothesis within the context of exploration. The six degrees of separation imply that you are six delegations away from ALL social information in the world. In such a world, a friend of your friend (a person you have never met) was likely competing in the 2024 Olympic Games, while a friend of a friend of a friend (whom you have also never met) might have been on the top of Mount Everest.

Concepts

Exploration through delegation. *The act of exploring aspects of the environment by delegating responsibility to another party (an individual or an organization).*

Under-/Overdelegation. *Delegating exploration to another person (entity) below/above optimal levels.*

Advice. *The act of extending or receiving opinions and recommendations from another person regarding a certain situation or a possible course of action.*

Judge–Advisor System (JAS). *An experimental design used to study advice giving and advice taking behavior. Participants enter the laboratory and are randomly assigned the role of a judge or advisor, where the judge makes the final decision and the advisor provides an advice under various circumstances.*

Delegation and Trust

Civilized society is based on trust. High levels of interpersonal trust in a community promote investment, exchange, and other forms of social interaction (e.g., Fukuyama, 1996; Guiso et al., 2004; Knack & Keefer, 1997). Kenneth Arrow famously noted that "[v]irtually every commercial transaction has within itself an element of trust" (Arrow, 1972). Delegation is not an exception. Every act of delegation is guided by some form of an explicit or implicit contract, and to enter this contract, every party needs to trust the other party. Indeed, JAS studies confirm that judges' trust in their advisors is positively related to advice taking (Sniezek et al., 1998; Van Swol & Sniezek, 2005).

Trust deficit could result in under-delegation. In this case, people could under-explore their environment, especially in cases where delegated exploration is valuable. For example, more introverted and risk-averse individuals would suffer more from their lack of trust compared to more extroverted and risk-taking individuals.

Too much trust, however, could result in over-delegation. First, as any form of exploration, delegation is expected to have diminishing returns. Since delegation is costly, over-using it when its benefits are small could be sub-optimal. Second, a person's trust in someone else makes them vulnerable because the other person might not live up to their expectation, even unintentionally. This is reflected in the expression "you always hurt the one you love." In some cases, the delegating person could also be intentionally expropriated by the other party.

Delegation defines an agency relationship between the person who delegates and the person accepting the task. As such, it is subject to a conflict of interest, commonly referred to as the principal-agent problem. The principal-agent problem refers to the idea that when one person or entity (the agent) acts on behalf of another (the principal), the agent might not act in the best interest of the principal (Grossman & Hart, 1983; Jensen & Meckling, 1976). In an exploration context, the advisor might not put in enough effort; demand excessive compensation, and over-state their expertise.

Conclusion

This chapter discusses exploration through delegation. By transferring responsibilities to others, people can explore states of the world that they are not aware exist. People can delegate responsibilities to others either directly or indirectly by accepting their recommendations and advice. The chapter argues that exploration could account for the growth and popularity of the advisory industry, both at the personal and the business level. In a complex world, companies are increasingly seeking consultants to explore emerging new technologies, industry trends, and new markets. The delegation of authority, however, could have a dark side, as the advisor might not always act in the best interest of the advisee.

References

Arrow, K. J. (1972). Gifts and exchanges. *Philosophy and Public Affairs*, 343–362.

Bonaccio, S., & Dalal, R. S. (2006). Advice taking and decision-making: An integrative literature review, and implications for the organizational sciences. *Organizational Behavior and Human Decision Processes*, *101*(2), 127–151.

Banford, C. G., Ronald Buckley, M., & Roberts, F. (2014). Delegation revisited: How delegation can benefit globally-minded managers. *International Journal of Physical Distribution and Logistics Management*, *44*(8/9), 646–654.

Fukuyama, F. (1996). *Trust: The social virtues and the creation of prosperity*. Simon and Schuster.

Goldsmith, D. J., & Fitch, K. (1997). The normative context of advice as social support. *Human Communication Research*, *23*(4), 454–476.

Grossman, S., & Hart, O. (1983). An analysis of the principal-agent problem. *Econometrica*, *51*, 7–45.

Guiso, L., Sapienza, P., & Zingales, L. (2004). The role of social capital in financial development. *American Economic Review*, *94*(3), 526–556.

Jensen, M. C., & Meckling, W. H. (1976). Theory of the firm: Managerial behavior, agency costs and ownership structure. *Journal of Financial Economics*, *3*, 305–360.

Johnson, T. R., Budescu, D. V., & Wallsten, T. S. (2001). Averaging probability judgments: Monte Carlo analyses of asymptotic diagnostic value. *Journal of Behavioral Decision Making*, *14*(2), 123–140.

Knack, S., & Keefer, P. (1997). Does social capital have an economic payoff? A cross-country investigation. *The Quarterly Journal of Economics*, *112*(4), 1251–1288.

Sniezek, J. A., Heath, C., Van Swol, L. M., & Nochimowski, M. (1998). Suspicious minds. In *Annual meeting of the society for judgment and decision making*. Dallas.

Soll, J. B. (1999). Intuitive theories of information: Beliefs about the value of redundancy. *Cognitive Psychology*, *38*(2), 317–346.

Timmons, J. A., & Bygrave, W. D. (1986). Venture capital's role in financing innovation for economic growth. *Journal of Business Venturing*, *1*(2), 161–176.

Treher, E., Piltz, D., & Jacobs, S. (2011). Increasing effectiveness through delegation. In *A guide to success for technical managers: Supervising in research, development, and engineering* (pp. 89–111). John Wiley & Sons, Inc.

Van Swol, L. M., & Sniezek, J. A. (2005). Factors affecting the acceptance of expert advice. *British Journal of Social Psychology*, *44*(3), 443–461.

Yaniv, I. (2004). Receiving other people's advice: Influence and benefit. *Organizational Behavior and Human Decision Processes*, *93*(1), 1–13.

CHAPTER 9

Deep Exploration

Habit is a second nature that destroys the first. But what is nature? Why is habit not natural? I am very much afraid that nature itself is only a first habit, just as habit is a second nature.

—Blaise Pascal

Source: Pascal, Blaise. (1966). Pensées. Translated by A. J. Krailsheimer. Baltimore, Maryland: Penguin Books. (**p. 30**)

Contents

Introduction

Primary preferences direct living organisms toward activities that are beneficial for survival and away from activities that diminish their chances for survival. If the environment is stable, one would expect that primary

C. A. Pirinsky, *A Theory of Dynamic Preferences*,
https://doi.org/10.1007/978-3-032-13334-2_9

preferences will be inevitably geared toward survival because preferences not aligned with survival would not be passed to the next generation. However, as the environment changes, individual preferences could become out of tune with survival. As a result, learning about the optimality of our own preferences becomes important. I refer to this learning process as deep exploration and the system of preferences that incorporates this knowledge as revised preferences.

This chapter analyzes deep exploration. It argues that social groups aggregate the knowledge generated through deep exploration in a system of social norms that are transferred from one generation to the next in oral and written forms. These norms effectively modify individual preferences. Meat tastes good, but if existing conditions make the consumption of meat unhealthy, societies will develop social norms banning the consumption of meat. Physical exercise could be unpleasant. But if the prevailing lifestyle makes exercise beneficial, then societies will develop social norms encouraging physical activity. Cultural beliefs serve the important purpose of fine-tuning individual preferences toward beneficial choices and away from harmful choices. I refer to this property of cultural beliefs as preference tuning. I also contend that preference exploration is asymmetric. Since people are naturally attracted to pleasant outcomes, they collect more information about the implications of high-reward options than the implications of low-reward options. Thus, society could benefit from deeper exploration of the potential benefits of low-reward alternatives.

When people start questioning the optimality of their primary preferences, they may start seeking feedback on their actions. I argue that this is one important reason people are prone to share their experiences, especially the ones they regard as positive or negative. Bragging and complaining, although prevailing in life, have been difficult to explain. One potential benefit of these activities is that they solicit feedback on actions with positively-valanced and negatively-valanced emotions.

Revised preferences inevitably require people to engage in behaviors that are not rewarded by the reward system and to abstain from behaviors that are highly rewarding. Thus, preference revision requires substantial discipline and mental strength. Habit formation is an important mechanism facilitating the process of preference modification. By making unpleasurable activities rewarding, habits can direct our lives toward beneficial behaviors and away from harmful behaviors.

Exploring Preferences

If the environment is relatively stable, the forces of natural selection would tend to align preferences with survival. The environment, however, is constantly changing for a variety of reasons. Some of them reflect changes in one's life situation. Getting married, starting a new job, or relocating to a new state could all trigger important changes in one's environment. Other changes are systematic and reflect major trends in the world. Technological development has fundamentally transformed the way we shop, learn, and communicate with each other. AI will further reshape all aspects of our lives. These developments are happening rapidly, and they could challenge the preferences that we currently have.

When the environment changes, preferences could become out of tune with survival. For example, over-eating could have been optimal when the supply of food was scarce and unpredictable. Such behavior, however, could become harmful when food is abundant. Along the same lines, aimless use of energy, such as exercise, was probably not encouraged when food supply was limited. Today, exercise is widely regarded as beneficial. Stress is a correct response to dangerous situations because it helps the organism mobilize resources to overcome a life-threatening situation. Stress, however, could be damaging in a safe environment.

All these developments create the need for deeper exploration of our innate preferences. I refer to this learning process as deep exploration and the system of preferences incorporating this knowledge as revised preferences. The objective of deep exploration is to obtain a better understanding of the "real" consequences of our actions, independently of the rewards they generate. To accomplish this, however, one needs information (observations) about the choices of different people and the consequences these choices entail. Personal experiences are important, but when it comes to survival, they generate very limited information. Thus, we cannot learn about the optimality of our own preferences through our personal experiences alone. Deep exploration requires breadth.

Deep exploration could take many forms. Some of it happens naturally, as people learn about the optimality of their reward system through everyday experiences. For example, people could learn about the health implications of smoking by observing the implications of smoking for the lives of people around them. Based on this information, they can build a "mental model" assessing the health risks of smoking. People could further communicate this information to some of their acquittances.

These activities lead to the aggregation of information within social networks. The resulting learning process is spontaneous and uncoordinated. This is how deep exploration has been evolving through history.

Given the existential importance of deep exploration, societies encourage collective efforts aimed at a better understanding of their primary preferences. Some of these explorations take place in specialized research units at universities, government agencies, and firms. For example, in the domain of nutrition, independent research has been conducted by universities, non-profit organizations, and the National Institute of Health. The main findings from this research are summarized in reports and disseminated to the public. The knowledge that collective exploration generates is aggregated in a system of beliefs that are transferred from one generation to the next in oral and written forms, i.e. it becomes part of society's culture.

Richerson and Boyd (2005) define culture as "*information capable of affecting individuals' behavior that they acquire from other members of their species through teaching, imitation, and other forms of social transmission.*" This definition implies that culture is impactful and persistent. The fact that deep exploration shapes individual behavior suggests that it becomes an important component of societal culture. The internalization of this knowledge, however, requires a great deal of trust in societal institutions. More specifically, the following hypothesis is expected to hold.

Preference Tuning Hypothesis. Cultural beliefs serve the important purpose of directing individual preferences towards beneficial choices and away from harmful choices. These beliefs accumulate knowledge from the collective experience of the group.

Primary preferences could be viewed as a classification mechanism mapping the physiological response of an action (the reward) to the survival likelihood of an individual. As such, this mechanism is prone to two types of errors. First, it could classify a dangerous outcome as pleasant and, as a result, expose an individual to risks (a false positive). Second, it could classify a beneficial outcome as unpleasant and, in the process, discourage individuals from beneficial actions (a false negative). Since people are naturally attracted to peasant outcomes, deep exploration would be more likely to correct Type 1 errors (pleasant outcome is harmful) than Type 2 errors (an unpleasant outcome is beneficial). Thus, the following proposition is expected to hold.

Asymmetric Exploration Hypothesis. High-reward (more attractive) options are explored deeper than low-reward (less attractive) options. Society could benefit from grater exploration of less rewarding outcomes.

The History of Smoking and Penicillin

This section illustrates how preference exploration has reshaped social attitudes toward two substances—tobacco and noble mold.

Smoking originated in American shamanistic rituals more than 5000 years ago. Following the arrival of the Europeans in the sixteenth century, the consumption, cultivation, and trading of tobacco quickly spread all over the world. Spanish and Portuguese sailors were perhaps the first Europeans to light up a cigar. They introduced tobacco to a Frenchman named Jean Nicot (from whose name the word nicotine derives) who brought tobacco to France. From there, it spread to England and subsequently to Asia. Tobacco consumption deeply infiltrated all cultures around the world. Smoking even became a part of the traditional Japanese tea ceremony.

Like coffee and opium, tobacco was originally seen as something that was beneficial in its healing properties. The concept of ingesting substances in the form of smoke was also met with curiosity and astonishment. Mass production quickly expanded the scope of tobacco consumption. In the late nineteenth century, automated cigarette-making carried out the mass production of cigarettes at low cost. Cigarettes became elegant and fashionable among men. But the main reason for the expansion of tobacco consumption was that tobacco is pleasurable and addictive.

With the arrival of information about the health hazards of tobacco, the public attitudes toward smoking gradually changed. Prior to World War I, lung cancer was a rare disease. With the postwar rise in cigarette smoking, however, the significant increase in lung cancer promoted investigations into the link between smoking and cancer. In 1929, the German scientist Fritz Lickint established a formal statistical connection between lung cancer and tobacco use. He also argued that tobacco use could explain the fact that lung cancer struck men more often than women (since women smoked much less). A series of breakthrough studies throughout the 1950s demonstrated convincingly that smoking could cause serious health damage. As a result of this research, smoking became stigmatized throughout Western societies. Since primary preferences were encouraging harmful behavior, a correction of these preferences seemed justifiable.

The story of mold is quite different from the story of tobacco. Mold is a microscopic fungus that can grow in moist areas. It causes biodegradation, which makes mold unwanted and particularly dangerous when ingested. Indeed, many strategies for food preservation (e.g., salting, pickling, and drying) prevent mold growth as well as the growth of other microbes. Not surprisingly, molds do not look appetizing and tend to be unpalatable (except for blue cheese).

In 1928, Scottish physician Alexander Fleming returned from a holiday to his lab in the St. Mary's Hospital in London. In the lab, he had left a few Petri dishes with strains of Staphylococcus bacteria. He noticed that one of the Petri dishes had a mold, Penicillium notatum, growing on it. His initial reaction was disappointment from the contamination. He also noticed, however, that the mold had a clear zone around it, indicating that its presence was inhibiting the growth of the bacteria. Upon further investigation, Fleming discovered that the mold produces chemicals that could kill bacteria by disrupting the synthesis of their cell walls. His discovery led to the development of penicillin, the first widely used antibiotic able to treat life-threatening bacterial infections.

Fleming's discovery shifted dramatically the public attitudes toward mold. From being unpleasant and potentially toxic, molds became a life-saving compound that revolutionized medicine. Exploration has transformed our preferences toward penicillin. This example also illustrates the idea that Type 2 errors of the reward system (false negatives) are more likely to be uncovered by chance than by directed exploration because unpleasant outcomes are naturally avoided. Indeed, Fleming was intentionally trying to prevent his Petri dishes from fungal contamination. Fortunately, he was not completely successful in his pursuit. His failure led to a deep exploration that transformed healthcare. The example also illustrates the profound effect of randomness on exploration and scientific discovery (see Chap. 11).

Concepts

Deep exploration. *The acquisition of knowledge about the implications of our primary preferences for survival. It is based on the critical examination of the behavior of a large group of people.*

Revised preferences. *A system of preferences that incorporates the knowledge accumulated through deep exploration.*

Preference tuning hypothesis. *The idea that cultural beliefs serve the purpose of directing (or fine-tuning) individual preferences toward beneficial choices and away from harmful choices.*

Asymmetric exploration hypothesis. *The idea that higher-reward (more attractive) options are explored deeper than lower-reward (less attractive) options.*

Type 1 error. *A situation in which primary preferences classify a potentially dangerous outcome as pleasant (false positive).*

Type 2 error. *A situation in which primary preferences classify a potentially beneficial outcome as unpleasant (false negative).*

Habit formation. *The process through which certain actions and behaviors become automatic,* i.e. *implementable with limited cognitive and emotional cost or effort.*

Learning by Sharing

Primary preferences provide information about the relative advantages of the options we face. When people start questioning the quality of this information, they start examining the optimality of their preferences. Since most experiences are private, this prompts people to start sharing their experiences.

There is extensive evidence that people are inclined to share experiences and the very act of doing so is rewarding. We structure our daily schedules to gather with others to eat meals, celebrate occasions, and engage in conversations. People do this even in situations where social interactions are minimal, such as watching a film or attending a presentation. There is also evidence that sharing experiences, even from afar, could bring people together. In one experiment, researchers arranged for college students to receive a personalized video message from a local celebrity—the school basketball coach (Shaddy et al., 2021). Students were then asked to choose a friend to receive a similar message and to decide whether the message should be sent on the same day or a different day. Almost all participants wanted the video message sent on the same day.

Shared experiences provide a sense of connection, validation, and enhanced enjoyment. The fact that sharing is rewarding suggests that it serves a purpose. I argue that a reevaluation of one's own preferences could be one such purpose. Sharing an experience allows an individual to compare their perceived reward of the experience with the perceived rewards of others.

Two well-documented properties of shared experiences—their amplification and synchronization—are consistent with this interpretation.

It is well-documented that sharing amplifies both positive and negative experiences. For example, a recent study found that sharing an experience with another person, even without communicating, intensifies the experience for both participants (Boothby et al., 2014). Yet, it is not clear why merely sharing an experience affects people's subjective evaluation of stimuli (Boothby et al., 2014). Shared experiences provide information about the tastes and preferences of another person. Even the very act of sharing is informative because it tells us that an experience we regard as positive is also regarded as positive by another person. This validation could intensify one's response to the experience.

There is also evidence that shared experiences elicit synchronized emotional responses. A recent study recorded the facial expressions and electrodermal activity (EDA) of participants as they watched four episodes of a TV show with another participant (Cheong et al., 2023). Participants displayed synchronized emotional facial expressions, and the degree of synchronization predicted the self-reported social connection between viewing partners. This evidence is also consistent with social learning. The reactions of other people provide information about the rewards they associate with particular stimuli. When people internalize this information, their reactions are expected to synchronize.

If people share experiences to receive feedback on their preferences, they would be more likely to share experiences they regard as extreme. The phenomena of bragging and complaining are evidence for such behavior. Both behaviors are prevailing and often displayed by the same people. It is difficult to develop a theory predicting that a person would engage in bragging and complaining at the same time. Learning about our own preferences provides one explanation.

Bragging (or self-praise) is an attempt to present favorable self-image by disclosing an attribute about the speaker or their in-group that the speaker believes is positively valued (Dayter, 2014). It is widespread in daily communications, especially on social media. Bragging is often interpreted as a mechanism to enhance one's self-esteem. Given that it elicits envy and other negative emotions in others, however, it is unclear how it benefits the bragging individual.

The exploration framework developed in this book suggests that one potential benefit of bragging is that it solicits feedback on actions with positively-valanced emotions. Since such actions are attractive and likely to repeat, a better understanding of their consequences is particularly important. Bragging invites commentary. A bragging individual is effectively asking—is this as good and useful as I think it is? Interestingly, envy makes the commentary even more informative because an envious person would try to discredit the positive news by finding some potential drawbacks of the shared experience. The absence of commentary is also informative. Bragging always generates useful information about the implications of pleasant outcomes people are naturally attracted to.

Similarly to bragging, complaining provides information about negatively-valanced emotions. People complain or vent to manage stress, seek validation, or express feelings of helplessness. However, excessive complaining seems unproductive (Norlock, 2018). Philosophers, most notably Aristotle and Kant, have also advocated the view that burdening others with one's pain is unethical and should be avoided. Yet, people continue doing it, very likely because it generates information. A complaining individual is effectively asking—is this as bad as I think it is? Complaining invites commentary. An empathic response reinforces the negativity of the outcome, while a comforting response suggests that the outcome should not be regarded as negatively as the complainer thinks. Complaining helps us revise our primary preferences.

Habit Formation

One of the most remarkable aspects of life is our ability to form habits. Habit formation is the process by which, through repetition, a behavior becomes automatic or habitual. In 1903, the *American Journal of Psychology* defined habit as follows: "A habit, from the standpoint of psychology, is a more or less fixed way of thinking, willing, or feeling acquired through previous repetition of a mental experience." During much of our waking lives, from the time we rise until we fall asleep, we act out habits.

One important function of habit formation is that it facilitates the revision of primary preferences. By making unpleasurable activities rewarding, habits could direct our lives toward beneficial outcomes. Thus, one possible response to Pascal's question at the beginning of this chapter "Why is habit not natural?" could be that inherited traits lack flexibility. The neuroplasticity of habits provides a valuable tool for individuals to "adjust" their innate preferences.

Numerous properties of habits are consistent with the idea that they are an effective mechanism for preference modification (see e.g., Graybiel, 2008).

For example, habits are largely learned and habit acquisition is often consciously directed by the person acquiring the habit. In the initial stages of habit learning, behaviors are goal-directed. With extended repetitions, however, individuals come to perform the behaviors automatically, and once established, habits can be very strong and persistent. The "habit loop" describes the process of habit formation as consisting of three components: a cue (trigger), a routine (behavior), and a reward (positive response). The reward reinforces the loop, making it more likely to be repeated. The behavioral patterns we repeat are imprinted in our neural pathways, which further increases their attractiveness (Balleine & Dickinson, 1998; Graybiel, 2008).

There is evidence that individuals use habit formation strategically to modify their preferences. Public health experts have developed numerous techniques for forming new healthy habits and breaking existing unhealthy habits (Lally & Gardner, 2013). Habit formation is also used strategically by firms. In his book "The Power of Habit," Charles Duhigg explains how companies leverage the "habit loop" (cue, routine, reward) to influence both customer behavior and employee performance (Duhigg, 2012). By manipulating these loops, businesses can change both their customer behavior and workplace culture.

Preference modification is related to the concept of plasticity in biology. Adaptive phenotypic plasticity refers to the ability of organisms to modify their traits during their lifetime to cope with changing environments (Maklakov et al., 2011; Snell-Rood & Steck, 2019). For example, muscle mass increases with exercise and decreases with inactivity. Plants like water lilies can produce different types of leaves (submerged, floating, and aerial) depending on whether they are below, on, or above the surface. Along similar lines, neuroplasticity refers to the ability of the nervous system to change its structure in response to various stimuli, including learning, experience, and disease. It involves the formation of new synapses (connections between neurons) and the strengthening or weakening of existing ones.

Habit formation has been applied in economic analysis to model how past consumption influences current and future consumption. This effect is often modeled by incorporating a "habit stock" component to the utility function. Habit formation models predict that habits cause consumption to adjust slowly to shocks to permanent income (Campbell & Deaton, 1989). Because habits increase the disutility associated with large declines in consumption, they may also provide a partial solution to the equity premium puzzle (Constantinides, 1990; Campbell & Cochrane, 1999). Habit formation in most of these models, however, is a mechanical artifact of repetition. The focus of this book is on individual preferences. Preference evaluation is a result of exploration, and habit formation facilitates the ability of individuals to modify their preferences.

Conclusion

The forces of natural selection tend to align individual preferences with survival. As the environment changes, however, preferences could become suboptimal, i.e., they could encourage harmful behavior and discourage beneficial behavior. Preferences could be viewed as a classification mechanism mapping the evolutionary advantages of an action to a physiological response (the reward). As such, this mechanism is prone to two types of errors. First, it could classify a dangerous outcome as pleasant and, as a result, expose an individual to risks (a false positive). Second, it could classify a beneficial outcome as unpleasant and, in the process, discourage individuals from survival-enhancing behaviors (a false negative).

This chapter introduces the concept of deep exploration, defined as the accumulation of knowledge about the optimality of primary preferences. I refer to a preference system that internalizes this knowledge as revised preferences. Deep exploration has the following properties: 1) it is data-intensive, i.e., it requires a large cross-section of observations; 2) the knowledge it generates is universal, i.e., it applies to most individuals in the group; 3) the knowledge it generates is aggregated in societal culture; 4) it is asymmetric, i.e., it explores deeper high-reward (more attractive) options than low-reward (less attractive) options; 5) it creates incentives for people to share their experiences, especially the ones they regard as extreme; and 6) it leads to modification of primary preferences, and habit formation facilitates this process.

References

Balleine, B. W., & Dickinson, A. (1998). Goal-directed instrumental action: Contingency and incentive learning and their cortical substrates. *Neuropharmacology, 37*(4–5), 407–419.

Boothby, E. J., Clark, M. S., & Bargh, J. A. (2014). Shared experiences are amplified. *Psychological Science, 25*(12), 2209–2216.

Campbell, J., & Deaton, A. (1989). Why is consumption so smooth? *Review of Economic Studies, 56*(3), 357–373.

Campbell, J. Y., & Cochrane, J. H. (1999). By force of habit: A consumption-based explanation of aggregate stock market behavior. *Journal of Political Economy, 107*(2), 205–251.

Cheong, J. H., Molani, Z., Sadhukha, S., & Chang, L. J. (2023). Synchronized affect in shared experiences strengthens social connection. *Communications Biology, 6*(1), 1099.

Constantinides, G. M. (1990). Habit formation: A resolution of the equity premium puzzle. *Journal of Political Economy, 98*(3), 519–543.

Dayter, D. (2014). Self-praise in microblogging. *Journal of Pragmatics, 61*, 91–102.

Duhigg, C. (2012). *The power of habit: Why we do what we do in life and business.* Random House.

Graybiel, A. M. (2008). Habits, rituals, and the evaluative brain. *Annual Review of Neuroscience, 31*(1), 359–387.

Lally, P., & Gardner, B. (2013). Promoting habit formation. *Health Psychology Review, 7*(supl), S137–S158.

Maklakov, A. A., Immler, S., Gonzalez-Voyer, A., Rönn, J., & Kolm, N. (2011). Brains and the city: Big-brained passerine birds succeed in urban environments. *Biology Letters, 7*(5), 730–732.

Norlock, K. J. (2018). Can't complain. *Journal of Moral Philosophy, 15*(2), 117–135.

Richerson, P. J., & Boyd, R. (2005). *Not by genes alone: How culture transformed human evolution.* University of Chicago Press.

Shaddy, F., Tu, Y., & Fishbach, A. (2021). Social hedonic editing: People prefer to experience events at the same time as others. *Social Psychological and Personality Science, 12*(7), 1233–1240.

Snell-Rood, E. C., & Steck, M. K. (2019). Behaviour shapes environmental variation and selection on learning and plasticity: Review of mechanisms and implications. *Animal Behaviour, 147*, 147–156.

CHAPTER 10

Evolving Preferences

The only true voyage of discovery ... would be not to visit new landscapes, but to possess other eyes, to see the universe through the eyes of another, of a hundred others, to see the hundred universes that each of them sees.

—Marcel Proust

Source: Proust, M. (1974). 'La Prisonnière', À la Recherche du Temps Perdu (1913–27). In Roger Shattuck, Proust (1974), (**p. 131**)

Contents

Introduction

When the environment changes, inherited preferences could become out-of-tune with survival. Some changes to the environment are external; others are systematically related to our preferences. This chapter analyzes one such case.

C. A. Pirinsky, *A Theory of Dynamic Preferences*,
https://doi.org/10.1007/978-3-032-13334-2_10

Humans naturally strive to maximize their interactions with pleasant outcomes and to minimize their interactions with unpleasant outcomes. This is the reason we have been growing crops, building shelters, and forming friendships. The increased availability of high-reward options, however, reduces the value of these options. As a result, the existing rewards or utilities of these options become unjustifiably high. I refer to this possibility as reward inflation. Reward inflation could result in over-consumption, some aspects of which could be harmful.

Reward inflation suggests that a hedonistic approach to life is not optimal because it puts too much emphasis on high-reward options. In response, societies are expected to develop social norms for abstinence from these options. However, a complete denial of pleasurable outcomes would not be optimal either because it bets against evolutionary processes. Thus, an optimal strategy in life would be to follow the middle path between two extremes—one of excess and the other of deficiency. I refer to this as the golden mean hypothesis because it aligns with the ancient philosophical doctrine carrying the same name.

The chapter also analyzes how reward inflation has reshaped societal attitudes toward food, security, social connections, and wealth. There is a certain irony in the way preferences evolve. Civilized societies work hard to secure access to the things they like and to avoid the things they dislike. The reward system, however, is slow in adjusting to these developments, which leads to overreaction. We are drawn to things we do not need and are fearful of things that do not harm us. The negative emotions are harmful. The positive emotions lead to over-indulgence, which itself could be harmful. A better understanding of our evolving preferences could help us better address the emerging challenges.

The Inflation of Rewards

As advocated in the previous chapter, when the environment changes, inherited preferences could become suboptimal. The environment changes for a variety of reasons. Some changes are exogenous. For example, a meteorite impact can trigger large changes in the Earth's atmosphere. Other changes are an artifact of human activity. For example, technological advances have transformed our physical and social environment in a short period of time. Since some of these developments are related to the prevailing preferences in the population, they could undermine the optimality of these preferences.

This section explores one such possibility. It is based on two assumptions. The first assumption is that scarcity enhances rewards. The reward system directs individuals toward outcomes that are beneficial for survival. Not all outcomes, however, are equally available. Given that the objective of rewards is to motivate reward acquisition, the rewards of scarcer options are expected to be higher than the rewards of more available options. The second assumption is about the increasing availability of high-reward options. The fact that we want to maximize contact with the things we like steers the path of economic development toward increased access to high-reward options. This is the reason people's ability to satisfy their basic needs has been increasing over time. Poverty, both globally and within the US, has also been declining rapidly in recent times.

The above two assumptions imply that by making high-reward options more available, people are effectively reducing the value of these options. As a result, the rewards of these options could become unjustifiably high. I refer to this possibility as reward inflation because it bears some resemblance to the phenomenon of average price increases in economics. More formally, the following proposition is expected to hold:

Reward Inflation Hypothesis. The increased availability of high-reward options reduces the value of these options. This makes their rewards (utilities) abnormally high relative to the rewards (utilities) of other options.

The above hypothesis suggests that reward inflation could lead to overconsumption of resources. Such overconsumption could be harmful because organisms might not be well-equipped to deal with it. The overconsumption of some resources could also lead to the underconsumption of others, which could also be harmful. For example, overconsumption of saturated fats would lead to underconsumption of non-saturated fats.

There are two ways people can address the tension arising from the inflation of high-reward options. The first one is preference revision. People could adjust the inflated rewards downward and artificially reduce consumption. Of course, this response requires a clear understanding of the effect and the discipline to implement the revision. Second, given the possibility, a person could lend some of the accumulated resources or exchange them for other resources in a marketplace. It has been well established in finance that liquid assets are more valuable than illiquid assets. The same logic applies to rewards as well: rewards that are easier to exchange would be more likely to be accumulated than rewards that are more difficult to exchange.

When the rewards of certain options are difficult to store or exchange, societies are expected to develop social norms advocating for abstinence from these options. In such a scenario, a hedonistic approach to life is not optimal because it puts too much weight on high-reward options. However, an ascetic approach to life would not be optimal either because it completely disregards the information in the reward system. Thus, the following hypothesis is also expected to hold:

Golden Mean Hypothesis. The optimal policy in life follows a middle path between two extremes – one of excess and the other of deficiency.

Societies are expected to develop social norms discouraging the "excessive" consumption of high-reward (pleasurable) options. For example, the ideas of moderation are ingrained in the seven deadly sins (also known as the capital vices) in Christianity condemning excessive pride, greed, wrath, envy, lust, gluttony, and sloth. Moderation ideas are also in line with the golden mean (golden middle) philosophical doctrine that could be traced back to antiquity. The maxim "Nothing in Excess" was inscribed on the Temple of Apollo in the ancient precinct of Delphi. Socrates emphasized that people should avoid extremes. Gautama Buddha (fl. Sixth century BC) famously taught of the Middle Way, a path between the extremes of worldly self-indulgence and religious asceticism. Confucious also taught in the Analects that excess is similar to deficiency.

Despite its popularity, the moderation philosophy is difficult to rationalize because it implies that inherited preferences are suboptimal. The reward inflation hypothesis provides one explanation. The rest of this chapter analyzes the evolution of attitudes toward some high-reward activities using Maslow's hierarchy of needs. Maslow (1943) classified human needs into five groups based on their level of importance as follows: at the bottom are the physiological (e.g., food and clothing), followed by security, love and belonging, recognition, and self-actualization (e.g., pursuit of meaning and purpose). According to Maslow, the basic needs at the bottom of the pyramid need to be fulfilled before the higher-level needs are fulfilled.

Concepts

Scarcity. *It refers to the gap between the demand (desirability) of a good and its supply (availability). It is hypothesized that the scarcity of a useful resource would tend to enhance its reward (utility).*

Reward inflation hypothesis. *Facilitating access to high-reward options reduces the value of being in contact with these options. This makes their existing rewards abnormally high relative to the rewards of other options.*

Golden mean hypothesis. *A philosophical doctrine advocating for moderation and a balance between two extremes: one of excess and the other of deficiency.*

Maslow's hierarchy of needs. *A motivational theory in psychology defining five tiers of human needs. The needs, from most basic to most advanced, are physiological, security, love and belonging, recognition, and self-actualization. Individuals must satisfy lower-level needs before progressing to higher-level needs.*

More Food

At the foundation of Maslow's hierarchy of needs are physiological needs (Maslow, 1943). These are the most basic needs for survival, including food, water, air, and shelter. These needs need to be satisfied first before higher-level needs are satisfied. This section analyzes the evolving preferences for food. I focus on food because historically it has been less abundant than other basic resources, such as water and air.

Food supply has been scarce and uncertain throughout most of human history. In hunter-gatherer societies, people relied on the natural availability of plants and animals. The supply of these resources was highly unpredictable and depended on factors, such as weather conditions and the success of a particular hunting or gathering operation. The development of agriculture around 10,000 years ago dramatically increased the availability of food and the predictability of food supply. Agricultural societies enabled food storage, which in turn facilitated settlement formation, population growth, and the development of specialized labor. The availability of food in these societies, however, also varied unpredictably depending on weather conditions, conflicts, and one's socio-economic status.

The scarcity of food supply throughout history has likely enhanced the pleasure (reward) associated with food consumption. Since hunger is the main driver to search for food, individuals who find food more rewarding would be more likely to find food and survive. The uncertainty of food supply is also expected to enhance the reward or utility of over-eating, particularly high-calorie foods. Overeating enables individuals to store calories in the form of body fat, which could be used in periods of low food supply. Indeed, fat storage has been recognized as an important factor for survival enabling animals to deal with food shortages during normal times as well as during migrations (Young, 1976). Human survival was also dependent on the capacity of the human body to store fat. It is not surprising that throughout history obesity was regarded as a sign of wealth and prosperity. Obesity was also often considered an indicator of health and a beauty standard (Marghoub et al., 2023).

The Industrial Revolution dramatically increased food supply by boosting agricultural output and facilitating food refrigeration and distribution. As expected, the increased supply tilted toward high-calorie foods, which are more satisfying and pleasurable to consume. The increased consumption of high-calorie foods likely contributed to overconsumption and systematic weight gain in society (Christakis & Fowler, 2007). This is an example of reward inflation. It happens because food availability changes at a higher pace than preferences.

One of the central ideas of this book is that when innate preferences are suboptimal, social norms emerge to "adjust" individual behavior. Consistend with this idea is the fact that societies started developing social norms promoting healthy diet and exercise. The beauty standards in society also gradually changed from valuing full-figured and larger bodies to valuing slim and slender body shapes. Some people have criticized the fact that modern society places enormous pressure on people, particularly women, to adhere to unrealistically high standards. This tendency, however, is natural and inevitable. As long as people are predisposed to consume more than necessary, cultural norms will emerge to restrain food consumption.

More Security

The second tier of needs, according to Maslow, is the need for security (Maslow, 1943). Once most of their physiological needs are met, people want to ensure that their lives are safe and secure. This includes physical safety, financial security, and emotional stability.

The feeling of security is highly psychologically rewarding. As a result, humans have made life increasingly more secure over time. Over the past two hundred years, life expectancy in the United States has risen from 40 years to around 80 years (Oeppen & Vaupel, 2002). The share of the world's population living in extreme poverty was cut in half just over the last 30 years alone (Sachs, 2005). The world of today is also more peaceful, less violent, and more predictable than the world of the past. While these recent developments have decreased the real value of security, its psychological rewards have likely remained high.

The possibility that increased security is not reflected in primary preferences has two behavioral implications. First, when people underappreciate security, they would tend to overreact to uncertainty. Stress could be a correct response in dangerous situations because it helps the organism mobilize resources to overcome a life-threatening situation. In safer environments, however, stress could be harmful. Second, when people underappreciate their safety and security, they would extend effort and resources to acquire more security than necessary. Thus, inflated rewards to security predict that people would tend to extend more resources for risk management and insurance than they need or can afford. Indeed, there is evidence that people tend to be over-insured (Shapira &Venezia, 2008).

To mitigate the negative effects of stress, modern (and safer) societies are expected to adopt cultural norms for stress reduction. This is not straightforward, however, because telling a person not to worry is not enough to change their behavior. The experience of stress and anxiety is also highly private. As a result, it cannot be regulated effectively through social norms.

More Social Connections

At the third level of Maslow's hierarchy of needs is the need for love and belonging (Maslow, 1943). These are social needs related to feeling loved, accepted, and connected to others (see also Baumeister & Leary, 1995).

The need for feeling connected and being a part of a group is the main driver behind the growth of social media. Social media enables users to connect with others, share content, and participate in online communities. Platforms allow users to connect with friends and family across geographical distances using diverse methods for engagement, such as text, images, and videos. Social media helps people maintain existing relationships and expand their social networks, creating a sense of belonging and support. All these developments, however, are not accompanied by a downward adjustment of the psychological rewards to social connections.

The abnormally high rewards to connectivity could lead to over-socialization. Consistent with this idea is the fact that social media addiction, characterized by excessive and compulsive engagement with social media platforms, is a major trend negatively impacting various aspects of life. As of the time this chapter is written, the average person spends 2 hours and 24 minutes on social media every day. The average American checks their mobile device 159 times a day and 46% of Americans say they watch more user-generated content on social media than they watch movies and television on streaming services.[1] The addiction effect seems particularly high among young people. For example, a recent Gallup survey found that teens spend on average 4.8 hours on social media each day.[2]

While the excessive use of social media could be potentially harmful, we still know relatively little about the nature of the harm. A 2020 systematic review suggests a link between social media use and the development of mental health conditions, such as depression and anxiety. According to the authors, this may occur because increased social media use may lead to sleep problems, lack of exercise, and peer pressure (Keles et al., 2020). Another recent study investigates the role of social media among young people hospitalized for suicide attempts or suicidal ideation. It finds that social media could exhibit a negative impact on young people due to a variety of factors, such as increased stress, triggering content, social comparisons, and high friendship expectations (Weinstein et al., 2021).

Limiting social media use may be difficult for people with social media addiction. However, it is an important step for the promotion of better public health. Considering these developments, new social norms could also emerge restricting the use of social media.

More Wealth

As discussed in Chap. 2, rewards could be intrinsic or extrinsic, depending on whether they are inherently pleasurable or pleasurable because they could be associated with desirable outcomes. One important extrinsic reward is the reward associated with wealth. Wealth accumulation does not bring positive emotions on its own, but only because it could be

[1] See https://explodingtopics.com/blog/social-media-usage.

[2] See https://news.gallup.com/poll/512576/teens-spend-average-hours-social-media-per-day.aspx.

associated with the acquisition of intrinsic rewards in the future. The possibility of converting money into goods and services makes money valuable and desirable.

The inflation hypothesis applies to extrinsic rewards as well. In the context of wealth, people are expected to accumulate liquid assets that could be exchanged for consumption in the future, such as real estate, bank deposits, and other financial assets. Once people accumulate more wealth, the value of wealth and its associated psychological rewards should decline. This is in line with the law of diminishing marginal utility (Bernoulli 1738; Easterlin 2005). Yet, the inflation hypothesis suggests that the reward system could be slow at adjusting the rewards of wealth downward.

Excessive wealth accumulation could be harmful for various reasons. First, wealth needs to be managed, which engages cognitive resources. Wealth also needs to be protected and one's ability to protect it is expected to decline with the accumulated amount. Wealth accumulation would inevitably attract people trying to appropriate some of the wealth through manipulation, misrepresentation, and even theft. For all these reasons, wealth could be burdensome for the individual. It is not surprising that a financial windfall, such as winning a lottery, often affects negatively the lives of the winners, leading to financial hardship, relationship problems, and even criminal activity (Nisslé & Bschor, 2002; Raschke, 2019).

The ability to lend and rent out assets mitigates the above costs of wealth accumulation. The yield that accumulated assets generate can compensate for some of the losses incurred. By lending, an individual is effectively sharing their intrinsic rewards with other people. This adds value to wealth that could compensate for the inflation effect. People could also value the opportunity to borrow or rent assets from others.

For all these conflicting reasons, it is not surprising that the social benefits of wealth accumulation have been widely debated. Even closely related religions tend to disagree. For example, some interpretations of Protestant theology, particularly Calvinism, often view hard work, frugality, and success as a religious duty. John Wesley, the founder of the Methodist church, famously stated, "gain all you can, save all you can, and give all you can." This perspective suggests that wealth accumulation can be compatible with faith, particularly when combined with charitable giving. However, some other Protestant traditions and religious denominations have openly opposed greed and excessive wealth accumulation.

Conclusion

This chapter provides an insight into the evolution of individual preferences. It is built on two assumptions.

The first one is that the reward (utility) associated with an outcome reflects both its usefulness as well as its scarcity. The second one is that by maximizing contact with high-reward options, societies are effectively reducing their scarcity. Both assumptions are intuitive. The central point of this chapter is that the greater availability of high-reward options reduces the value of these options. As a result, their inherited rewards could become unjustifiably high. I refer to this possibility as the reward inflation hypothesis. Reward inflation leads to overconsumption, which could be harmful.

One way of addressing the potentially harmful effects of inflated rewards would be to adjust these rewards downward. In this regard, societies are expected to develop social norms restricting the consumption of high-reward options. However, eliminating high-reward options completely would not be optimal either. Thus, an optimal policy in life would be to follow a golden middle way: the middle path between two extremes—one of excess and the other of deficiency. The golden middle philosophical doctrine has existed for thousands of years. The framework developed in this book provides one justification for its existence.

The framework also predicts the possibility for a reward deflation. This could happen for resources that have been abundant historically and experience sudden depletion. The increased scarcity increases the value of these options. Yet, the reward system could be slow in upgrading its rewards upward. For example, clean air and water have been abundant throughout history. As a result, humans do not attach extra utility to air and water quality. This could explain why people fail to recognize many environmental and ecological problems as serious threats (Poortinga et al., 2011; Hornsey et al., 2016).

References

Baumeister, R. F., & Leary, M. R. (1995). The need to belong: Desire for interpersonal attachments as a fundamental human motivation. *Psychological Bulletin*, *117*, 497–529.

Bernoulli, D. (1738). Specimen Theoriae Novae de mensura sortis. *Commentarii Academiae Scientiarum Imperialis Petropolitanae*, *5*, 175–192.

Christakis, N. A., & Fowler, J. H. (2007). The spread of obesity in a large social network over 32 years. *New England Journal of Medicine, 357*(4), 370–379.

Easterlin, R. A. (2005). Diminishing marginal utility of income? Caveat emptor. *Social Indicators Research, 70*(3), 243–255.

Hornsey, M. J., Harris, E. A., Bain, P. G., & Fielding, K. S. (2016). Meta-analyses of the determinants and outcomes of belief in climate change. *Nature Climate Change, 6*(6), 622–626.

Keles, B., McCrae, N., & Grealish, A. (2020). A systematic review: The influence of social media on depression, anxiety and psychological distress in adolescents. *International Journal of Adolescence and Youth, 25*(1), 79–93.

Marghoub, S., Sanaie, S., Sullman, M. J., Nejadghaderi, S. A., Safiri, S., & Mohammadinasab, R. (2023). Obesity from a sign of being rich to a disease of the new age: A historical review. *Health Science Reports, 6*(11), e1670.

Maslow, A. H. (1943). A theory of human motivation. *Psychological Review, 50*(4), 370.

Nisslé, S., & Bschor, T. (2002). Winning the jackpot and depression: Money cannot buy happiness. *International Journal of Psychiatry in Clinical Practice, 6*(3), 183–186.

Oeppen, J., & Vaupel, J. W. (2002). Broken limits to life expectancy. *Science, 296*(5570), 1029–1031.

Poortinga, W., Spence, A., Whitmarsh, L., Capstick, S., & Pidgeon, N. F. (2011). Uncertain climate: An investigation into public scepticism about anthropogenic climate change. *Global Environmental Change, 21*(3), 1015–1024.

Raschke, C. (2019). Unexpected windfalls, education, and mental health: Evidence from lottery winners in Germany. *Applied Economics, 51*(2), 207–218.

Sachs, J. D. (2005). Can extreme poverty be eliminated? *Scientific American, 293*(3), 56–65.

Shapira, Z., & Venezia, I. (2008). On the preference for full-coverage policies: Why do people buy too much insurance? *Journal of Economic Psychology, 29*(5), 747–761.

Weinstein, E., Kleiman, E. M., Franz, P. J., Joyce, V. W., Nash, C. C., Buonopane, R. J., & Nock, M. K. (2021). Positive and negative uses of social media among adolescents hospitalized for suicidal behavior. *Journal of Adolescence, 87*, 63–73.

Young, R. A. (1976). Fat, energy and mammalian survival. *American Zoologist, 16*(4), 699–710.

CHAPTER 11

Collective Exploration

It's hard to believe in coincidence, but it's even harder to believe in anything else.

—John Green and David Levithan

Source: Green, J. and Levithan, D. (2012). Will Grayson, Will Grayson. Penguin UK. (**p. 72**)

Contents

Introduction

Exploration is a collective effort. Social insect colonies, birds, and other species work together to explore and exploit resources in their environment. Firms engage in exploration to discover profitable opportunities and

C. A. Pirinsky, *A Theory of Dynamic Preferences*,
https://doi.org/10.1007/978-3-032-13334-2_11

gain competitive advantage. Many economists believe that the very success of an economic system is rooted in its ability to explore new product lines, technologies, and organizational structures (Schumpeter, 1942).

This chapter develops the idea that a group of individuals exhibits a greater potential for exploration than a single individual. Exploration is about discovering something unique. This could be a resource, a piece of a puzzle, or the missing link in a thought process. The laws of probability theory imply that, under a general set of assumptions, as the number of independent opinions increases, a random observation in the sample will get arbitrarily close to the best outcome. I refer to this regularity as the ingenuity of crowds. It is different from the wisdom of crowds-idea that the collective (average) judgment of a large group of people is often more accurate than the judgment of any individual in the group. The exploration potential of the crowd is not an aggregation phenomenon; it is the outcome of a game of chance. A large group of players is more likely to win a lottery than a single player.

There are numerous accounts that some of the most influential discoveries in human history were greatly influenced by chance (some are reviewed below). However, while the impulses contributing to the discovery are random, the people acting upon these impulses are not. They are capable of recognizing, appreciating, and developing the opportunities that are presented to them. In one of his lectures, Louis Pasteur famously noted that "in the fields of observation, chance favors only the prepared mind."[1] Yet, chance would be more likely to favor a group of prepared minds than a single one.

Societies and organizations can design mechanisms fostering the creative potential of their group members. I argue that the exploration success of a group is determined by two factors—its ability to generate a large set of diverse opinions and the expertise of evaluating these opinions. The chapter presents evidence that the collective exploration efforts of social animals and humans follow these principles. It also discusses how our inherent tendency to refocus our attention based on external and internal stimuli could be used productively to enhance the creativity of individuals and teams.

[1] See https://www.nhlbi.nih.gov/directors-messages/serendipity-and-the-prepared-mind.

The Wisdom of Crowds

The term wisdom of crowds refers to the idea that the aggregation of information in groups could result in better decisions than the decisions made by individual group members. The term was coined by James Surowiecki in his book with a similar title (Surowiecki, 2005). The book illustrates the idea with an anecdote about a competition at a county fair in Plymouth, where participants were trying to guess the weight of an ox. According to the story, the accuracy of the average guess of the attendees exceeded substantially the accuracy of the best experts at the fair.

The wisdom of crowds-phenomenon can be well explained in terms of probability theory. Although the weight of the ox is fixed, the guess of an outside observer could be viewed as a realization of a random variable. Figure 11.1 below depicts the probability distribution of a hypothetical random variable centered around its expected value $\bar{x}$. The figure also depicts one random assessment—x_n.

The Law of Large Numbers (LLN) in probability theory states that given a sample of independent and identically distributed random variables, such as individual assessments, the sample mean converges to the true mean of these variables when the sample size increases. In the context of the competition, this implies that the average assessment of a large number of participants would converge toward the true weight of the ox. In terms of the notations on Fig. 11.1, the LLN implies that the following convergence holds:

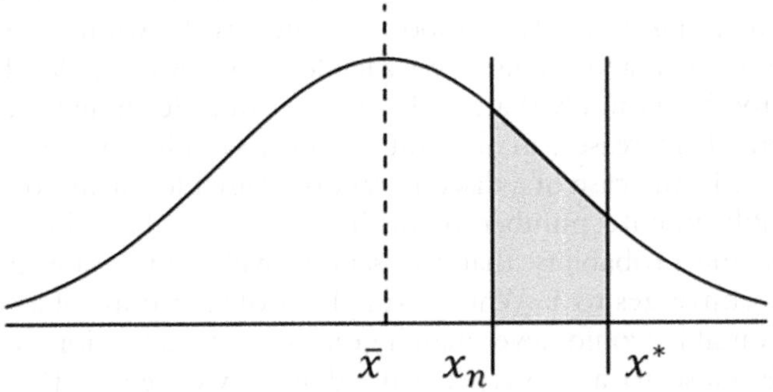

Fig. 11.1 Probability distribution. The figure plots the probability density function of a random variable

$$\frac{x_1 + x_2 + \ldots + x_N}{N} \underset{N \to \infty}{\longrightarrow} \bar{x} \tag{11.1}$$

Note that the assumption of independence is important for the validity of (Eq. 11.1). Imagine that in the county fair competition, everybody decides to follow the assessment of the first participant. There are various reasons this could happen. For example, the opinion of this person could be highly regarded. In the social media space, such people are referred to as influencers. Initial assessments could also skew subsequent assessments subconsciously. For example, the well-documented anchoring effect refers to the fact that individuals tend to rely too heavily on the first piece of information they encounter when making a decision (the "anchor"). In all these cases, the average assessment of the participants would converge toward the assessment of the first person and not necessarily toward the true weight of the ox. Thus, signal independence is an important prerequisite for the aggregation of information.

The Ingenuity of Crowds

The wisdom of crowds-effect is about the average of many independent observations of a random variable. A large sample of observations, however, has another interesting property: an observation from the sample will get arbitrarily close to any pre-specified realization of the random variable.

In terms of the notations on Fig. 11.1, let's denote with x^* one possible realization of the random variable. We can think about this outcome as being something particularly important, such as the winning outcome of a lucky draw or a random discovery à la Fleming (see Chap. 9). The laws of probability theory imply that, as the number of independent observations of the variable increases, an observation in the sample would get arbitrarily close to x^*. In the case of a discrete random variable (taking on a finite or a countably infinite number of distinct values), when the sample size increases, the probability that the sample will contain any prespecified outcome converges to 1. While a sample of observations of a continuous random variable would never match perfectly any realization, it would get arbitrarily close to any prespecified value. If we denote the sample of observations with x_n, for $n = 1, 2, \ldots, N$, then the following convergence holds:

$$\min_{1 \le n \le N} |x_n - x^*| \underset{N \to \infty}{\longrightarrow} 0 \qquad (11.2)$$

I refer to the property in (Eq. 11.2) as the ingenuity of crowds. It represents the idea that chance alone could get a person arbitrarily close to any outcome, as long as they try long enough and all trials are independent.

Chance has been an essential element of many scientific discoveries. For example, it is widely believed that Isaac Newton's inspiration for his theory of the law of gravity came from witnessing an apple falling from a tree. His mind at the time was already contemplating the laws governing the motion of celestial bodies and other objects. Only within the context of this mindset can the fallen apple trigger a sequence of thoughts leading to the formulation of his theory of gravity. Would have Newton discovered the laws of gravity if he hadn't witnessed the falling apple at this very moment? The answer is not clear. For sure, luck played an important role in his discovery.

Many other scientists have also acknowledged the role of fortunate luck or serendipity in their discoveries. The Danish scientist Hans Christian Ørsted discovered the relationship between electricity and magnetism by accident. In 1820, during a lecture, Ørsted was demonstrating the heating of a wire with electric current. He observed that any time the current was switched on, a nearby compass needle was deflected by the current. This led Ørsted to the discovery of the link between electricity and magnetism. The German physicist Wilhelm Conrad Röntgen discovered X-rays in 1895 by accident while experimenting with cathode ray tubes. He noticed that a fluorescent screen glowed even when shielded from the tube, indicating a new type of radiation. He named the radiation "X-rays" because of their unknown nature.

Serendipity plays an important role in creative exploration. Random factors seem as important as routine training. Einstein developed his groundbreaking theories while working at the Swiss Federal Office of Intellectual Property. His job involved examining patent applications, which in Switzerland at the time often involved watches and timepieces. It is plausible that this work directed Einstein's attention toward the concept of time and some of the thought experiments that set up the theories of relativity. He might have never developed his theories if he was somewhere else.

The ingenuity of crowds is particularly relevant for exploration, where the objective is the discovery of a scarce resource, rather than the estimation of a particular property. Since randomization is at the heart of most explorations, the ingenuity of crowds implies that a large number of independent attempts will ultimately lead to the best outcome. In particular, the following proposition is expected to hold.

Proposition [Ingenuity of Crowds]. The quality of the best opinion generated in a group increases with the number of independent opinions.

The proposition implies that the exploration success in a group increases with the number of independent opinions generated by the group. Note that the assumption of independence here is also important. It is also crucial that the group is able to compare and assess objectively the generated opinions. Only then would the best opinion be recognized.

You are a Crowd

The exploratory potential of a crowd depends on its ability to generate independent assessments (opinions). Such opinions, however, are not necessarily expressed by different people, as the same person has the potential to judge a problem differently depending on the situation.

One's thought process is heavily influenced by circumstances. Human attention is easily drawn to random factors in the environment. For example, existing research shows that individuals tend to overweight salient information when making decisions (Bordalo et al., 2013; Dessaint & Matray, 2017; Guthrie et al., 2001). Memories also surface involuntarily in response to random cues in the environment. They are generally referred to as involuntary autobiographical memories (IAMs) (Berntsen, 1996). For these reasons, even small changes in the environment could result in completely different perceptions and thought processes for the same person. Perhaps a better characterization of a person is as a being having multiple personalities that are activated by the environment. You are a crowd. This instability of human judgment might seem as a disadvantage. Yet, the awareness of these effects and the ability to use them strategically could enhance tremendously individual and organizational creativity. Thus, the following proposition is expected to hold.

Proposition [Ingenuity of Circumstances]. The quality of the best opinion generated by a person in a series of trials increases with the diversity of the settings where the opinions are generated.

The idea that diversifying our experiences can improve creativity is not completely new. For example, Gocłowska et al. (2018) review a range of diversifying experiences that have been found to influence creativity, such as multicultural exposures and unexpected adversity. Even subtle changes, however, could exhibit significant effects on creativity. Furthermore, these effects could be used strategically to enhance the creative output of individuals and groups.

Concepts

Wisdom of crowds. *The idea that the average assessment of a group of individuals is more accurate than the assessment of individual group members.*

The Law of Large Numbers. *The Law of Large Numbers (LLN) in probability theory states that the average of independent and identically distributed random variables converges toward the expected value of the variables, as the number of variables increases.*

Ingenuity of crowds. *The idea that the quality of the best opinion generated in a group increases with the number of independent opinions.*

Ingenuity of circumstances. *The idea that the quality of the best opinion generated by a person in a series of trials increases with the diversity of the settings where the opinions are generated.*

Brainstorming. *A technique used for the generation of creative ideas in a group by encouraging free and spontaneous sharing of ideas.*

Fostering Exploration

The ideas in this chapter have implications for the design of mechanisms fostering exploration in groups. According to the analysis, the exploration success of a group is determined by two factors. The first one is the ability of the group to generate diverse opinions. The second one is its ability to evaluate critically these opinions and identify the best ones. The analysis also suggests that even small changes to the setting of a decision process could enhance the creative output of individuals and groups.

There is evidence that groups across a wide range of domains tend to follow these principles. For example, social insect colonies are often divided into scouts who explore independently for new food sources, and workers who are recruited to exploit what others find (Frisch von, 1967). Individuals of many bird species also specialize as either producers, who search for food, or as scroungers, who join the birds that have already found food (Giraldeau & Lefebvre, 1986). Furthermore, social animals frequently rotate different members of the colony across scout and worker positions, which effectively delegates exploration to a diverse set of individuals (Beekman et al., 2007; Hills et al., 2015). Rotation also allocates resources within the colony where they are needed the most. If there are not enough existing foraging locations for the workers to exploit, the proportion of a colony participating in exploration increases. Vice versa, when local resources are abundant, some of the scouts could become workers to help the colony harvest the available resources.

Exploration in teams is also centered around the generation and selection of ideas. The creativity theorist Alex Osborn introduced the concept of brainstorming as a creative problem-solving process (Osborn, 1953). He outlined four basic brainstorming rules. The first one is to generate as many ideas as possible, emphasizing the quantity rather than the quality of the ideas. The second rule is that no one criticizes an idea. The third rule is the encouragement of wild or unreasonable ideas. The fourth rule is that participants are permitted to combine ideas or improve on each other's ideas. The brainstorming process quickly became popular among America's largest corporations and society at large (Besant, 2016).

Although Osborn's rules have been shown to improve group brainstorming performance (Meadow & Parnes, 1959), many have questioned the communication aspect of the process, or its fourth rule. Researchers have identified some factors limiting the creative output of interacting groups, such as anxiety (Camacho & Paulus, 1995; Nijstad et al., 2002), low accountability (Karau & Williams, 1993), and the cognitive interference of unproductive ideas and distractions (Diehl & Stroebe, 1991; Nijstad et al., 2003). Communication in brainstorming is also expected to reduce the ingenuity of crowds-effect in the team by reducing the level of independence of the generated ideas. Interactions could create pressure on group members to agree with the majority opinion even if they disagree privately. Some people could also feel uncomfortable contradicting an expert or a person of authority. Such effects are expected to be the strongest among novice members of the team, which could potentially generate the most original ideas.

Organizations also utilize various mechanisms to enhance creative exploration. One such mechanism is flat organizational hierarchies. Flat hierarchies have few or no levels of management between staff and executives, emphasizing collaboration over more bureaucratic power structures. It is not surprising that most startups, particularly in highly innovative industries, tend to adopt a flat organizational structure. Even in large organizations, exploration units tend to be small and decentralized, while exploitation units tend to be larger and more centralized (Benner & Tushman, 2003). Exploration units also tend to have less formal process management and a looser culture (Hidma et al., 2020).

Professionalization and Creativity

Creativity feeds on originality. An increasingly large number of creative endeavors, however, take place in large organizations, which themselves are parts of well-orchestrated professions. Can professionalization suppress creativity?

One of the first cases of professionalization was the accounting profession, which emerged in England with the design of laws about formal audits of the new joint-stock companies in the late 1800s. During the twentieth century, the accounting profession consolidated into a few large firms (Abbott, 1988). Professionalization gradually emerged in other areas such as law, engineering, and medicine. Most of these areas, however, are not innovative and exploratory in nature. Indeed, the term "creative accounting" has a negative connotation and refers to fraudulent accounting practices. Engineers and medical doctors utilize innovative products in their practice, but the researchers generating these products are not under the umbrella of these professions.

One of the main functions of professions is to protect human capital accumulation of the group from outsiders (Abbott, 1988; Larson, 1977; Parsons, 1954). Professionalization, however, inevitably leads to the standardization of human capital in the corresponding fields. Employees would like to acquire standardized skills because these skills are deployable across firms. Firms are interested in hiring employees with standardized skills because such skills are easier to verify and contract upon (Caplow, 1954). Standardization is often facilitated by universities and professional training institutions engaged in developing the corresponding skills (DiMaggio & Powell, 1983; Perrow, 1974). Yet, while practically useful, standardization also reduces the diversity of available skills for exploration (Pirinsky & Togan, 2025).

Over time, professionalization also expanded into the creative sectors of the economy, such as film, music, and academia. Currently, the music labels and the production studios tend to hire people who were trained in the same schools, use similar equipment, and were exposed to the same ideas. Hollywood is dominated by five major studios: Disney, Universal, Sony Pictures, Paramount, and Warner Bros. Collectively, these studios command approximately 85% of U.S. box office revenue. They also have the financing and distribution mechanisms to generate projects much faster than the independent entertainment companies. But are these projects more creative?

Professionalization has also permeated into the academic fields. Obtaining a PhD degree is costly and when job market opportunities are limited, very few people would be willing to invest in a PhD degree. To protect this investment, most universities commit to employ predominantly faculty members with PhD degrees in the corresponding disciplines, and accrediting organizations monitor the compliance with this requirement. Some people have expressed concerns about the dramatic decline of important scientific discoveries in fundamental sciences (Caudwell, 2018). Smolin (2006) argues that string theory, the dominant paradigm in theoretical physics over the last 50 years, has failed to establish a coherent theoretical framework with testable empirical predictions. Although not everybody would agree about the deficit of creative ideas in fundamental sciences, the unintended consequences of the professionalization of academic fields could be a legitimate concern.

Conclusion

Exploration is a collective effort. This chapter argues that the exploration potential of a group could be enhanced by two factors. The first one is its ability to generate a large number of independent ideas. The objective of exploration is to discover a unique resource. The laws of probability theory imply that as the number of independent opinions increases, a random observation in the sample will get arbitrarily close to the best outcome. Thus, a larger pool of ideas contains better ideas than a smaller one. The second factor facilitating exploration in a group is its ability to evaluate critically the generated ideas and identify the best ones.

The chapter presents evidence that groups across numerous domains tend to follow these principles when they explore their environment. The chapter also argues that some recent developments in society could inhibit creative exploration. Numerous creative fields, such as film, music, and even academia, have become increasingly professionalized. The initial motivation of professionalization was to establish norms and qualification standards protecting professionals from the entry of outsiders. Professionalization, however, leads to the standardization of human capital in the corresponding fields, which in turn could hinder their ability to generate independent and original ideas.

References

Abbott, A. (1988). *The system of professions. An essay on the division of expert labor*. The University of Chicago Press.

Beekman, M., Gilchrist, A. L., Duncan, M., & Sumpter, D. J. (2007). What makes a honeybee scout? *Behavioral Ecology and Sociobiology, 61*(7), 985–995.

Benner, M. J., & Tushman, M. L. (2003). Exploitation, exploration, and process management: The productivity dilemma revisited. *Academy of Management Review, 28*(2), 238–256.

Berntsen, D. (1996). Involuntary autobiographical memories. *Applied Cognitive Psychology, 10*(5), 435–454.

Besant, H. (2016). The journey of brainstorming. *Journal of Transformational Innovation, 2*(1), 1–7.

Bordalo, P., Gennaioli, N., & Shleifer, A. (2013). Salience and consumer choice. *Journal of Political Economy, 121*, 803–843.

Camacho, L. M., & Paulus, P. B. (1995). The role of social anxiousness in group brainstorming. *Journal of Personality and Social Psychology, 68*(6), 1071.

Caplow, T. (1954). *The sociology of work*. University of Minnesota Press.

Caudwell, C. (2018). *The crisis in physics*. Verso Books.

Dessaint, O., & Matray, A. (2017). Do managers overreact to salient risks? Evidence from hurricane strikes. *Journal of Financial Economics, 126*, 97–121.

Diehl, M., & Stroebe, W. (1991). Productivity loss in idea-generating groups: Tracking down the blocking effect. *Journal of Personality and Social Psychology, 61*(3), 392–403.

DiMaggio, P. J., & Powell, W. W. (1983). The iron cage revisited: Institutional isomorphism and collective rationality in organizational fields. *American Sociological Review, 48*, 147–160.

Frisch von, K. (1967). *The dance language and orientation of bees*. Harvard University Press.

Giraldeau, L. A., & Lefebvre, L. (1986). Exchangeable producer and scrounger roles in a captive flock of feral pigeons: A case for the skill pool effect. *Animal Behaviour, 34*(3), 797–803.

Gocłowska, M. A., Damian, R. I., & Mor, S. (2018). The diversifying experience model: Taking a broader conceptual view of the multiculturalism–creativity link. *Journal of Cross-Cultural Psychology, 49*(2), 303–322.

Guthrie, C., Rachlinski, J., & Wistrich, A. (2001). Inside the judicial mind. *Cornell Law Review, 86*, 777–830.

Hidma, A., Küchler, S., & Sandström, V. (2020). *The present-focused, future-ready r&d organization*. McKinsey & Company.

Hills, T. T., Todd, P. M., Lazer, D., Redish, A. D., & Couzin, I. D. (2015). Exploration versus exploitation in space, mind, and society. *Trends in Cognitive Sciences, 19*(1), 46–54.

Karau, S. J., & Williams, K. D. (1993). Social loafing: A meta-analytic review and theoretical integration. *Journal of Personality and Social Psychology, 65*(4), 681–706.

Larson, M. S. (1977). *The rise of professionalism: A sociological analysis*. University of California Press.

Meadow, A., & Parnes, S. J. (1959). Evaluation of training in creative problem solving. *Journal of Applied Psychology, 43*(3), 189–194. https://doi.org/10.1037/h0046040

Nijstad, B. A., Stroebe, W., & Lodewijkx, H. F. (2002). Cognitive stimulation and interference in groups: Exposure effects in an idea generation task. *Journal of Experimental Social Psychology, 38*(6), 535–544.

Nijstad, B. A., Diehl, M., & Stroebe, W. (2003). Cognitive stimulation and interference in idea generating groups. In P. B. Paulus & B. A. Nijstad Eds., *Group creativity: Innovation through collaboration* (pp. 137–159). Oxford University Press.

Osborn, A. (1953). *Applied imagination*. Charles Scribner's Son's.

Parsons, T. (1954). *Essays in sociological theory*. The Free Press.

Perrow, C. (1974). Is business really changing? *Organizational Dynamics, 3*(1), 31–44.

Pirinsky, C., & Togan, A. (2025). *Silos*. Working paper.

Schumpeter, J. A. (1994). *Capitalism, socialism and democracy*. Routledge. 1942.

Smolin, L. (2006). *The trouble with physics: The rise of string theory, the fall of a science, and what comes next*. Houghton Mifflin Harcourt.

Surowiecki, J. (2005). *The wisdom of crowds*. Vintage.

CHAPTER 12

Exploration and Social Choice

Institutions are the rules of the game in a society; more formally, they are the humanly devised constraints that shape human interaction. … Institutional change shapes the way societies evolve through time and, hence, is the key to understanding historical change.

—Douglass North

Source: North, D. C. (1990). Institutions, Institutional Change and Economic Performance. Cambridge University Press, New York. (**p. 3**)

Contents

C. A. Pirinsky, *A Theory of Dynamic Preferences*,
https://doi.org/10.1007/978-3-032-13334-2_12

Introduction

The interactions in every social group are governed by a set of rules or policies. Social scientists usually refer to these rules as institutions. Similarly to the way individuals explore their environment, societies explore the institutional space in search of better policies. Policy exploration is challenging because policies could exhibit unintended consequences on group behavior. Experimenting with new courses of action could be also politically risky. Notwithstanding these challenges, societies engage in policy exploration.

The framework developed in this book provides a perspective on institutional change. According to the framework, the likelihood that a person supports a policy would depend on the expected benefits and costs of the policy, as well as the person's openness to change (propensity for exploration). Once people evaluate a policy proposal, they vote for or against it based on both their perceived benefits of the proposal as well as their openness to change. If the proposal receives a majority vote, then it becomes a law.

This section argues that institutional change is more likely to favor the preferences of liberal political ideologies. The logic is as follows. It is well-established that people who are more open to change tend to associate with left (liberal) ideologies, while people who are less open to change tend to associate with right (conservative) ideologies (Jost et al., 2009). As a result, liberal voters are unconditionally more likely to support new policies than conservative voters because they are more open to change. In such an environment, right-leaning proposals would be difficult to pass because their ideas are unpopular with the left, and the changes they entail are generally unpopular with the right. Left-leaning proposals are more likely to get close to the 50% majority threshold, and some of them could exceed the threshold just by a matter of chance. I refer to this property of institutional change as the Liberal gradient hypothesis. Note that the liberal direction of institutional change is not an artifact of the values of liberal voters; but only of their openness for change.

The proposed framework also suggests that when innate attitudes are disadvantageous, people could use their belief system to adjust their behavior. Given that institutional change favors liberal ideologies, people holding conservative views are expected to adopt beliefs exaggerating the social benefits of conservative policies and the social costs of liberal policies. This distortion creates additional incentives for conservative voters to support change. It is a fine-tuning process of their innate attitudes toward change.

At the end, the chapter discusses the relative advantages of various political arrangements with respect to social exploration. It notes that representative democracies often fail to represent well the views of the entire population. The chapter also argues that some organizational structures, such as the federal government system and the franchise business model, could promote exploration by allowing their constituencies to experiment with alternative courses of action. The knowledge generated in this process could be shared among the whole population.

Institutions

Economic activity is structured within a set of formal and informal norms of behavior or institutions. Formal norms are written down and formally enforced (e.g., laws and codes); informal norms are rules that people follow in everyday life (e.g., values and moral obligations). North (1990) advocates the view that informal institutions tend to be slow-moving and generally exogenous to the formal institutions in society. Social norms, however, exert a powerful influence on individual and group behavior (Greenfield, 2000; Hofstede, 2001).

Institutions determine the economic performance of the group and its members. They define and enforce social norms that enable people to work together, organize activities, and achieve common goals. Institutions play a vital role in fostering economic development by defining and protecting property rights, enforcing contracts, and promoting fair competition. All these factors incentivize entrepreneurs and businesses to invest, innovate, and engage in productive exchange. Strong institutions are also crucial for protecting the fundamental freedoms of individuals.

Similarly to the way individuals explore their environment, social groups explore the rules and policies governing their behavior. When considering a new policy, group members factor in the individual rewards they are expected to collect from the implementation of the policy. Note that these rewards might not be entirely monetary and could include various non-pecuniary considerations, such as prestige and recognition. Based on this information, the group makes a choice. Although there are different ways for a group to reach a decision, it is convenient to think about public choice in terms of voting. When the majority votes for a particular policy, it gets implemented.

Since the rewards associated with a particular policy are uncertain, societies are trying to understand the effect possible rules have on the welfare of their citizens. Thus, societies explore the institutional space the same way individuals explore their surroundings. Policy exploration is challenging for a variety of reasons. For one, group dynamics are highly complex. Implementing a new policy for the sake of experimentation could be also politically risky. Even if some groups experiment with a particular policy, to assess its effect, one needs to compare the group to other similar groups that did not adopt the policy. Such groups usually do not exist.

Society is a complex system, whose internal logic is difficult to understand. In such systems, small changes in initial conditions can lead to dramatically different outcomes over time. This effect is often illustrated with the hypothetical scenario in which a butterfly flapping its wings in one part of the world could cause a hurricane on the other side of the globe (i.e., the butterfly effect). The ultra-sensitivity of complex systems to initial conditions was first analyzed in meteorology (Lorenz, 2017).

Policies also often exhibit unintended consequences. These consequences can be either positive or negative, and they may not be related to the original goal of the policy. One popular example is the so-called cobra effect (Siebert, 2001; Warczak Jr., 2020). The British governor of Delhi, India, implemented a bounty on cobras to reduce their population. However, the bounty led to farmers breeding cobras in order to sell them for the bounty. This, in turn, had the effect of increasing the number of cobras overall. Another example of unintended consequences is the Prohibition. The prohibition of alcohol in the United States in the 1920s was intended to reduce crime and social problems. Instead, it led to the growth of organized crime and an increase in the illegal production and consumption of liquor (known as "bootlegging"). As a result, Congress adopted a resolution that ended the Prohibition in 1933 (Behr, 1996).

Policy Exploration

Policy exploration can be analyzed within the framework developed in this book. Every policy generates some aggregate rewards (or net benefits), which are then redistributed among the members of the group. Policies generally govern both the aggregate reward and its redistribution. If we denote the total number of individuals as N, the aggregate reward for the group as R, and the reward for individual n as R_n, then the aggregate reward could be expressed as $R = R_1 + R_2 + \ldots + R_N$.

Considering the ABC-model of exploration, the likelihood that a person would support a particular policy can be modeled with the quantity P(Vote) = (PPEX*β)*(PB—PC), where *PB* and *PC* are the estimated personal benefits and costs of the policy, *PPEX* is the propensity for policy exploration; and β is a belief distortion parameter about the net benefits of the policy. The parameters *PPEX* and β are not policy specific; they are also different across individuals.

On the surface, political ideologies around the world appear random and eclectic. A closer look at the political landscape, however, reveals that most political doctrines could be classified along a single left-right dimension, where the left side (liberal) exhibits strong preference for social change, openness to new experiences, and tolerance for uncertainty, while the right side (conservative) exhibits preference for stability, intolerance of ambiguity, and "personal need for order, structure, and closure" (Jost et al., 2009). Indeed, the terms "left" and "right" first appeared during the French Revolution of 1789 when members of the National Assembly divided into supporters of the Ancient Régime to the president's right and supporters of the revolution to his left.

The fact that the liberal-conservative dimension correlates strongly with propensity for policy exploration (PPEX) has important implications for our understanding of institutional change. Let us consider the following stylized model. The entire population is split into two equally-sized groups. The Left (liberal) represents people with a high propensity for exploration, the Right (conservative) represents people with a low propensity for exploration (see Fig. 12.1 below). Both political ideologies

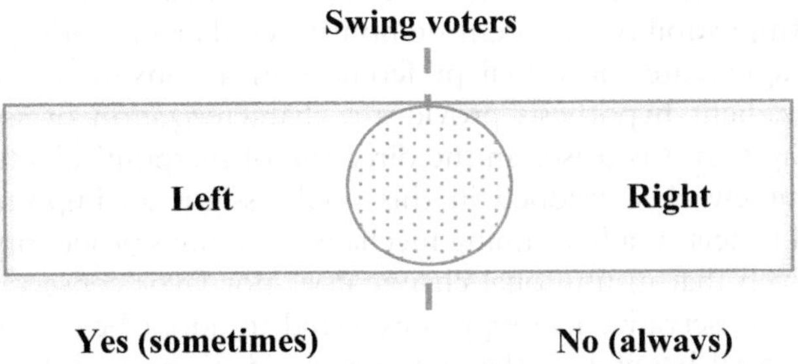

Fig. 12.1 Voting for change. The entire population is split into two equally sized groups. The Left (liberal) represents people with high propensity for exploration. The Right (conservative) represents people with low propensity for exploration

have distinct policy preferences. There is a small group of swing voters with balanced views in the middle.

Policy proposals arrive randomly. The ones that are too far left or too far right alienate swing voters and cannot get passed. Thus, only moderate proposals would be considered. Every policy proposal instigates some changes of the status quo. Regardless of the specifics, a conservative voter is more likely to vote against the proposal than a liberal voter. For the sake of simplicity, let us assume that conservative voters always vote NO to preserve the status quo. Let's consider one specific proposal. If it is tilted to the right, both liberals and conservatives vote NO. If it is tilted to the left, however, liberals vote YES, while conservatives vote NO. The decision now is in the hands of the swing voters. If they act completely randomly (e.g., flip a coin), this implies that 50% of the liberal proposals will pass. Thus, the following proposition is expected to hold.

Liberal Gradient Hypothesis. Institutional change is gradual and favors the views of people who are more open to change. In most political systems, these views are represented by the political left.

Liberal ideologies appear more progressive because institutional change follows their preferences. This trend, however, is not related to the nature of liberal values. Institutional change moves to the left simply because the left is more tolerant of change. In optimization theory, the gradient of a function is a vector that indicates the direction and the rate of the fastest increase of the function. If we think about institutions as a function of various factors, their gradient characterizes the direction of institutional change. Considering this, I refer to the above proposition as the Liberal gradient hypothesis.

The Liberal gradient hypothesis echoes the analysis of Arrow (2012). Arrow's Impossibility Theorem demonstrates that no voting system can perfectly aggregate individual preferences in a consistent manner. The Liberal gradient hypothesis provides a characterization of social choice by showing that it is biased in the direction of the political left.

The framework developed in this book assigns an important role to individual beliefs, as a fine-tuning mechanism of one's propensity for exploration. Given that institutional change does not favor conservative preferences, the conservative ideology is expected to adopt beliefs exaggerating both the social benefits of the conservative ideology as well as the social costs of the liberal ideology. As in the individual exploration case, these beliefs have to be biased; otherwise, they would not be able to "correct" inherited dispositions. Thus, the theory predicts that, ceteris paribus, conservative voters are more likely to develop biased perceptions about the relative benefits of their ideology compared to liberal voters. Note that these biases emerge to encourage political participation. As such, they will be insensitive to information. They exist to ensure that the conservative views are adequately represented in the political discourse.

Relationship to North

Every policy needs to restrict or inconvenience somebody. A rule that is voluntarily observed in society is unnecessary. Rules always restrict somebody's freedom of choice. Even the laws against theft, as natural as they seem, restrict the freedom of thieves. Thus, every rule has an opposition. When the opposition is a minority, the rule is adopted. When the opposition becomes a majority, the rule is repealed.

According to North, economic agents continuously assess their expected gains in the existing institutional framework relative to their gains in alternative frameworks. When entrepreneurs perceive the existing institutions as disadvantageous, they start lobbying for institutional change. The likelihood of change reflects the perceived opportunities of economic agents and their bargaining power. Thus, the process of institutional change is generally slow and highly contested (North, 1990).

According to North, the economic agents that have come into existence in the current institutional framework have an incentive to perpetuate it. The existing investments and contractual obligations tend to bias institutional change in favor of the interests of incumbents and legacy organizations. They can instigate formal changes (e.g., laws and codes) through the courts, regulatory agencies, and the US Congress. Changes in informal norms (e.g., values and conventions) are less coordinated and occur gradually and often subconsciously. Even in this case, however, legacy organizations can direct cultural change by manipulating societal narratives (Shiller, 2020).

The framework developed in this book also predicts that institutional change will be slow and incremental. The driving force behind this change, however, is the people with greater tolerance for change and uncertainty. The institutional framework of North has a conservative bias, i.e., it tends to emphasize the impediments to social change. In contrast, the framework developed in this book has a liberal bias, i.e., it tends to emphasize change, particularly in the direction of liberal political ideologies.

The Problem with Representative Democracies

If citizens need to choose among a known set of policies, then they could vote directly for their preferred option. This is referred to as direct democracy. Most of the time, however, people do not know what the set of available options is. As a result, they appoint representatives to explore on their behalf. Representative democracies delegate policy exploration and design to a small number of elected officials. This reduces the policy exploration in society to meta exploration, where people need to choose among a set of available representatives the ones that would explore best on their behalf. Most modern Western-style democracies function as some form of a representative democracy.

A potential problem with representative democracies is that their effective level of representativeness could be very low. Since in an election people can vote for any person on the list, this creates the perception that elections are representative. Yet, the average voter cannot influence the composition of the list. As a result, their choice set is severely limited. In Ancient Athens, the birthplace of democracy, elections were regarded as highly non-democratic and biased in favor of the more popular and privileged members of society. Elections also appeared vulnerable to manipulation and corruption. For all these reasons, Athenians rarely used elections for the selection of public officials.

In Athenian democracy, the traditional and primary method for appointing political officials was through a random allocation (sortition). The Athenians believed that since elections tend to favor candidates with greater status or popularity, they contradict the principle of equal rights for all citizens (Hansen, 1999). As a result, they viewed random allocations to public office as fairer and more democratic than elections. The random allotment of positions also served as a deterrent to vote-buying and corruption, as it was impossible to predict who would be elected in a random draw. The Athenians employed a special machine to generate random numbers for this purpose, called *kleroterion*. The practice of sortition later transferred to some of the Italian states, most notably, Florence and Venice. Random selection is still used today for the allocation of judges and jurors in common law countries.

This book suggests that every exploration has an element of randomization. If political candidates are not selected randomly, this could significantly reduce the novelty and diversity of policy ideas. Thus, representative democracies could hinder policy exploration.

The Benefits of Federalism

Policy exploration is challenging partly because of the lack of adequate counterfactuals. The effect of a policy on a group needs to be evaluated relative to other similar groups that do not have the policy, and such groups could be difficult to find. Institutional exploration could benefit from a cross-section of groups or societies with similar characteristics. In this section, I argue that some organizational structures, such as the federal system of government and the franchise business model, naturally promote policy exploration at the local level.

A federal system of government divides power between a central (federal) government and regional local governments. Such a system creates space for exploration, where local governments experiment with alternative policies. The generated knowledge could be used by all members of the federation.

Justice Louis Brandeis coined the term "laboratories of democracy" in his dissenting opinion in the 1932 Supreme Court case *New State Ice Co. v. Liebmann* to describe the capacity of US states for social innovation. In his own words: "It is one of the happy incidents of the federal system that a single courageous state may, if its citizens choose, serve as a laboratory; and try novel social and economic experiments without risk to the rest of the country." Once a few states adopt the new policy, additional states could follow the example of these early adopters in a process known as policy diffusion.

One example of policy diffusion across states is the Amber Alert laws. Amber Rene Hagerman (November 25, 1986—January 15, 1996) was a nine-year-old girl abducted while riding her bike in Arlington, Texas. Within days of her tragic death, Amber's parents established the People Against Sex Offenders (PASO) organization. The organization started immediately raising awareness about the importance of the media for the dissemination of timely information about missing children. In response, the Dallas police chief launched the first ever Amber Alert. Other states followed, and by 2005, all 50 states had Amber Alert Programs. Today, this program operates successfully across state and jurisdictional boundaries.[1]

The franchise business model exhibits similar characteristics to the federal system of government. In this model, a franchisor grants

[1] See chrome-extension://efaidnbmnnnibpcajpcglclefindmkaj/https://www.ojp.gov/sites/g/files/xyckuh241/files/media/document/amberfaq.pdf

a franchisee the right to operate under the franchisor's brand and support, while maintaining a certain degree of independence. The franchise model, while emphasizing consistency and standardization, also provides franchisees with the flexibility to experiment with new products and advertising strategies in different locations.

The coexistence of multiple organizational structures could also provide insights into the effectiveness of the cultural norms governing these organizations. The fact that culture is slow-moving makes it difficult to assess the causal effect of cultural norms on societal outcomes. In a recent article, Guiso et al. (2015) advocate the view that the effect of culture could be easier to identify in simpler, more controlled, environments, such as corporations. Thus, corporate culture could be used as a natural laboratory to study the role of societal culture and the way it can be changed.

Conclusion

Similarly to the way individuals explore their environment, societies explore the rules and policies governing their behavior. A person is more likely to support a policy when they (1) have a high tolerance for change (propensity for policy exploration) and (2) estimate a relatively high personal benefit from its implementations. Since in a democracy people have the right to vote, more popular policies are expected to be implemented, and less popular policies are expected to be rejected.

This chapter argues that institutional change is more likely to favor the preferences of people who are more open to change. In most democracies, these people tend to associate with liberal political ideologies. Thus, institutional change would tend to move in the direction of liberal policies. This is the reason they appear progressive. This progressiveness, however, is not related to the nature of the policies, but rather to the greater willingness of their proponents to tolerate change. In response, conservative voters are expected to adopt beliefs overstating the social benefits of their platform to achieve competitive influence on institutional change.

References

Arrow, K. J. (2012) [1951]. *Social choice and individual values.* (Vol. 12). Yale University Press.

Behr, E. (1996). *Prohibition: Thirteen years that changed America.* Arcade Publishing.

Greenfield, P. M. (2000). Three approaches to the psychology of culture: Where do they come from? Where can they go? *Asian Journal of Social Psychology, 3*(3), 223–240.

Guiso, L., Sapienza, P., & Zingales, L. (2015). Corporate culture, societal culture, and institutions. *American Economic Review, 105*(5), 336–339.

Hansen, M. H. (1999). *The Athenian democracy in the age of Demosthenes: Structure, principles and ideology. Bristol Classical Paperbacks.* Bristol Classical Press. ISBN 978-1-85399-585-9.

Hofstede, G. (2001). *Culture's consequences: Comparing values, behaviors, institutions, and organizations across nations* (2nd ed.). Sage.

Jost, J. T., Federico, C. M., & Napier, J. L. (2009). Political ideology: Its structure, functions, and elective affinities. *Annual Review of Psychology, 60*, 307–337.

Lorenz, E. N. (2017). Deterministic nonperiodic flow 1. In *Universality in chaos* (2nd ed., pp. 367–378). Routledge.

North, D. C. (1990). *Institutions, institutional change and economic performance.* Cambridge University Press.

Siebert, H. (2001). *Der Kobra-Effekt. Wie man Irrwege der Wirtschaftspolitik vermeidet (in German).* Deutsche Verlags-Anstalt.

Shiller, R. J. (2020). *Narrative economics: How stories go viral and drive major economic events.* Princeton University Press.

Warczak Jr, P. (2020). The cobra effect: Kisor, Roberts, and the law of unintended consequences. *Akron Law Review, 54*, 111–157.

CHAPTER 13

The Exploring Human

We need more understanding of human nature, because the only danger that exists is man himself – he is the great danger, and we are pitifully unaware of it. We know nothing of man – far too little.

—Carl Jung

Source: *An interview for the BBC program 'Face to Face' in 1959*

Contents

C. A. Pirinsky, *A Theory of Dynamic Preferences*,
https://doi.org/10.1007/978-3-032-13334-2_13

Introduction

From the moment they are born till their last breath, people need to navigate unfamiliar territories and make choices that improve their chances for survival. These territories encompass different realms, including the physical world, the social environment, and our own mentality. The exploring human is guided by two forces. The first one is an innate system of preferences that attaches positive responses to beneficial outcomes and negative responses to disadvantageous outcomes. It is shaped by evolutionary processes. The second one is accumulated knowledge generated by our own experiences as well as the experiences of our peers (past and present). Both forces are important, yet imperfect. Sometimes they also contradict each other.

Classical utility theory assumes that the rewards associated with every single action in any possible context are known or automatically attached to an individual at birth. Inheriting complete information about every aspect of the environment is impossible, especially when the environment changes unpredictably. Since people cannot inherit the sensory responses associated with every single action, they need to explore their environment to discover what their primary preferences are. Thus, the choices that preferences entail are embedded in a more fundamental choice of whether and what to explore. If we denote the set of explored options from an action space with E and the revised preferences from this exploration with P(E), then individual choice could be expressed as CHOICE = C (P(E), E).

When exploration is exogenously fixed, individual choices could be reduced to a static utility function. Such scenario would naturally emerge when the environment is relatively simple and stable. In this case, primary preferences would stabilize over time toward an optimal level. Exploration stops, and choice is confined to a small number of familiar options. Evidence from animal foraging supports this idea. When animals reach a non-depleting patch, it is common for them to occupy it permanently (Beachly et al., 1995). However, when the resources in the currently selected patch are depleted and the likelihood of finding a better patch increases, exploration becomes important (Stephens et al., 2008).

Building on recent advances in biology, neuroscience, and psychology, this book develops a framework for human behavior centered around the important role of exploration and self-discovery. Below, I summarize how the exploration-centered view on individual behavior could provide insights into numerous phenomena, such as biased perceptions, inconsistent preferences, irrational behavior, economic (hyper)activity, the nature versus nurture debate, and free will.

Biased Perceptions

Individual beliefs are motivationally biased, i.e., people tend to make judgments and interpret information based on what they want to be true, rather than what is objectively accurate. These biases have been documented in thousands of scientific studies, but a simple self-reflection should convince most people that they exist. Yet, biased perceptions would be difficult to justify if we regard people as beings who know who they are, where they want to go, and how to get there. How could biased perceptions help us navigate our life journey better if everything we want is to get from point A to point B?

In life, we are starting at point A without knowing with certainty what the next point will be. We need to figure it out, given where we are and what is given to us. We are choosing our path, while simultaneously walking on it. Furthermore, the path we choose is changing us. We are making our choices as much as the choices are making us.

Encounters with the unknown, or explorations, play an important role in life. They provide information not only about our environment but also about our innate preferences over the explored territories of our lives. As such, exploration creates a strong path-dependence in life, accentuating early life experiences. The people (and organizations) who explore earlier and better their environment would be significantly advantaged. Striking the right amount of exploration, however, is difficult. Exploring too little could limit severely our choices. Exploring too much could be risky and counterproductive.

Exploration is inherently dangerous, and the risks of over-exploration outweigh the risks of under-exploration. As a result, the forces of natural selection tend to under-incentivize exploration genetically. In this situation, beliefs are important because they could motivate, and if necessary, discourage, exploration. Their main purpose is not to be factually correct but to "adjust" inherited traits toward a more optimal level. For example, people who exhibit low propensity for exploration would be more likely to adopt positive illusions to achieve a competitive level of exploration in their lives. Similarly, people prone to over-exploration would be more likely to develop beliefs constraining their exploration drive, such as pessimism and distrust.

Inconsistent Preferences

To an outside observer, the exploring human exhibits inconsistent and sporadic behavior. Broadly speaking, preferences are inconsistent if someone is choosing A to B and later B to A, or if a person prefers A to B, B to C, and C to A. When people are exploring their preferences, inconsistencies are not only expected; they are a logical consequence of learning and self-discovery. Every act of exploration is changing the actor engaging in it. Our preferences evolve with the choices we make.

The theory developed in this book predicts that preferences would appear more inconsistent earlier in life or a new situation because in these cases, people need to explore more aggressively their environment. Furthermore, preferences would be more inconsistent when the environment changes. It is also important to note that exploration is embedded in every choice we make, even when we are choosing among familiar outcomes. Every interaction with the world generates knowledge, which inevitably changes our preferences.

Currently, researchers agree that one of the most powerful ways of learning is through experience, or "learning by doing." The concept of learning through experience could be traced back to the works of Aristotle, who wrote in the Nicomachean Ethics that "for the things we have to learn before we can do them, we learn by doing them." (Chase, 1998). In this process, a person experiments with different courses of action and learns firsthand, instead of hearing or reading about others' experiences. Experience, however, allows people to learn not only about the outside world but also about their own preferences.

Irrational Behavior

The exploring human also often appears irrational. Exploration has a self-sabotaging element because it sacrifices an immediate reward to engage in a random action. By exploring, however, people anticipate that the information gained would enable them to collect more rewards in the future. Yet, many attempts at exploration fail, and from the perspective of an outside observer, such attempts could be interpreted as irrational.

Numerous seemingly irrational behaviors, such as context-dependent effects and divination, could be rationalized as effective mechanisms for exploration. Exploration can also explain the propensity of people to engage in pure gambles, or situations where success or failure is primarily a matter of chance, with little or no influence from skill. Gambling is widespread in most cultures, even though it has been recognized as a significant public health concern (Dellosa & Browne, 2024). Exploration resembles pure gambles—it is guided by chance, and it has no expected reward beyond the learning experience. In this respect, gambling could be rationalized as an activity allowing people to stretch their exploratory muscle.

It is not surprising that the demographic groups that can benefit the most from exploration, such as younger individuals and men, are also more likely to take risks (Deakin et al., 2004; Dellosa & Browne, 2024). Exploration is more beneficial earlier in life because the information gained could be used multiple times in the future. The reproductive success of men also depends more on exploration and risk-taking than the reproductive success of women (Barrett et al., 2002; Wilson & Daly, 1985). Indeed, this could explain why men exhibit a greater propensity for risk taking than women (Byrnes et al., 1999; Kruger & Nesse, 2004).

The theory suggests that seemingly irrational beliefs could carry a deeper purpose for the person holding these beliefs. As a result, behavior modification needs to be approached with caution. For example, existing research suggests that people do not save enough for retirement, and the effect is stronger for lower income and minority households (Karlan et al., 2014; Lusardi & Mitchell, 2007). Lower income and minority households, however, could be severely disadvantaged in early life exploration, given that they have limited resources. In order to overcome these limitations and achieve a competitive exploration in life, these individuals need to engage all available resources. These resources could enable them to develop important skills and establish valuable social connections they could utilize later in life. Thus, the low propensity to save of under-privileged individuals could be completely rational from an exploratory perspective, even if *ex post* some of these exploratory efforts do not pay off.

Economic (Hyper)Activity

One striking artifact of economic activity is that there seems to be too much of it. People pursue goals and activities that do not appear to bring any tangible benefits to them. One "hidden" benefit of these activities could be the accumulation of knowledge about our own dispositions.

Many have argued that entrepreneurial activity is excessive, given that the failure rates of entrepreneurs seem unusually high (Dunne et al., 1988; Camerer & Lovallo, 1999; Moskowitz & Vissing-Jørgensen, 2002). The literature usually does not recognize that failure is highly informative. It teaches a person that they are not particularly good at something. As a result, they could direct effort in different directions—start a new venture or abandon entrepreneurial activity completely. Failure provides self-knowledge, and so does success. The steep learning curve of entrepreneurial activity could justify the relatively high entry rates of entrepreneurs.

There is also evidence that people tend to consume beyond their basic needs (Brown & Cameron, 2000; Kjellberg, 2008). At the personal level, excessive consumption can lead to dissatisfaction, excessive leverage, and stress. At the macro-level, overconsumption contributes to resource depletion, pollution, and reduction in biodiversity. Status considerations could explain some of these effects. For example, the idea that people emulate the consumption patterns of their peer groups could be traced back to the works of Smith (1776) and Veblen (1899). Yet, over-consumption extends beyond positional goods, i.e., goods whose value could be tied to status.

Preference exploration provides a simple explanation of the overconsumption phenomenon. We buy things not only to consume them but also to see how we would like them. Product exploration is ultimately rooted in consumption, even when this is the consumption of a friend, a reviewer, or a random person. When the number of products and services in the marketplace increases, so does the need for exploring them. The more differentiated the product space, the greater the need for its exploration. If there is only one brand and type of yoghurt in the market, one's consumption of yogurt would be very stable. If there are 50 different brands, then a person would be tempted to try different options and switch between brands. It is likely that in this environment, a person will buy more yogurt. A great deal of purchases in this market would be also wasteful because when the number of options increases, it becomes more difficult for people to plan their consumption. The "excess" in consumption could be related to the "excess" in product differentiation.

Product differentiation is an artifact of competition. It is a marketing strategy that allows companies to distinguish themselves in a crowded market and to gain competitive advantage by attracting new customers. Product differentiation is ubiquitous. Currently, there are approximately 2735 bottled water companies in the U.S.[1] Most of them market themselves as being unique and different, and most of them are not. Product

[1] See https://www.beveragemarketing.com/shop/the-beverage-marketing-bottled-water-operations-database.aspx.

differentiation inevitably deepens with more complex products, which also provokes the need in consumers to explore these products.

To this end, product exploration could facilitate the operation of many markets. In a highly influential paper, Akerlof (1970) argues that when firms are better informed about their products than customers, inferior quality products (or lemons) would invariably replace good quality products in the market. If customers value exploration, however, their demand would be less sensitive to quality, which in turn would allow producers to charge higher prices. Markets would be less likely to break down when customers are more eager to learn about a product. This effect would be stronger for newer and less familiar products and technologies.

If competition drives product differentiation and over-consumption, this suggests a potential negative externality of competition. Economists have recognized the social cost of monopoly arising from the tendency of a monopolist to restrict output and raise prices. This, in turn, leads to reduced consumer surplus and overall societal welfare. Henry Ford famously said that he will produce cars with "any color the customer wants, as long as it's black." For an extended period, Ford offered one model (Model T), which was only available in black. The consumer choice in this market was severely restricted. Yet, the exploration of this market was straightforward. There is no need to try the new Model T because it is the same as the old one. There were no car collectors either. Why would anyone store in a garage a fleet of the same cars!? Competition has great social benefits, but its potentially harmful effect on over-consumption should be considered in welfare analysis.

Firms also tend to be hyperactive. For example, the merger and acquisition activity in the market seems abnormally high. The average acquisition destroys value for the shareholders of the acquiring company. Despite this, managers continue to pay high acquisition premiums for target firms. The framework developed in this book suggests that a great deal of firm activities, including mergers and acquisitions, could be rationalized as explorations. Every firm has some unique advantages in the marketplace, yet it does not know well what these advantages are. It is up to the firm to discover them.

Exploration could explain some of the abnormal trading activity in capital markets (Odean, 1999). Odean (1998) and Statman et al. (2006) propose that abnormal trading activity could be linked to investor overconfidence. Barber & Odean (2008) test this prediction by partitioning investors by gender. Psychological research demonstrates that men are more overconfident than women. Consistent with the idea that overconfidence drives trading, Barber and Odean find that men trade more than women, and trading reduces men's investment performance. Overconfidence, however, also drives exploration. Trading generates knowledge about the market and the trader's ability to generate returns.

Exploration is also expected to influence investment decisions. Financial economists usually characterize security payoffs in terms of probability distributions and are agnostic with respect to the underlying technologies generating these distributions. New technologies could be more attractive to investors than old and better-established technologies because they enable the exploration of new products, production processes, and career opportunities. As a result, the equity of new industries is expected to trade at a premium compared to the equity of old industries. Consistent with this prediction is the fact that major technological innovations are generally associated with increased investor interest and relatively high valuations (Shiller, 2000).

Is Nurture Fine-Tuning Nature?

Nature versus nurture refers to a long-standing debate about the relative importance of genetic inheritance (nature) vs. environmental conditions (nurture) for personal characteristics. Some authors have emphasized nature, or the idea that human behavior is directly controlled by an individual's genes. For example, Francis Galton advocated the view that behavioral traits such as alcoholism and criminality are inheritable (Allen, 1984). The biologist W. D. Hamilton even suggested that genes could be underlying altruism (Hamilton, 1964). Other authors have emphasized nurture, or the idea that cultural influence dominates heredity in shaping personal characteristics (Watson, 2017).

One way to determine the contribution of genes and environment to a trait is to study twins. Twins share the same genes (nature) but could be exposed to different environments (nurture). This allows researchers to design different tests decomposing the variability of a given trait in a population into a genetic and an environmental component (Rende et al., 1990; Meaney, 2004). Some studies also estimate the effect of genetic factors using data on identical and fraternal twins (e.g., Barnea et al., 2010). Most of the research on twins estimates the effect of heritability to be between 40% and 50%, thus, leaving a significant room for nurture to shape individual behavior.

The framework developed in this book suggests a complementary view of nature and nurture. Inherited traits reflect long term evolutionary processes. Yet, they are imperfect and inflexible. Cultural traits evolve to correct the deficiencies of genetic traits. They are flexible and adjust as both the environment and our knowledge about it evolve. Nurture plays a correcting role of nature. It mitigates the effect of genetics on individual behavior.

The adaptability of nurture resembles the concept of plasticity in physiology. Adaptive phenotypic plasticity refers to the ability of organisms to modify traits during their lifetime to better suit their surroundings (Snell-Rood & Steck, 2019; West-Eberhard, 2003). For example, the muscle mass of most species increases with exercise and decreases with inactivity. Similarly, neuroplasticity refers to the brain's ability to change its structure in response to changing conditions. It involves the formation of new synapses (connections between neurons) and the strengthening or weakening of existing ones. Nurture also provides an element of plasticity to personal traits, allowing individuals to cope with changes in their environment.

Free Will

Free will is a concept about our ability to choose free from past and current circumstances. Philosophers have debated the nature of free will for centuries, with some arguing for its existence, while others arguing against it.

Primary preferences create the illusion of a Free will, because the choices embedded in these preferences are completely predetermined. If a person prefers A to B, then given the choice between A and B, they will always choose A. This contradicts the idea that free choice is the result of a conscious act of deliberation. It seems that freedom of choice resides in the action space of exploration. Since affinity for exploration takes the form A = PEX*Beliefs, and PEX is also predetermined, the freedom of choice is effectively reduced to our freedom to form beliefs about the unexplored.

Conclusion

This chapter discusses implications of the theory of dynamic preferences for economic analysis. The theory can explain a wide range of cognitive biases and seemingly irrational beliefs. It points toward the evolutionary advantages of optimism and positive illusions. It identifies many hidden benefits of inter-personal conflicts, self-sabotaging behaviors, and superstitious beliefs. The theory can also explain the appeal of art and our interest in narratives. The analysis has implications for our understanding of cultural evolution. It suggests that cultural traits evolve, at least in part, to correct the deficiencies of genetic traits. This flexibility helps individuals to cope with changes in their environment. Nurture plays a correcting role of nature.

References

Akerlof, G. A. (1970). The market for 'Lemons': Quality uncertainty and the market mechanism. *The Quarterly Journal of Economics, 84*(3), 488–500.

Allen, G. E. (1984). The roots of biological determinism: Review of the mismeasure of man by stephen jay gould. *Journal of the History of Biology, 17*(1), 141–145.

Barber, B. M., & Odean, T. (2008). All that glitters: The effect of attention and news on the buying behavior of individual and institutional investors. *Review of Financial Studies, 21*(2), 785–818.

Barnea, A., Cronqvist, H., & Siegel, S. (2010). Nature or nurture: What determines investor behavior? *Journal of Financial Economics, 98*(3), 583–604.

Barrett, L., Dunbar, R., & Lycett, J. (2002). *Human evolutionary psychology.* Palgrave.

Beachly, W. M., Stephens, D. W., & Toyer, K. B. (1995). On the economics of sit-and-wait foraging: Site selection and assessment. *Behavioral Ecology, 6*(3), 258–268.

Brown, P. M., & Cameron, L. D. (2000). What can be done to reduce overconsumption? *Ecological Economics, 32*(1), 27–41.

Byrnes, J. P., Miller, D. C., & Schafer, W. D. (1999). Gender differences in risk taking: A meta-analysis. *Psychological Bulletin, 125*, 367–383.

Camerer, C., & Lovallo, D. (1999). Overconfidence and excess entry: An experimental approach. *American Economic Review, 89*, 306–318.

Chase, D. P. (1998). *Nicomachean Ethics.* Courier Corporation.

Deakin, J., Aitken, M., Robbins, T., & Sahakian, B. J. (2004). Risk taking during decision-making in normal volunteers changes with age. *Journal of the International Neuropsychological Society, 10*(4), 590–598.

Dellosa, G., & Browne, M. (2024). The influence of age on gambling problems worldwide: A systematic review and meta-analysis of risk among younger, middle-aged, and older adults. *Journal of Behavioral Addictions, 13*(3), 702–715.

Dunne, T., Roberts, M., & Samuelson, L. (1988). Patterns of firm entry and exit in US manufacturing industries. *Rand Journal of Economics, 19*, 495–515.

Hamilton, W. D. (1964). The genetical evolution of social behaviour. I. *Journal of Theoretical Biology*, *7*(1), 1–16.
Karlan, D., Ratan, A. L., & Zinman, J. (2014). Savings by and for the poor: A research review and agenda. *Review of Income and Wealth*, *60*(1), 36–78.
Kjellberg, H. (2008). Market practices and over-consumption. *Consumption, Markets and Culture*, *11*(2), 151–167.
Kruger, D. J., & Nesse, R. M. (2004). Sexual selection and the male:female mortality ratio. *Evolutionary Psychology*, *2*, 66–85.
Lusardi, A., & Mitchell, O. S. (2007). Baby boomers retirement security: The role of planning, financial literacy and housing wealth. *Journal of Monetary Economics*, *54*, 205–224.
Meaney, M. (2004). The nature of nurture: Maternal effects and chromatin remodeling. In J. T. Cacioppo & G. G. Berntson (Eds.), *Essays in social neuroscience*. MIT Press.
Moskowitz, T. J., & Vissing-Jørgensen, A. (2002). The returns to entrepreneurial investment: A private equity premium puzzle? *American Economic Review*, *92*(4), 745–778.
Odean, T. (1998). Volume, volatility, price, and profit when all traders are above average. *Journal of Finance*, *53*(6), 1887–1934.
Odean, T. (1999). Do investors trade too much? *American Economic Review*, *89*(5), 1279–1298.
Rende, R. D., Plomin, R., & Vandenberg, S. G. (1990). Who discovered the twin method? *Behavior Genetics*, *20*(2), 277–285.
Shiller, R. J. (2000). *Irrational exuberance*. Princeton University Press.
Smith, A. (1776). *An inquiry into the nature and causes of the wealth of nations: Volume one*. printed for W. Strahan & T. Cadell.
Snell-Rood, E. C., & Steck, M. K. (2019). Behaviour shapes environmental variation and selection on learning and plasticity: Review of mechanisms and implications. *Animal Behaviour*, *147*, 147–156.
Statman, M., Thorley, S., & Vorkink, K. (2006). Investor overconfidence and trading volume. *Review of Financial Studies*, *19*(4), 1531–1565.
Stephens, D. W., Brown, J. S., & Ydenberg, R. C. (Eds.). (2008). *Foraging: Behavior and ecology*. University of Chicago Press.
Veblen, T. (1899). *The theory of the leisure class: An economic study of institutions*. Penguin.
Watson, J. B. (2017). *Behaviorism*. Routledge.
West-Eberhard, M. J. (2003). *Developmental plasticity and evolution*. Oxford University Press.
Wilson, M., & Daly, M. (1985). Competitiveness, risk taking, and violence: The young male syndrome. *Ethology and Sociobiology*, *6*, 59–73.

CHAPTER 14

The Exploring Gene

Our own physical body possesses a wisdom which we who inhabit the body lack. We give it orders which make no sense.

—Henry Miller

Source: Miller, Henry (1956). A Devil in Paradise. New Directions (**p. 51**)

Contents

Introduction

Exploration happens at multiple levels. Social groups engage in collective exploration of their environment. Individuals explore the outside world as well as their own dispositions. Organ systems within the body also explore the environment to optimize their performance. This chapter hypothesizes that exploration could happen even at the level of individual genes.

C. A. Pirinsky, *A Theory of Dynamic Preferences*,
https://doi.org/10.1007/978-3-032-13334-2_14

There are several indications that genes could be exploratory. Genes often experience mutations, i.e., permanent changes in their deoxyribonucleic acid (DNA) sequence. Although the nature of genetic mutations appears random, the timing of mutations is not. Mutations are more likely at times when the organism is under stress; for example, due to exposure to mutagens or viruses. The very state of stress indicates that the existing genetic structure is incapable of neutralizing successfully an emerging threat. This, in turn, suggests that an exploration of alternative gene structures could be highly beneficial. Randomization is an effective exploration mechanism. Thus, random gene mutations are consistent with exploration. Recent research in genetics suggests that some gene mutations could be even strategically directed toward more advantageous configurations.

Evolutionary Dynamics

Modern evolutionary analysis is built on Darwin's theory of natural selection (Darwin, 2004 [1859]). According to the theory, when living organisms replicate themselves, they undergo some random copying errors. These errors create naturally occurring variation of individual traits in the population. Since some of the traits are better suited to their environment, individuals carrying these traits are more likely to survive, reproduce, and pass those traits to their offspring. Over generations, advantageous traits become more common in the population, leading to the evolution of the species.

The prevalence of favorable traits in the population creates the illusion that these traits were purposefully designed to aid the survival of individuals. However, according to Darwin, they were merely the product of accumulated copying errors. This surprising outcome is a result of the cumulative effect of numerous generations of replications. If copying errors were not random, i.e., they were the result of a strategic selection, then this selection would make natural selection superfluous.

The brush of evolution has touched the shapes and colors of all species. For example, flowers may evolve to have a more colorful appearance and pleasant scents to attract pollinators and ensure successful reproduction. Animals may evolve to run faster to escape predators. The ability of humans to digest milk as adults, also known as lactase persistence, is one example of how our genes adapt to environmental changes. This trait became advantageous as humans began domesticating animals for milk production. As a result, people who were better able to tolerate lactose were also more likely to survive and pass their genes to the next generation. The forces of natural selection spread lactase persistence throughout Central Europe in only a few 1000 years (Burger et al., 2020).

Randomness plays an important role in modern evolutionary theory. Evolution involves both natural selection and a random variation that provides the material for the selection. Most such variations are caused by random mutations, i.e., genetic changes in the structure of the DNA (Wagner, 2012). The environment does not create mutations that are specifically beneficial; rather, it selects among mutations that already exist and happen to be advantageous.

Although Darwin formulated natural selection at the individual level, subsequent research has suggested that selection could take place at higher levels (e.g., groups) or at lower levels (e.g., genes). Group selection was proposed to explain the evolution of cooperation and other altruistic traits (Boyd & Richerson, 2009; Nowak, 2006; Wilson & Sober, 1994). From the point of classic evolutionary theory, selfish individuals would have an evolutionary advantage over altruistic individuals. Thus, the widespread presence of cooperative behavior presents a puzzle for classic evolutionary theory. Group selection could resolve this puzzle. Groups of cooperative individuals would have an evolutionary advantage over groups of selfish individuals (Boyd & Richerson, 2009). Thus, in the case of cooperation, there is a tradeoff between what is advantageous to any given organism and what is advantageous to a group of organisms.

Another strain of literature has suggested that genes are the primary units of selection in evolution, i.e., natural selection acts on genes rather than individuals or groups. The gene-centered view on evolution, also known as the "selfish gene" theory, argues that natural selection favors genes that are better at replicating and being passed on to future generations (Dawkins, 1976). Proponents of this viewpoint argue that, since heritable information is passed from generation to generation almost exclusively by DNA, evolutionary processes are best considered from the perspective of genes. The gene-centered view also allows for altruism, but only among genetically related individuals (kin selection). Altruism, from this viewpoint, is not true selflessness but a way for genes to propagate themselves by ensuring the survival and reproduction of individuals carrying copies of those genes. Kin selection theory, however, seems incapable of explaining the prevalence of cross-familiar, cross-racial, and cross-species acts of altruism (see e.g., Wilson & Wilson, 2007).

Multi-Level Exploration

Similar to evolutionary processes, exploration also happens at multiple levels. Individuals face the exploration-exploitation dilemma in many of their decisions (Hills et al., 2015). Research from biology, psychology, and neuroscience has analyzed extensively how individuals balance the exploration-exploitation tradeoff (reviewed in earlier chapters).

Living organisms also explore collectively at the group level. Social animals often exercise division of labor, where some organisms specialize in exploration and others in exploitation (Frisch von, 1967; Giraldeau & Lefebvre, 1986). Humans also collaborate to tackle exploration challenges in organizations and teams (see e.g., March, 1991). Exploration has been also recognized as an important factor for the development of firm competitive advantages (see e.g., Kerr et al., 2014).

There is evidence that exploration takes place even within different systems of the human body. The human body is comprised of several organ systems that work together to maintain life, such as the nervous, cardiovascular, respiratory, digestive, and immune systems. For example, the immune system explores by continuously patrolling the body, searching for and eliminating potential threats like pathogens, damaged cells, or cancer cells. The immune system distinguishes between self and non-self-cells by recognizing unique molecules called antigens on the surface of foreign invaders. These antigens, typically proteins on bacteria, viruses, or other pathogens, act as identifiers that trigger an immune response. This exploratory process is often referred to as immunological surveillance.

In addition to identifying threats, the immune system also uses resources to fight identified threats, as well as to maintain itself. These activities are equivalent to exploitation. For example, when immune cells encounter a threat, they initiate immune responses to eliminate the threat, such as destroying infected cells, clearing damaged tissue, or mounting an adaptive immune response. After encountering an antigen, the immune system remembers it, so that it can respond more quickly and effectively the next time it encounters the same antigen. The immune system also continuously deploys resources to maintain itself, for example, by generating white blood cells like lymphocytes and phagocytes.

The Exploring Gene

Genes are the basic units of heredity that are passed from parents to offspring and determine a variety of traits, including our innate preferences. Genes consist of DNA; a long molecule made up of smaller units called nucleotides. DNA replication is the process by which a DNA molecule is copied to produce two identical DNA molecules during cell division.

Most sexually reproducing organisms begin their lives as a single cell. This single cell, called a zygote (a fertilized egg), then divides and differentiates to form the complex multicellular structures of the adult organism. The zygote contains half of its genetic material (DNA) from one of the parents and the other half from the other parent. The recombination process, however, is not entirely deterministic and undergoes changes or mutations. Germline mutations (that occur in eggs and sperm) can be passed on to offspring, while somatic mutations (that occur in body cells) are not passed on. Mutations are the "action space" for the genes.

There are several indications that gene mutations could be exploratory. First, mutations do not happen arbitrarily. Mutations are more likely at times when the organism is under threat, such as exposure to mutagens or viral infections. The very fact that the organism experiences distress in these situations suggests that its current genetic composition is incapable of dealing effectively with the threat. Because of this, a change in the gene structure of the organism could be beneficial. The only point in time when an organism can change its gene structure, however, is at the initial fertilization stage. Thus, the survival of the gene depends on the ability of the organism to mutate the genetic structure of its reproductive cells (sperm and ova). Every single cell of the new organism then will contain the initial mutation of the zygote.

Second, although the timing of genetic mutations is not arbitrary, the nature of the mutations appears random. Random mutations have been recognized as an important element of evolutionary processes. They introduce random variation that natural selection acts upon. Organisms with traits that are better suited to their environment are then more likely to survive and reproduce, passing those advantageous traits to their offspring. Randomization is also a defining characteristic of exploration. The fact that both gene mutation and exploration are centered around randomization suggests that the two phenomena could be indeed related.

The random element of mutations raises the question of how this randomness is realized in practice. Generating a random outcome is not trivial. A spontaneous reaction is not inherently random because it could be influenced by non-random local factors. This suggests that some randomization mechanisms could be embedded in the structure of most genes.

The possibility that gene mutations are exploratory also suggests that some of these mutations could be strategically directed (i.e., directed exploration). Recent research in genetics provides supporting evidence for this conjecture. For example, some studies find that essential genes exhibit lower mutation rates than less essential genes to protect themselves from harmful mutations (Domingues, 2023; Monroe et al., 2022). These results challenge the traditional view of mutations as entirely random, non-strategic processes.

Conclusion

Exploration is ubiquitous, and it takes place at different levels. Social groups explore collectively both their surroundings and the rules governing their social interactions. Individuals explore their environment on a daily basis. Different systems within the human body also explore their surroundings. This chapter asks whether exploration takes place even deeper at the level of individual genes.

Genes mutate, and there are several indications that these mutations could be exploratory. Gene mutations are often triggered by exposure to mutagens like UV radiation, various chemicals, and metabolic processes. All these developments indicate that the existing genetic composition is unable to respond adequately to an existing threat. As a result, a change to the existing structure of the genes could be evolutionary beneficial. Existing patterns of gene mutations are consistent with the idea that genes explore various configurations in order to improve their chances for survival and reproduction.

References

Boyd, R., & Richerson, P. J. (2009). Culture and the evolution of human cooperation. *Philosophical Transactions of the Royal Society B: Biological Sciences, 364*(1533), 3281–3288.

Burger, J., Link, V., Blöcher, J., Schulz, A., Sell, C., Pochon, Z., Diekmann, Y., Žegarac, A., Hofmanová, Z., Winkelbach, L., & Reyna-Blanco, C. S. (2020).

Low prevalence of lactase persistence in Bronze Age Europe indicates ongoing strong selection over the last 3,000 years. *Current Biology, 30*(21), 4307–4315.
Darwin, C. (2004). *On the origin of species, 1859* (Vol. 2). Routledge.
Dawkins, R. (1976). *The selfish gene*. Oxford university press.
Domingues, V. (2023). Mutations are not random. *Nature Ecology and Evolution, 7*(1), 5.
Frisch von, K. (1967). *The dance language and orientation of bees*. Harvard University Press.
Giraldeau, L. A., & Lefebvre, L. (1986). Exchangeable producer and scrounger roles in a captive flock of feral pigeons: A case for the skill pool effect. *Animal Behaviour, 34*(3), 797–803.
Hills, T. T., Todd, P. M., Lazer, D., Redish, A. D., & Couzin, I. D. (2015). Exploration versus exploitation in space, mind, and society. *Trends in Cognitive Sciences, 19*(1), 46–54.
Kerr, W. R., Nanda, R., & Rhodes-Kropf, M. (2014). Entrepreneurship as experimentation. *Journal of Economic Perspectives, 28*, 25–48.
March, J. G. (1991). Exploration and exploitation in organizational learning. *Organization Science, 2*(1), 71–87.
Monroe, J. G., Srikant, T., Carbonell-Bejerano, P., Becker, C., Lensink, M., Exposito-Alonso, M., Klein, M., Hildebrandt, J., Neumann, M., Kliebenstein, D., & Weng, M. L. (2022). Mutation bias reflects natural selection in Arabidopsis thaliana. *Nature, 602*(7895), 101–105.
Nowak, M. A. (2006). Five rules for the evolution of cooperation. *Science, 314*(5805), 1560–1563.
Wagner, A. (2012). The role of randomness in Darwinian evolution. *Philosophy of Science, 79*(1), 95–119.
Wilson, D. S., & Sober, E. (1994). Reintroducing group selection to the human behavioral sciences. *Behavioral and Brain Sciences, 17*(4), 585–608.
Wilson, D. S., & Wilson, E. O. (2007). Rethinking the theoretical foundation of sociobiology. *The Quarterly Review of Biology, 82*, 327–348.

CHAPTER 15

Exploration and Intelligence

We have to continually be jumping off cliffs and developing our wings on the way down.

—Kurt Vonnegut

Source: Vonnegut, K. (2013). If this isn't nice, what is? Advice for the young. Seven Stories Press. (**p. 131**)

Contents

Introduction

Life is a collection of choices, and the individuals who make better choices are more likely to survive, reproduce, and ingrain their values into the fabric of society. The choice process goes through two stages. At stage one, people review the rich set of available alternatives and focus their limited attention on a subset of them. At stage two, they select one of the

C. A. Pirinsky, *A Theory of Dynamic Preferences*,
https://doi.org/10.1007/978-3-032-13334-2_15

explored options. Sometimes people explore directly the options they face by trying them, and sometimes they explore them indirectly by inferring their rewards based on the available information. In both cases, individuals' ability to acquire and analyze the relevant information is an important determinant of exploration quality.

Intelligence directs the choices of many living organisms. One could even make the case that this is the very reason intelligence exists. Intelligence, however, is a multifaceted phenomenon. The theory of multiple intelligences (MI) posits that human intelligence consists of various distinct modalities. For example, Gardner (1983) identified eight dimensions, such as verbal-linguistic, logical-mathematical, and interpersonal intelligence, among others. Other authors have proposed alternative classifications. Although people could disagree on how intelligence could be classified, most of them would agree that the understanding of different aspects of our reality requires a different set of skills and abilities.

This chapter argues that the exploration strategies of an individual depend crucially on his or her intellectual abilities. For example, people who score high on Interpersonal (Emotional) intelligence would find social exploration more attractive. People who score high on Logical-mathematical (Analytical) intelligence would be more successful at building mental models and simulations. The relative importance of different forms of intelligence is also expected to vary across societies. Agricultural societies would tend to favor Naturalistic intelligence, or the ability to recognize and categorize animals, plants, and other objects in nature. Industrial societies would tend to favor Interpersonal intelligence, or one's capacity to detect and respond appropriately to the moods, motivations, and desires of others.

What type of intelligence drives exploration in the modern world? Information technologies, in general, and artificial intelligence (AI), in particular, are transforming all aspects of our lives. Exploration is not an exception. One's ability to develop, understand, and utilize AI algorithms becomes an important factor for the prosperity of individuals, organizations, and even countries. I refer to this ability as AI intelligence, or AI2.

What is Intelligence?

The word intelligence derives from the Latin verb *intelligere*, which means to comprehend or perceive. Currently, the term intelligence is widely used yet not rigorously defined across disciplines. It generally refers to an individual's ability to acquire and process information to their advantage.

The Merriam-Webster Dictionary defines intelligence as "the ability to learn or understand, the skilled use of reason, the ability to apply knowledge to manipulate one's environment or to think abstractly as measured by objective criteria." The APA Dictionary of Psychology defines intelligence as "the ability to derive information, learn from experience, adapt to the environment, understand, and correctly utilize thought and reason."

The modern study of intelligence began with the work of the British psychologist Charles Spearman, who introduced the term general intelligence (Spearman, 1904). After using factor analysis to examine mental aptitude tests, Spearman observed that the scores on these tests were very similar. People who performed well on one cognitive test performed well on other tests, while those who scored poorly on one test tended to score poorly on others. He concluded that intelligence is a general cognitive ability that researchers can measure and express numerically.

While empirical research often supports the existence of a general intelligence factor (Deary, 2020), a growing body of research suggests that intelligence exhibits important nuances. The theory of multiple intelligences (MI) posits that human intelligence is not a single general ability but comprises of various distinct modalities, such as linguistic, logical-mathematical, musical, spatial, and other intelligences. Although some authors have expressed concern that the proposed dimensions appear arbitrary, the popularity of the idea has been increasing over time. For example, Google Ngram Viewer shows that while the term "multiple intelligences" did not exist in the 1970s, its use increased exponentially throughout the 1980s and 1990s.[1]

One widely referenced intelligence classification was developed by Howard Gardner (Gardner, 1983). Gardner proposed eight forms of intelligence based on skills and abilities that are valued in various cultures, as follows:

Bodily-kinesthetic intelligence: The ability to control body movements and handle physical objects. People with strong kinesthetic abilities are good at sports, acting, and dance.

Visual-spatial intelligence: The capacity to think in images and visualize accurately spatial objects. High visual-spatial intelligence can be expressed practically (e.g., in construction), artistically (e.g., in sculpture), or as a combination of both (e.g., in architecture and design).

[1] The Google Books Ngram Viewer is an online tool that visualizes the frequency of words and phrases (n-grams) appearing in a massive corpus of digitized books.

Verbal-linguistic intelligence: The ability to write, read, and communicate in written language. People with high verbal ability are typically good at articulating concepts and ideas, composing and telling stories, and memorizing text.

Logical-mathematical intelligence: The ability to understand the underlying, often causal, principles of a system. It is related to one's ability to formulate, analyze, and solve a problem. People with high logical-mathematical intelligence are good at finance, engineering, and the sciences.

Interpersonal intelligence: The capacity to detect and respond appropriately to the moods, motivations, and desires of others. People with high interpersonal intelligence have an insightful understanding of other people's point of view, which makes them good leaders, counselors, and teachers.

Intrapersonal intelligence: The capacity to be self-aware and in tune with inner feelings, beliefs, and thought processes. Through introspection, people with high intrapersonal intelligence are able to achieve an understanding of their personal advantages and limitations. Such understanding is crucial for achieving high level performance in most highly competitive professions, such as management, competitive sports, and politics.

Musical intelligence: The ability to produce and appreciate musical harmonies. Musical traditions have been an integral part of human existence for thousands of years. People with high musical intelligence can sing, play musical instruments, or compose music.

Naturalistic intelligence: This category was not part of Gardner's original seven dimensions and was added by him later to the list (Gardner, 1995). It refers to one's ability to recognize, categorize, and relate to animals, plants, and other objects in the natural world. People with high naturalistic intelligence have a deeper, holistic understanding of the ecosystem and its complexity.

Researchers have also proposed a series of additional dimensions and classifications of human intelligence over the last 40 years. For example, the psychologist Daniel Goleman introduced the concept of emotional intelligence, which refers to a person's ability to understand and regulate their own emotions as well as the emotions of others (Drigas & Papoutsi, 2018). The psychologist Robert Sternberg defined three meta-components of intelligence—componential, experiential, and practical—also called triarchic components (Sternberg, 1985). In totality, this research reaffirms the view that autonomous domains of intelligence exist. However, as noted by

Demetriou et al. (2011), theories that overemphasize the autonomy of the domains are as simplistic as the theories that overemphasize general intelligence and ignore the domains.

Intelligence and Exploration

Intelligence is inherently linked to exploration. Higher intelligence is associated with better ability to analyze information, weigh options, and predict outcomes, all of which are essential elements of the exploration process. The fact that one's ability to explore and make better decisions is crucial for evolutionary survival (e.g., Schultz, 2015), also suggests that the very existence of intelligence could be rooted in exploration. Indeed, some of the definitions of intelligence explicitly identify such a connection. For example, Stemberg (2012) defines intelligence as "the ability to learn from experience and to adapt to, shape, and select environments."

Exploration encompasses a wide range of decisions, such as whether, when, and what to explore. Importantly, it is also about what type of exploration strategies to implement. Exploration could be either direct or indirect, depending on whether an individual assesses the attractiveness of an option by engaging directly with it or by approximating it based on the available information. All these approaches utilize different techniques and require the collection and analysis of different pieces of information.

The diversity of exploration methods and the multiplicity of intellectual capabilities suggest that individuals are likely to select exploration methods that match their relative advantages. For example, people who score high on interpersonal intelligence and emotional intelligence would be more likely to engage in social exploration. People who score high on logical-mathematical (analytical) intelligence would be more successful at building mental simulations. People with high verbal-linguistic intelligence could be more successful at delegating exploration and persuading people to explore on their behalf. Finally, people who score low on the above qualities would be more likely to rely on random exploration.

Different societies are also likely to favor different intellectual capabilities. Agricultural societies would naturally promote bodily-kinesthetic and naturalistic intelligence. People in these societies tend to live in extended families focused on farming and agriculture. The self-reliance of the family minimizes social interactions outside of the family circle. In such cultures, connection to nature is more important than connection to people outside of the kin.

Industrial societies are characterized by mass production fueled by automation and a high degree of division of labor. In these societies, specialization naturally led to urbanization and the conglomeration of people with different qualifications in the same geographic area. The concentration of people from different backgrounds and occupations demands greater interpersonal intelligence, or the ability to detect and respond appropriately to the moods, motivations, and desires of others. The increased complexity of urban life and the need for communication also stimulated the development of verbal-linguistic intelligence.

AI Intelligence

Society is currently experiencing major structural changes characterized by the widespread use of information and communication technologies, the most transformative of which is artificial intelligence. Here, I argue that the successful development, implementation, and utilization of these technologies requires the cultivation of a new mindset. I refer to it as AI intelligence, or AI2.

Defining artificial intelligence is at least as challenging as defining natural intelligence. Most views on AI tend to center around the ability of a machine or an algorithm to engage successfully in tasks that require human intelligence. For example, McKinsey & Company defines AI as "a machine's ability to perform some cognitive functions we usually associate with human minds."[2] The leading American research and advisory firm Gartner, Inc. defines AI as the application of "advanced analysis and logic-based techniques, including machine learning (ML), to interpret events, support and automate decisions, and take actions."[3]

An interesting feature of most AI systems is that the designers of the system do not have a clear understanding of its properties ex ante. AI technologies are developed spontaneously in a highly competitive and largely unregulated environment. Each algorithm is designed and trained on a large amount of data, and its performance is evaluated ex post. In most cases, the designers do not know how the algorithm will perform, what its main advantages and disadvantages are, and why it performs the way it does. For the first time in history, we are engineering a system, the

[2] See https://www.mckinsey.com/featured-insights/mckinsey-explainers/what-is-ai.

[3] See https://www.gartner.com/en/topics/artificial-intelligence.

properties we are trying to understand after it has been already built. In this respect, AI creations resemble a real person. It is capable and mysterious, and it is up to us to understand its full potential. Thus, before we engage AI to explore the world, we need to explore the AI first.

AI could be a promising tool for exploration. Exploration is based on information, and AI algorithms utilize vast amounts of information. Even if their ability to process this information is limited, they could provide valuable insights that are complimentary to the insights provided by human intelligence (Pothos & Widdows, 2025).

Another important application of emerging information technologies is for building sophisticated simulations. Generative AI can realistically recreate hypothetical situations that could be highly beneficial for exploration. As discussed earlier in the book, computer simulations provide an alternative solution to complex exploration problems. While until now computer simulations have been a prerogative of highly specialized scientific teams, AI technologies promise to democratize simulations and make them accessible to a wide group of people.

Let's revisit the discussion of one important personal exploration—career choice. This is a highly complex decision encompassing a wide range of pecuniary and non-pecuniary considerations. Furthermore, when choosing a career, people also need to factor in their personal abilities and preferences. Yet, people need to make this decision early in life based on very limited information about both the outside options they face, as well as their preferences. Emerging technologies, such as Generative AI and Virtual Reality, can simulate realistically the environment of any possible career, thus, allowing an individual to gain valuable insights about potential career choices.

At the end, I would like to note that AI will challenge and transform societal culture. AI gradually is becoming an important member of society. It gets involved in an increasingly large number of situations and decisions. Yet, AI is not a real person. Interactions with it are based on rules that often contradict the existing rules governing human interactions. For example, saying "please" and "thank you" are widely recognized social norms, promoting positive social interactions in most cultures. Yet, saying "please" and "thank you" to an AI system is not recommended.[4] Can AI

[4] https://www.usatoday.com/story/tech/2025/04/22/please-thank-you-chatgpt-openai-energy-costs/83207447007/.

make society ruder? It could. AI algorithms are also incredibly fast. Does this mean that AI can make us impatient? It might. If we would like to preserve our existing human norms, we might need to teach AI algorithms to follow these norms.

Conclusion

The exploration of the unknown is an important factor for personal development and survival. Individuals who can better explore their environment will win in evolution. This chapter argues that intellectual capabilities are one of the main determinants of exploration quality. Most exploration techniques, such as directed exploration, social exploration, and simulations, are based on the analysis of a large amount of data. These techniques also require different skill sets. As a result, people could choose to specialize in different types of exploration, depending on their relative advantages. Furthermore, the relative importance of different forms of exploration (and types of intelligence) is expected to vary over time and across societies. The chapter also argues that emerging AI technologies provide new means for exploration, and the people and societies that are able to utilize these technologies better will be significantly advantaged.

References

Deary, I. J. (2020). *Intelligence: A Very Short Introduction.* Oxford University Press.

Demetriou, A., Spanoudis, G., & Mouyi, A. (2011). Educating the developing mind: Towards an overarching paradigm. *Educational Psychology Review, 23*(4), 601–663.

Drigas, A. S., & Papoutsi, C. (2018). A new layered model on emotional intelligence. *Behavioral Sciences, 8*(5), 45. https://doi.org/10.3390/bs8050045

Gardner, H. (1983). *Frames of mind: The theory of multiple intelligences.* Basic Books.

Gardner, H. (1995). Reflections on multiple intelligences: Myths and messages. *Phi Delta Kappan, 77*, 200–209.

Pothos, E. M., & Widdows, D. (2025). Natural, Artificial, and Human Intelligences. arXiv preprint arXiv:2506.02183.

Schultz, W. (2015). Neuronal reward and decision signals: From theories to data. *Physiological Reviews, 95*(3), 853–951.

Spearman, C. (1904). "General intelligence," objectively determined and measured. *The American Journal of Psychology*, *15*(2), 201. https://doi.org/10.2307/1412107

Stemberg, R. J. (2012). Intelligence. State of the art. *Dialogues in Clinical Neuroscience*, *14*(1), 19–27.

Sternberg, R. J. (1985). *Beyond IQ: A Triarchic Theory of Intelligence*. Cambridge University Press.

CHAPTER 16

Epilogue

This book proposes a new dynamic framework for analyzing individual preferences. Adopting a dynamic view of preferences is important because preferences change. A simple self-reflection suggests that the things we like and aspire to today are different from the things we liked and aspired to a year ago. The values and aspirations of societies also change. The concept of preferences plays a central role in economics and other social sciences. Without understanding why preferences change, it would be impossible to gain a deeper understanding of economic change.

The theory provides a series of insights into individual preferences. First, preferences are linked to survival. We are inherently attracted to things that improve our chances for survival and pushed away from things that are disadvantageous for our survival. Second, preferences are shaped by both long-term evolutionary processes and short-term experiences. Third, to access the information encoded in innate preferences, individuals need to explore their environment to learn the relative attractiveness of the options they face. Fourth, the information contained in innate preferences is imperfect. As a result, individuals engage in deeper exploration of their own preferences.

Given its importance, most living organisms have developed mechanisms incentivizing exploration. One such mechanism is an innate propensity for

C. A. Pirinsky, *A Theory of Dynamic Preferences*,
https://doi.org/10.1007/978-3-032-13334-2_16

exploration (PEX), which makes exploration intrinsically rewarding. Since exploration is inherently risky, however, inherited dispositions would tend to under-incentivize exploration. This opens space for a second, more flexible mechanism for incentivizing exploration—individual beliefs. The adoption of biased perceptions of reality fine-tunes one's propensity for exploration. For example, when people feel more optimistic about existing opportunities, they would tend to explore more; when they feel more pessimistic about them—they would tend to explore less.

One of the main insights of the theory is that beliefs correct our innate deficiencies. Similarly to the way a pair of glasses restores one's vision by distorting the visual perceptions of reality, beliefs adjust individual behavior through biased perceptions. To be an effective adjustment mechanism, beliefs need to be biased. Yet, not all beliefs are equally flexible. Some beliefs are more fundamental and deeply ingrained in one's mind. These beliefs are formed early in life and significantly affect our thoughts, feelings, and behaviors. I refer to them as core beliefs. Other beliefs, in contrast, are more superficial and easier to change and adjust. I refer to them as higher-level beliefs.

The fact that beliefs exhibit different levels of plasticity, or ability to change, suggests that the dichotomy between nature and nurture is more nuanced. Indeed, the borderline between nature and nurture is not clearly defined. Since not all beliefs are equally flexible, one could make the case that higher-level beliefs could be used to correct lower-level beliefs, which in turn could be used to correct inherited traits, or nature (see Fig. 16.1). Thus, the Exploration Tuning Hypothesis that beliefs fine-tune individual PEX (Chap. 3) could be generalized by recognizing that higher-level beliefs exhibit greater fine-tuning flexibility than lower-level beliefs.

At the end, I would like to note that the analysis in this book has some practical implications for individuals seeking to improve their well-being and quality of life. It suggests that exploration is vitally important, yet it is under-incentivized. There are different ways people could overcome this deficiency. They could use exploration techniques that fit best their personality. More social individuals could explore more of the resources in their social networks, while more introverted individuals could rely more on their analytical abilities. Embrace your biases. Our tendencies to

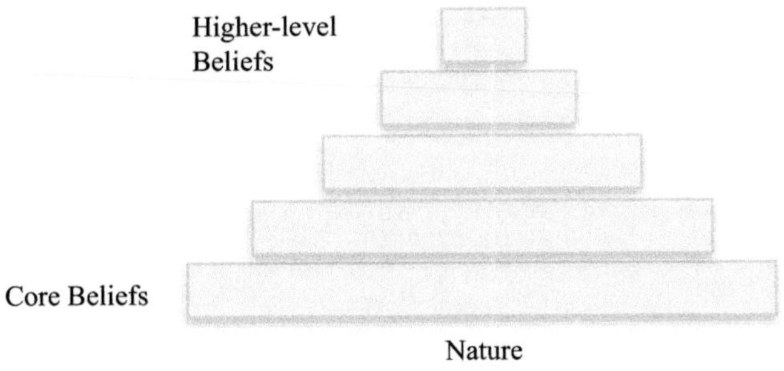

Fig. 16.1 Nature versus nurture. The figure illustrates the hierarchical structure of beliefs, where core beliefs are more fundamental and difficult to change, while higher-level beliefs are more flexible and easier to change

procrastinate, share our experiences, and follow superstitions could be more beneficial than we think. And remember, bad decisions often pave the way for better ones.

Index

C. A. Pirinsky, *A Theory of Dynamic Preferences*, https://doi.org/10.1007/978-3-032-13334-2

9783032133335